TRAVELS WITH
A HUNGRY
BEAR

◆

Books by Mark Kramer

INVASIVE PROCEDURES
A Year in the World of Two Surgeons

THREE FARMS
Making Milk, Meat and Money
from the American Soil

MOTHER WALTER AND
THE PIG TRAGEDY

LITERARY JOURNALISM
(coeditor)

TRAVELS
WITH A
HUNGRY
BEAR

———— ◆ ————

A JOURNEY TO THE
RUSSIAN HEARTLAND

Mark Kramer

A Richard Todd Book
HOUGHTON MIFFLIN COMPANY
BOSTON • NEW YORK
1996

For information about permission to reproduce selections
from this book, write to Permissions, Houghton Mifflin Company,
215 Park Avenue South, New York, New York 10003.

For information about this and other Houghton Mifflin trade
and reference books and multimedia products, visit
The Bookstore at Houghton Mifflin on the World Wide Web
at http://www.hmco.com/trade/.

Library of Congress Cataloging-in-Publication Data
Kramer, Mark.
Travels with a hungry bear: a journey to the Russian
heartland / Mark Kramer
p. cm.
"A Richard Todd book."
ISBN 0-395-42670-7
1. Russia (Federation) — Rural conditions. 2. Russia
(Federation) — Description and travel. 3. Agriculture —
Russia (Federation) I. Title
HN530.2A8K725 1996
914.704 — dc20 95-50609 CIP

Printed in the United States of America

Book design by Robert Overholtzer
Maps by Leslie Evans

MP 10 9 8 7 6 5 4 3 2 1

For my wife, SUSAN EATON,
who is strong on content and style,
and for our young WILL,
who revised everything

———————

The Czar himself is powerless against the bureaucratic body: he can send any one of them to Siberia, but he cannot govern without them . . .

JOHN STUART MILL, *On Liberty*, 1859

CONTENTS

PREFACE

I'VE BEEN FASCINATED for decades with how the ancient trade of farmer fits into high-tech society. I worked on farms in my twenties and started writing about farming in my thirties. At the height of *perestroika* in 1988, I went to the Soviet Union for the *New York Times Magazine* and wrote about why a nation whose farms stretched from Norway to Korea across eleven time zones suffered nearly empty food shops. Farming there had gotten so badly broken that city dwellers often had no choice but to grow much of their own food on private plots, as they still do. The spectacle of an empire that could loft astronauts or blow up the planet but couldn't supply its bakers was troubling and puzzling.

So I began this book in 1989, studying a bit of Russian, but sure I'd be done writing long before gaining skill sufficient to free me from interpreters. I finished a draft in August 1991, which was the month seven plotters attempted a coup, precipitating the end of the Soviet Union and the collapse of the Communist Party — and the scrapping of my manuscript. I waited a year. The dust settled some, and I went back.

The extensive field notes of all of my outings — in every year from 1987 to 1993 — contributed to this chronicle of wanderings in the Soviet and post-Soviet outback. The intriguing details of farmers' work reveal much about the substance of any government. In the case of the Soviet Union, a vastness of bureaucrats enforced collectivization and obligatory crop deliveries, in the name of egalitarianism, upon a demoralized peasantry it had decimated and made landless. Daily life on the farm and contrasts between Soviet and Western farm conditions showed up the intricate connections between selfhood and statehood.

The reformulated *Travels with a Hungry Bear* begins in the Belgorod region in 1990, a time and place where *perestroika's* best results were on display. Then the book goes back to 1987 and proceeds chronologically to 1992.

On all my trips, I worked closely with interpreters. I found such reporting challenging every day because I couldn't casually comprehend side conversations or glance at documents, and even direct conversation took patience, cooperation, and a skilled third party. I thought at first that it might be like doing fine cabinetwork using only tools with ten-foot-long handles. But I found I could get the job done. The obstacle made it tougher, and changed the work; some choices closed off, but many opened.

I eventually gathered a stack of trip diaries full of translated quotations. I could have reproduced the fragmented, broken English of some of my interpreters, as transcribed directly onto the laptop computer I'd toted from Lithuania to Siberia. Instead, following the convention of foreign correspondents, I've rendered fractured sentences as "translation transparent." Neither method, of course, can convey raw utterance to readers as direct quotation does when translation isn't needed. Unsnarling translators' sentences no doubt occasionally shaded meanings. But I had several ways of mitigating that difficulty. In the field, I discussed matters doggedly when I needed to, until misunderstanding yielded to repeated explanation. I also gave the three principal translators (all are characters in the narrative: Pavel P. Sorokin, "the other Mark," and Sergei Sossinsky) draft copies of the parts of my travels each shared in, then puzzled out remaining confusions. I discussed ambiguities with Soviet experts. And finally, on return visits I cleared up points with many of the characters themselves. In the end, I'm satisfied that this process of translation did not cause much more distortion than inevitably bends the authenticity of translation-free journalism.

A note on the transliteration of Russian words: I've followed the Library of Congress method for the most part, but have changed some spellings in favor of variants likely to be more familiar or less intrusive when encountered by American or British readers outside the discipline of Soviet studies.

PART I

BELGOROD

1990

SCALE OF MILES

0   200   400

Moscow●

•Belgorod

BLACK SEA

CASPIAN SEA

1

LET US TRUDGE down a well-worn garden path toward a lavish rose patch planted in the middle of a Russian town. Fat flowers — red, white, yellow and pink, gaudy as cupcakes — wavered in file behind the burly shoulders of the delegation marching forward to greet us in the dooryard of the Belgorod Sausage Factory. The factory director, Andrei Mikhailovich Kozulin, held out a ham-sized hand. He had an expression on his broad face at once sincere and official. Nodding in agreement with himself about some unsaid point, he gripped my fingers in a long handshake. He seemed to consider me fragile. He guided me, even though I stood in place. He held on to my elbow to prevent toppling and shouted in my right ear as if it barely worked, "Please note that we have one thousand five hundred rose plants here in the yard in front of the cutting floor." In a sorrowful stage whisper, he added, "Regretfully, the production site is closed today. It is impossible to view it. But you will sample our excellent product."

He meant, I realized with dread, that we'd have lunch. Kozulin was hollering further regrets when a side door of the closed plant flew open, displaying, for a moment, a fluorescent-lit room full of busy workers. Three disheveled butchers in bloody shopcoats stepped out of the door for a smoke in the rose garden. A knife in a tattered scabbard flapped from the belt of the tallest, wiriest fellow. They squinted across the garden at our executive presence, and, cigarette packs still in hand, hustled back inside. Official assertion was, in this case, at odds with fact: the production site surely was not closed today.

Even on opening day, Russian factories often must have appeared Dickensian. The sausage factory was a long shed that had sprawled across the lot in stages, first through a brick era and then a galvanized-metal era. I inhaled the rich summer afternoon, the hot, humid perfume of roses, and of disinfectant, offal, acrid singed hair and rusty blood. No one acknowledged the uttering of an obvious lie. A fly buzzed past my nose.

"You smell only flowers. You do not smell meat because we have neutralizer, catalyzers. We have no flies. We have chemical spray with chlorofers," the director, Kozulin, said, nodding concurrence with his points as he issued them. He shot his cuffs, folded his hands across his belly, and smiled, a patient teacher observing as his wisdom filtered into his student's mind.

A large billboard loomed above the factory wall behind him:

> **OUR HEARTS, OUR LABOR,**
> **FOR YOU OUR DEAR PARTY**

It was summer, 1990, and the hopefulness of *perestroika* had faded elsewhere in Russia. Belgorod remained a special case. Around Moscow, such billboards were being taken down, and smaller, portable versions were already entering the black market as antiques. However, three hundred miles to the south in Belgorod, near the Ukrainian border, the paint had been freshly renewed, perhaps by the grounds crew that also weeded the roses. Its message still fit this place, although it no longer fit all workplaces in Russia. Five years of *perestroika* had made citizens' lives harder, not simpler.

I looked around uneasily, experimentally nodding to myself (the gesture is as contagious as winking). I probably shifted from foot to foot. My host waited expectantly for me to join his stroll toward lunch. His pressure on my arm increased. I figured protest was futile, but I had to try. His Party bosses had set up the visit. I was not about to be stonewalled without a tussle. Pointing toward the big billboard, I made a sensible proposal: "Those butchers we just saw — why don't we go peek at them doing their labor? I know they're in there." Kozulin's reluctance was familiar to foreign correspondents. Over the decades, visiting writers often had been presented Soviet show farms and show factories, rarely normal farms and factories.

I recalled a Brezhnev-era joke and weighed telling it as we stood there — I was looking for a way to imply that I knew the game and could laugh about it:

A train has stalled in the Russian countryside. Lenin clambers down from his car and shouts, "The passengers will shoot the engineer and take over the train!" They do so, but in spite of this, the train stays stalled. Then Stalin gets out and gives his guards orders: "Shoot every third passenger and the rest will stop slacking off." They do so, but the train stays stalled. Finally Brezhnev descends and says, "Close the curtains on the train windows, and everyone pretend the train is running."

Andrei Mikhailovich Kozulin of the Belgorod sausage factory was simply practicing Brezhnev-era public relations, I realized. I thought better of reciting a joke that showed him up. He was just doing his job, and seemed, from the little I'd glimpsed, to be doing it well. And while officials at his level had started openly blaming Stalin for perverting the wholesomeness of socialism, they still spoke ambivalently about Brezhnev — agreeing he'd allowed economic "stagnation," but recalling that before *perestroika*, food shops had been better stocked. And Lenin still lay in his mausoleum before the Kremlin wall. Standing by the rose garden, I felt famished. Kozulin's face stayed blank. "I'll be heading back to the hotel," I said, and turned toward the car.

"But," Kozulin said, leaning right into my elbow, pushing me a few steps toward the dining hall, "we have prepared the special lunch." He glanced imploringly at Igor, my translator, a scholarly graduate student in economics from Moscow. The officials behind Kozulin looked concerned.

"Let's glance into the factory for just a few minutes before lunch," I said, as though it were a brand-new idea. And maybe it was. This really was a time of increased *glasnost* (openness), even if *perestroika* (restructuring) was proving more troublesome. And to my surprise Kozulin relented, with a quick, extra-resolute nod. Would I excuse him — he hadn't realized his guest's interest. He had upset past foreign guests by taking them into the unpleasant interior of an animal factory, although this was a well-run facility. Would I step this way, please, right past the roses?

We went in, not through the side door from which the butchers had disappeared, but properly, through the front door. We walked down corridors past many offices, and at last into a large cement-floored room. Cow carcasses, quarters, flanks, shanks, combs of ribs, mounds of steak, slabs of fat — meat, meat, meat — were piled on worktables all across the factory floor. Igor grinned and shook his head in wonder. As we stood in the corner of the room he whispered to me that he hadn't beheld a big, honest-to-goodness roast in a long time. It was a festive, overwhelming sight for him.

I'd visited a modern American meat-packing house, shiny, ceramic, chilly and spotless, full of power saws and forklifts, where workers had dressed like nurses and carnage was a distant afterthought. The production line at the sausage factory was gruesome territory. Were workers of the world to unite anywhere, this would be a likely place. The butchers spent their days amid the stench of slit guts, damp with blood and slimy with fat. Few machines eased the labor; perhaps that's what Kozulin hadn't wanted me to see. Crews worked with knives and cleavers and handsaws. Grease waxed the cement floors. Blood splattered the brick and tin walls. Carcasses rode an overhead trolley on long hairpin curves past the stainless-steel and tile cutting tables. Workers wearing white hats surrounded each table. They'd created a kind of house style, slinging their white coats loosely over street clothing in token conformity to hygiene regulations. At each workstation, a cow was disappearing, lopped away in hunks. Cutters flashed knives and smiled shyly, whispering together. We strolled past, and several eyed Kozulin furtively.

Here, at the beginning of a dark corridor between workrooms, a tiny, quick old lady with a flensing knife, whose job was to stand on a crate and split shoulders off the huge carcasses, set a headless half cow swaying down the rail. I'd turned away to write a few words in my notebook, and the carcass batted me on down the hall. I caught my balance and looked back at her. She met my gaze. Behind her, workers watched. Those farthest laughed. Open-mouthed smiles animated a few of the sullen, sweating, dark-browed faces.

I felt embarrassed and annoyed, but I also felt that perverse gladness journalists experience when an official chaperone's scripted event collapses and the real world shows itself. The workers weren't afraid to boff Kozulin's American guest. This was something new and free. The boss scurried up and slapped at me a few times, brushing off scraps of fat. He escorted me on along the corridor.

In the next workroom more teams of cutters broke down the meat slabs. At a stainless table thirty men and women rubbed elbows, their knives flicking amid haunches, in the ghostly gleam of greenish fluorescent bars. They trimmed the fat off steaks and stew beef, and filled twenty-five-kilo plastic sacks.

Igor and I looked at the abundance of good meat. Here was the place that separated out meat of a quality that state stores back in Moscow had rarely sold in recent years, a sort distributed, in these supposedly reformed times, office by office to officials and enterprise managers, to the new *nomenklatura* — which was most often the same as the old *nomenklatura*. Igor studied the bags. Red stew chunks, America-lean steaks. This ever-growing stack of sacks of fine meat was the muscle of privilege itself. It represented control and compensation as precisely as cigarettes did in a jailhouse economy. This was worth not showing an outsider, although that was probably not what had been on Kozulin's mind. It was the distinction, made manifest in flesh, between lumpen and patrician.

Workers wheeled trolleyloads of the meat sacks off to a freezer. We walked on down the production line. Finally I recognized the sort of meat for which citizens were lining up in front of state shops; women heaved fat, with little tatters of muscle remaining, into bins. They spilled the bins' contents into grinders — lungs, noses, hearts, aortas tumbled in with the fatty slabs. Men tugged carts of sausage in and out of big ovens. The tile floor was full of holes and slick with fat. The smell here was savory.

"The recipes for our sausage come from the All-Union Research Institute of the Ministry of Meat and Dairy Industry. They give us all recipes," the director's voice sang. Was there a tone of wonder to it, suggesting his enjoyment of being part of something strong, uniform, greater than even this wealth of carrion before us? "The same recipe is used all over the country!" Igor said. "Everywhere different sausages used to be made from local recipes."

"We are near production sites of sixty thousand pigs," Kozulin said. Meat grinders full of pig parts groaned behind him. "Production costs: 145 rubles a metric ton. We are near farms where thousands of bulls are fattened for three years. Production costs: 500 rubles a ton. This proves our big, specialized farms are more productive. Meat complexes are clean and organized, with good life for the workers — no one standing around leaning on his pitchfork, all operations mechanized."

This sounded Brezhnev-era. Kozulin was still sheltered enough from news of the fast world beyond the USSR to boastfully raise the subject of productivity. If I'd coached his debating team, I'd have advised him to tiptoe past that subject. Soviet collective farms had built Western-style hog barns during the 1980s, but for want of good breeding stock, medicines, improved feed and application of nutritional know-how, Soviet piglets took three hundred days to get as fat as American pigs did in one hundred fifty. Soviet pig barns were half as productive, and they used five times the labor in getting that half. I asked if the *zakaz* — the state central planners' mandatory quota for farm-by-farm and factory-by-factory production — still applied in Belgorod. It did. "We must provide twelve thousand tons of meat, three thousand tons of sausage, and five thousand blocks of meat without bone. We must send a thousand tons of fat to Fidel in Cuba every year." Does the factory produce more than this quota? "Yes." How much more? "It's difficult to say."

The grand design of a national Five Year Plan remained, and the factory was still a small part of it. Igor, my translator, quietly suggested that the place probably had a large "informal commercial life" besides — one that helped explain its position in the system and the advantage of keeping a job in spite of the grimness of the place. It was likely that some portion of the factory's production headed out the back door into the growing de facto marketplace. Igor said such factories typically diverted meat to hard-currency trades, to barter exchanges, and to semiofficial deals with other factories. Bosses and workers themselves privately must have found ways to market some, too.

This shadow economy persisted through the last days of *perestroika* and then burst into the market free-for-all that followed. The gray market had helped the nation get by with its creaky system. It was a common channel both of supply and compensation, one that must have paradoxically given workers and managers alike reason to shy away from change. The butcher trading a steak for a motorcycle part and the plant manager trading a carload of steak for *dacha* building materials both always had a few private transactions in the works which change would disrupt. The Belgorod Sausage Factory launched a disciplined flow of meat that yielded political control as well as sausage. Andrei Mikhailovich Kozulin was an influential local personage, and his meat cutters must have felt fortunate to have jobs there.

"A good cutter will earn 180 rubles a month," Kozulin shouted over the grinders — a low wage about equal to what a Moscow secretary made, but hardly a cutter's entire reward for working there. "We also provide lunch for our 526 workers for only 25 kopeks." That was a meaningful advantage for them in a time of scarce meat and rising prices, but still not the whole story. "And," the director went on as he turned me by the elbow and finally headed me toward our lunch, "workers have access to a special meat market. What they do with their purchases is their own business." That was the rest of the story. They could buy cheap and sell dear.

It was midafternoon. We strolled back past the cutting tables, out the corridor past the offices, back up the garden path by the roses and the billboard into a bare cement dining hall. A squad of old women peered out at us through the serving window, awaiting this moment. Kozulin sat down at the head of the one set table. His deputies clustered around him. He poured a first toast — the one to international friendship. The women carried out lunch. The deputies smiled like cherubs.

Meat. Meat was lunch.

Neither potatoes nor cukes nor even scallions disturbed the purity of the offering. This was a meat place. This was brash, *ap-*

paratchik opulence. Here was red sausage and here purple sausage, here sausage with big blebs of fat and sausage with fine blebs, and to round out the menu a platter of *shashlik*-style grilled steaks. Slivers of cured ham. Slabs of half-raw bacon with cloves of raw garlic. In a meat-starved time, we fed in the Temple of Meat. I'd had little in the month I'd been in the USSR. Igor had tasted little in a year. I recalled the tale of Lady Astor at the Connaught, instructing the waiter, "Bring me whatever's out of season," but I didn't tell that one either.

The vodka bottle and cognac bottle competed for the honor of standing empty first. Cognac won. The cherubs repeated the contest. Vodka won. The half-dozen officials, each the shape of a fireplug, honored the visitor by offering and executing further elaborate toasts to my nation, mother, work, and finally to my hound — we were getting friendly by then. The assistant director gnawed at a beef chop. He held it like a lollipop and told a joke about religion — before *perestroika*, religion would have been unmentionable around a foreign journalist. Igor provided a slurred but nearly simultaneous translation:

"The archbishop wrote an angry letter. 'Dear Pope, this local bishop of ours is a drunk. He drinks almost everything.' The cardinal was sent for a visit, to check if the letter was correct. The bishop laid out only food and fruit juice for the cardinal's meal. After a time the cardinal had to ask, 'So, Father, will we not have a drink?' So they had one, and the cardinal had to keep saying, 'Let's have one more.' They drank to the archbishop who had sent the letter to the pope. They drank to Our Heavenly Father. Then they drank a third, and a fourth, to various saints, and the cardinal says . . ."

My translator trailed off, perhaps chagrined at obscenities that followed. Humor is the culminating intercultural mystery. I enjoyed not getting the joke, but just watching the cherubs guffaw. Kozulin, glass raised toward me in that arrested gesture of after-dinner oration, commenced the next joke, and, glass aloft, I listened:

"I was on a farm once, drinking at a good meal, and an ancient creature, an old man, stands and says, 'Drink for a woman without a man. She is like a fish without water.' So a fat woman stands, glares at him and answers, 'I have lived all my life without a man.' My host stands too, and apologizes to me, saying, 'Sorry, Director. I was going to drink for a *wet* fish, not a *dry* fish.'"

Our table of meat men, now slumped onto their elbows and far off duty, grinned and belly-laughed in unison. This one I got. The bottles emptied. Everyone felt well disposed, at least toward fellow drinkers. The director smiled a silly smile as his gaze settled on the spectacle of his woozy pals. "A Russian man is a Russian man," he mumbled philosophically.

Eventually we toddled, squinting, into the sunshine. In an outburst of drunken hospitality, the director stuffed my satchel with yard-long bars of fragrant sausage and blocks of ham — they would be treasures for friends in Moscow. I wafted back to the Belgorod Tourist Hotel and stored them under my bed. For the remaining days of my stay in town they perfumed the room.

♦

A high-level Party connector-upper and Gorbachev adviser on agricultural reform named Viktor Lishchenko had pointed me toward Belgorod. First educated as a veterinarian, then as an academic, he'd gone on to become chief agricultural economist at the Institute for the Study of the USA and Canada (established originally by the Communist Party Central Committee to probe the enemy's weakness). A few weeks earlier, in Moscow, Lishchenko had sounded downright excited: history was being made down there in Belgorod! I'd see firsthand that a strong and enlightened regional administration could do well with Russian workers and a socialist dream. Belgorod was a special place, a sort of laboratory for Gorbachev's *perestroika*, which Lishchenko called "reform Communism." Certainly, his nation had experienced some economic problems. It was 1990, and the food lines in Moscow had been world news for a couple of years. Past leaders' policies had led to stagnation. But things were improving — long-distance supervision from Moscow of every last administrative detail had been relaxed. That fixed a big part of what had been wrong, so at last regions could run themselves efficiently. And the government was backing big capital investments, industrializing super-sized farms in Belgorod with new technology and tough, talented managers. Why attack the basis of socialism? This experiment in Belgorod was working out. Other regions were threatening to abandon the planned economy far too quickly, and they would slide toward nationalism and economic chaos. "You'll see!" he'd said.

Belgorod had a good leader, too, according to Lishchenko, "a commanding governor named A. F. Ponomarev. He makes things work. *Perestroika* increased his power — now he doesn't report to Moscow. He's a dictator! I don't like him, personally. He's a bully. He's too loud, crude, brutal to be a friend. But Moscow has bread lines and cigarette lines; Belgorod has bread and cigarettes just when you walk into the store. Ponomarev is rude — you have to be rude to be a businessman. I have worked with him on a model soy-milling project and a grain storage center. I saw he's a *boss*." Lishchenko described the old guard given a freer hand than ever. Ponomarev ran things Soviet-style — with two hats. He was first secretary of the Belgorod Oblast (Region) Communist Party Committee and also chairman of the Soviet Executive Committee — the "civil," non-Party half of the government. He was also on the Central Committee in Moscow. *"Belgorod is the best place we have right now, the best for agriculture in the Soviet Union,"* Lishchenko said. "You Americans have two hundred years of nice government, and that gives you a wonderful, flexible food system that responds to the needs of the people. In our conditions, we need a Belgorod, and a Ponomarev." I was interested to see if there was really a "best place." Lishchenko had insisted I go, arranged my trip, and found me a native guide.

Nikolai Sergeievich Kvitchenko was his name. He picked up Igor and me at the Belgorod Tourist Hotel the next morning. Kvitchenko gravely shook my hand, handed me his card, and pardoned his beat-up white Lada sedan. His official title, the card said, was Chief of Division of Scientific Provision, Oblast Agricultural Committee of Agroprom Soyuz. He'd recently been assembling a catalog of local technical resources that collective-farm* chairmen could call upon, he told me. In other words, he

---

*I use the term "collective farm" in this book to indicate both *kolhozy* and *sovkhozy*, collective and state farms, respectively. There surely were differences between them, in history and governance, but they did not much affect the everyday life of these communes by the period of my travels.

was a middle-level agri-bureaucrat familiar to the heads of the enterprises we'd visit, nonessential enough for high command to pack off for a week, but of sufficient consequence to censor officials as needed.

I was a tad woozy from the meat fest the previous afternoon, and for a confused moment I thought he was one of the sausage factory director's cherubs. My trip notebooks are full of descriptions of graying, barrel-chested men of middling height with bushy eyebrows, whose fleshy arms framed solid, portly bellies. Russian bureaucrats shared this physique, sculpted of potatoes, sausage, and vodka. But unlike most of them, Kvitchenko seemed, at the start of a tough schedule, cheery and gracious company. In the next few days the American journalist was destined to visit two meat farms, a chemical dealership, the Belgorod Dairy Combine, a tractor dealership, and a seed-corn plant. "They are expecting you," said Kvitchenko. Our agenda had been centrally planned at a meeting of Party officials, and was even approved by the mythic boss, Ponomarev himself.

A keeper such as Kvitchenko was necessary. *Perestroika* had not brought an end to Soviet restrictions on travel. Western tourists had to book through Intourist, get visas for each city visited, stay in designated hotels, and go on arranged tours. Business travelers were a bit freer, booked in by sponsoring Soviet enterprises responsible for each alien presence. The foreign press was closely watched, and travel still had to be cleared through a central office. I was officially a guest of the Writers' Union and Viktor Lishchenko's organization, the Institute for the Study of the USA and Canada, part of the Academy of Sciences. But even were there no restrictions on independent travel, it would have been difficult to tour the Soviet food system without a keeper. The nation was a dictatorship, not of the proletariat but of timid bureaucrats. I was far off the tourist track. Kvitchenko would more often authorize than encumber. In most places, I couldn't have booked a room, much less been received at a farm or factory (each a part of the large state bureaucracy), without the high Party approval he vouchsafed.

However, an oddity of the nation's piecemeal reform effort dampened any keeper's restrictive effort. All enterprises were ranked; there were records of everything — albeit politicized ones. Party officials invariably steered the Western journalist toward the best of every category. But the restructuring that leaders had imposed in their efforts to make an idealistic system function in the real world had lashed the worst to the best, that the one might be improved by the other. So the "best" Soviet enterprises were patched-together conglomerates, barely tautened by economic necessity, and were places from which I could steer toward affiliated worst places.

◆

"Meat farm first," Kvitchenko announced. We climbed into the little white car. He glanced at his watch as he drove, and chatted about his daughters and granddaughters, his sore-back theories, and his enthusiasm for new grain-mixing machinery he'd cataloged but which he wasn't sure anyone could really order. He seemed disposed to enjoy our few days' excursion. Half an hour later we stood by a feedlot, watching animals fetlock-deep in mud. This was the feedlot mentioned back at the sausage factory. It housed five thousand "bulls" (many of which were steers). The chairman, Alexei Ivanovich Amismov, was one of those people who signaled right away that nonsense was out of his line and made sure one stood accused of triviality the whole conversation long. The farm seemed appropriately named "Dzerzhinsky," after the stern "Golden Heart of the Revolution," founder of Lenin's secret police.

Amismov was master of ten villages, "four thousand one hundred citizens, including women and children." Standing before his small office building, he gestured as needed with darting finger, boxing a compass as he spoke. The farm's work was growing feed for the thousands of beef animals ("There!") and for three thousand dairy cows and calves ("There!"). The farm covered twenty thousand acres (his arms circled) — Soviet collective farms were gigantic compared to Western farms. This one had perhaps forty times the acreage of a large, efficient, Iowa family farm. The feedlot, except for the mud, was well set up. Three thousand cows were milked by machine (one hundred would make for a good-sized Western dairy farm) in tie-stall barns like those in Wisconsin, except for size — and results. These Russian cows averaged about eight thousand pounds of milk a year — half of average American production, but twenty-five percent above Soviet average and therefore a feat of management. The farm was modernizing, he said, by importing bulls from Sweden and Austria.

Amismov also ran a sewing shop that expanded from 30 workers in summer to 130 in winter ("Over there!"). Jealous ministries of Soviet industry and agriculture had, for the most part, prevented such sensible arrangements as a seasonal factory in a farm village. The sewing shop's presence was a sign that the chairman had unusual clout. To resist rival ministry bosses, he'd have needed protection high in government.

"I was born here," the chairman said. "My ancestors lived here. I studied here." Amismov had risen through the ranks — not of farmers but of Party bureaucrats: "I went to study agriculture at an institute specializing in economics, a Party school. I was Party secretary at a neighboring farm for ten years. I have been back for ten years. As a boy I was orchestra leader here, and the soccer coach. I still play in the farm orchestra. Last Sunday we held a music competition between streets of the villages."

His farm was governed in the traditional Soviet style: "There is still a Party secretary on this farm. That role hasn't changed. In the short term of *perestroika*, it's hard to reject the influence of the Party on staff selections. At the same time, the people now elect their leaders." Had he been elected? "Yes, certainly!" Was there an opposing candidate, then? a secret ballot? "No — no other candidate, because it's a hard job and not many people would take it. But I'm reelected every three years."

Wouldn't this smart man know that running unopposed made him less "the people's choice" than defeating an opponent would have? I didn't belabor the point. His seeming naiveté about political reform, in this penultimate year of *perestroika*, suggested that reform did not go far enough to threaten existing powers. I asked if he could fire useless workers — drunks, slackers, troublemakers; an enterprise that could not fire workers surely could not develop an efficient work force. Firing was still "very difficult" in this workers' paradise. "It's always hard to rid the farm of drunkards — they steal as much as they earn. We don't pay them bonuses. We publish their names in the farm newspaper to shame them. We provide wholesome activities that people like, in order to prevent drinking. Sports help a lot. We also have amateur costumed folk-music groups and four orchestras." The reform by "talented managers" that I had been sent to witness in the Belgorod area seemed, at the outset, to deviate little from Soviet business as usual.

Might private farmers, I asked, run farms better than bosses who couldn't fire drunkards? "I don't believe in it at all," Amismov said, "because I visited Finland, where the younger generation refuses to farm. Men on their own farms have trouble marrying. Young ladies don't like to go in there and milk cows. I visited private owners in Poland, and they had trouble. And we won't be able, anytime soon, to produce the mini-machines small farmers would need."

I said that an Iowa farmer with five hundred acres did often find time to marry, and worked not with mini-machines but with the same scale of 300-horsepower tractors that Soviet collective farmers favored. Amismov nodded, his face blank. End of discussion. He had serious business on his mind, and no need to consider this unlikely prospect for long.

We drove in his jeep to the far corners of the farm. It had been tamed more than most; he'd paved a road through it — unusual even in this developed part of rural Russia. We passed fields, some carelessly and many well planted. Amismov's vision of reform was in the mainstream of reform Communism: "We need help. We need technology. Implements. The equipment for a brick factory. The equipment for a new meat-packing plant. And my main problem these days, good instruments for the farm orchestras." Amismov laughed cheerfully with my guide, Kvitchenko — like two tubas tuning.

◆

Some of Belgorod's infrastructure (*infrastruktura* was a word relished by Soviet agri-bureaucrats) was on the day's itinerary. We headed out to view what Igor translated as "the chemical dealership." The name literally was "Belgorod Production Association Belgorod-Agriculture Chemistry Department." It was not a dealership in the sense of a place that sold a certain brand of product. It was a distribution center, and it was the only game in town. It received agricultural supplies, did some processing of chemicals, and sent materials on as ordained in the Five Year Plan.

The newish cement office building echoed and clacked with the sounds of a few workers scurrying about far off. It smelled of sour black tobacco, strong disinfectant, and mold. Even the endless corridors of power in the Kremlin itself had the same dismal odor. Behind the office building stretched a patchwork of factory buildings of tin and gray brick, a storage yard full of vats and tractors and sprayers, and a muddy field with some workers' cottages huddled in it.

The director of this "chemical dealership" fit the default description — he was a fireplug, bulky and balding, in his fifties. He had a serene mood about him, an air of irony and bemusement. He got people to open up by presenting himself almost as a co-conspirator, and was one of the few officials I had encountered who immediately and avidly asked for news of the world beyond his own. He wanted to know just how American factories like his worked. He pressed me right away with questions about brands and wholesale costs and bankers and who determined customers' needs. He really wanted to know.

We strolled along, talking about Iowa. In offices like this, which at first seemed to me so constrained by alien rules and exotic history, I often was surprised to see clerks and department heads laughing and gossiping in the hallways and secretaries clicking along in heels in the mundane fashion of office workers anywhere. But what organizations actually *did* in their office buildings often remained exotic to me. Even appropriately named enterprises had always grafted on dozens of unexpected sideline functions over the years, in this economy where administrative dominion was power, and profit and efficiency had almost no influence on how work was organized.

This was a large empire with many parts. Four thousand people worked at the "chemical dealership," distributing a million metric tons of farm chemicals a year, all the chemicals that all the farms in the state-sized region used. Peculiarly, the "dealership" also rebuilt so many thousands of engines of a certain type, and so many thousands of another certain type — the director had shops that disassembled and reconstructed engines. Another division built so many hundred farm buildings a year.

The director's legions did this much on-farm soil testing, that much soil-map making, and lime spreading, and scouting out and trucking in heavy equipment from elsewhere in the country, and making ecological impact investigations. They'd set up a production line to modify all the standard manure spreaders for the region, because Soviet manure spreaders "only parodied the real task." The director left me feeling that he tried to do things well and might indeed be talented at it.

He was enough of a honcho to speak critically in front of my keeper, Kvitchenko: "We make good spaceships but bad manure spreaders. We make tractor attachments ourselves — we can't get ones that work from the factories. We recommend less fertilizer than the Plan calls for, but still three times what American farms do. You apply liquids and pellets and coated granules, but we just have the chemical powders themselves. Our quality is worse than yours — sometimes half as much nutrient is available in ours. If we had more sophisticated equipment, our poor seeds and materials would give fifteen percent better yields. Then we lose half our fertilizer during storage or transport — we need buildings and better trucks. We have to store fertilizer outside, and rain soaks it."

Why doesn't he have better equipment? "Because we have monopolies — it's a condition of socialism. Our factories don't modernize or adopt new inventions even if they know about them. Our science is good, but the manager knows there's no competitor. Competition would make for cheaper and more careful service. In the new program, we're developing direct links — not through a ministry in Moscow, for the first time — with fertilizer factories. Nothing like that yet exists with equipment factories, though. We need several fertilizer producers in our system, and competition between them." This sounded new and wholesome to me. But I had a hard time imagining both central planning and competition between major agri-chemical manufacturers.

He didn't get competition between farms either. "We have competition. A fifty-thousand-hog farm where the cost of production is two hundred rubles a ton of animal competes with a five-thousand-hog farm where pigs cost two thousand rubles a ton — ten times as much. This is good competition. It's our future." I did not point out that the two farms both had guaranteed sales to the state, nor that there was no process for closing down the less efficient hog farm, which the government subsidized.

Kvitchenko kept nodding agreement, to my surprise. The director was a senior Party member; his irreverent views would not be blamed on Kvitchenko. The director hadn't criticized the Party or the ideology justifying its "leading role"; he'd recommended merely tinkering with organization. A final answer of his did surprise me, because it called into doubt the legitimacy of Belgorod as a model of reform Communism. I'd asked if his large enterprise was inconvenienced by the scarcities that, according to the newspapers, cramped manufacture everywhere.

"This whole region has no scarcity of anything," he replied. "We have priority in the factories. No other region has such priority. Leaders chose us because we have a pretty good infrastructure here, so we can carry out the experiment." I was amazed: the new system worked not because of good technology and "talented" management, but because national officials had declared Belgorod a pocket of plenty — a state-sized show farm. Its success was evidence only of the power of the system to enforce uneven distribution of scarce resources.

His vision of further reform seemed confused. Enterprises, he said, should be able to order supplies, not just accept stipulations from planners in Moscow. Inputs should be offered competitively, "by several state enterprises." He said such changes "will not disarrange Soviet authority." They would not disrupt central planning.

Did he see a place for private land? *"Nyet."* Private factories? *"Nyet* — why do we need more big bosses and landlords?"* He fell back on slogans of an earlier era: "Belgorod is freeing science and engineering to work wonders for the people."

◆

Next on our itinerary was the spectacle of science and engineering working wonders at a large dairy processing plant, the Belgorod Dairy Combine. Its director (yes, robust and fiftyish), Nikolai Ivanovich Maslennikov (whose name meant "butterer"), ran an imposing factory that smelled of fresh milk. Maslennikov also sounded tough, frank, "talented," and in charge. Kvitchenko again sat quietly while Maslennikov said critical things, such as: "We have Indian machinery, East German, Yugoslavian, Czech machines — and they are the reliable ones. We are hungry for cream separators, pasteurizers — things that have been standard for half a century in factories elsewhere in the world. But our Soviet stuff is always lower quality than in the West. They break down. Why? The factories that produce them are monopolies. I don't feel any changes from *perestroika*."

He settled back into his office chair, enjoying himself. "Well, one change," he said. "You couldn't even have visited five years ago. Another: individual factories had no right to hold or spend hard currency. My boss is in Moscow, trying to get permission to export milk powder to Pakistan. We'd get eight hundred thousand dollars. Thirty percent would disappear as taxes, but we'd get the rest.

"There is more. Our media have opened my eyes now; the leaders of the Party — of which I've never been a member — have done a lot of wrong things during all these years . . ."

I wondered how he'd risen so far without Party membership. He'd found the edge of Kvitchenko's comfort. "Mark," Kvitchenko said, interrupting, "this man isn't competent to answer political questions. He's only a director."

The director got fired up at this. "The Party doesn't influence this enterprise anymore," he shouted. "Before, a director was very afraid of an *apparatchik* such as you. But now I rely on my conscience. Command methods are losing force because my fear is gone." It was a sharp exchange.

Kvitchenko glowered and said to me, "It's better to have such talks with politicians. It's hard to have them with managers who wake up at six A.M. and come home late. I've told this director not to stray from your questions." Maslennikov didn't return to his argument. He offered production numbers, plant-capacity numbers, construction costs, and goals.

We put on lab coats and hard hats and peered about the plant, which was larger — with eight hundred workers — and cleaner, and more modern, he said, than it used to be. The visit had gotten stiff and demoralized after the exchange between chairman and keeper. Kvitchenko hurried me away. I still had a white mustache from sampling sour cream and yogurt and the kefir, which I liked especially.

♦

Kvitchenko had a second meat farm on the itinerary, Collective Farm Rossiya, whose chairman was "famous," said Kvitchenko, "lauded nationally for proving good management can make collective farms run well." Farm Rossiya was established more than thirty years after most collective farms, in 1966, probably custom made — an amalgam of parts of nearby farms — for this then-young, impressive boss. It produced "about five thousand metric tons of meat a year." Chairman Alexei V. Gamaly came out spraying numbers before him, as a model chairman surely should. "We have represented a new philosophy," he said, "the specialized industrialized farm." The farm "bought" surplus dairy animals, dairy bull calves, and meat animals from neighboring farms, grew feed grain, and fattened them "using very good technology."

The farm was indeed a showplace among showplaces. It took a lot to rise to, and remain in, such a visible position. Gamaly was tough and competent. His farm was paved over and kempt. It looked downright American, except that instead of a handful, scores of laborers ran about — "eleven hundred in all," said Gamaly, "including fifty-two persons with university degrees." They hired three hundred more during harvests. "Office workers are seven percent of the staff. We have three bookkeepers in accounting and a commandant responsible for guest living facilities and housing assignments. We have a chief of division, an engineer, a comptroller in six additional divisions. We have reduced the management here by a third in the last few years."

Gamaly favored one management change that *did* add sense to the workplace. I was especially interested in it, because if reform Communism shifted authority for some decisions down to regional bosses, this one actually moved the authority — for some decisions — from these bosses down to the individuals doing the work. It seemed potentially substantive and dangerous to the system, although at the time it was rare. "We adopted

Gorbachev's new strategy — lease brigades. A small team of workers takes over a task that used to be done by more workers. The team minimizes the number of workers doing a job. We allow it, and keep paying the old total salary for the new, smaller team to share. This makes people want to cut the numbers of workers on their work teams, even though the farm spends just as much paying workers. More work gets done. In our feed-mixing shop, we cut down from fifteen to ten workers. They kept one hundred percent of the old salary. The teams are happy and work hard. This was decided by the board of the collective farm — eleven specialists are on it, and I'm leader and chairman. It's a socialist board."

"It's a socialist board" meant "we're not rocking the boat either." But here was a "model" boss, trying out an experiment in dealing with the problem of absurdly low productivity per worker by tying high pay and workplace autonomy to good performance. This obvious remedy had been heresy since the 1930s. Bosses had died in prison for suggesting it — and for a reason not hard to comprehend: their logic, carried out on an effective scale, would have unraveled the Communist system. But now Gorbachev himself (who had toyed with the idea back when he was Party boss in the Stavropol region) had recommended lease brigades in a speech. Having crews bid on jobs they'd then manage themselves was a clumsy first try at getting the right number of the right workers to the right jobs at a motivating pay level. This was a goal Western business achieved with not one but a hundred methods, steps, plans, and programs, automatically, with no need for backing from national leaders. But in theory, it was a potent remedy. Gamaly said the lease-brigade workers' pay in the feed-mixing shop had doubled. Still, he had allowed just one tiny lease brigade, ten of eleven hundred workers. It was not a concept that could expand to an entire Soviet collective farm, or even a large portion of one — where would the dismissed workers go? It depended on unequal pay — a riveting heresy in the psychology of a collective-farm community. And it denied the need for the supervisory structure that towered over each worker, stretching clear up to the Kremlin.

Gamaly was as "talented" in managing the rest of the farm, too: he claimed crop yields of twice the national average — four tons of grain and eleven tons of sugar beets to the acre. His cows' annual yield averaged ten thousand pounds of milk — two thirds the West's average but nearly double the Soviet average. His political clout must have helped win these results. He'd had the influence to gather construction supplies and good technology and erect modern buildings. He said he'd received superior foreign breeding stock and the best imported equipment. Every region ran a farm or two like this. The evidence favored Kvitchenko's reform-Communist theme: good technology and "talented" management made collective farms work. The collective-farm system itself was fine; it just needed cash. "The problem is technical," Gamaly said. "We need good money to buy good supplies. If we were provided good herbicides and machines and chemicals and seeds and livestock, our efficiency would soar. We could produce milk and meat and build a processing factory that would give us high profits."

I asked Gamaly about the Party's role on his farm. "It's decreased. Just three years ago, an 'instructor' — a low-ranked Party officer — came here and ordered me around, and local soviet deputies and Party administrators came and ordered me around, even though I knew better than they did. They had to show who was important. Prosperous farms such as this are managed by people with the strength to resist Party orders. I didn't come from their circles. A real leader must resist the Party *apparatchiks*, ministries, special bosses. Every one of them wants to visit the farm and show me he is a real boss." Gamaly portrayed himself as independent and unwired, but he did not stand so far from such bosses that he could manage rationally. He also could not, for example, fire even a single worker — "unless there was bad behavior. Then, I still have to settle with union bosses."

The new technocrats used terminological contortions to invest their reform moves with Leninist magic: "What is leasing but a socialist association of entrepreneurs?" he asked. He looked at me as though he'd led me to high ground. He dreamed about being able "to deal with the West." He couldn't do that either, yet. Mundane but exotic dreams — of proper supplies, eager workers, an ample bank account of hard currency — poured from his mouth: "I've had an idea! We have some unused fields. I think a private foreign business could come here and till it. We could process their meat. A Danish specialist told us it was hard to invest here, because the laws changed every day. But McDonald's has done it."

The frustrating present seemed to Gamaly just a few bureaucratic obstacles away from a bright future: "The problem is, the ministry in charge of processing would grab at the profits. Right now if we did our own meat processing, we could make eight million rubles profit. But the sausage factory you visited takes it instead. If we could do it, and shift production entirely to lease brigades, and allow salary to depend on results, we could make a big profit." He came down to earth. "Instead, we can't find the material or equipment for even a small factory of our own. With *perestroika*, we have the right to build one, but we still can't do it."

We strolled through what to my eyes was a jury-rigged but sizable feed-mixing facility. He shrugged and said, "No money." Had he thought about *why* rubles were soft, and *why* factories turned out manure spreaders that wouldn't spread manure, and *why* the laws under which foreigners might invest shifted unreliably? Kvitchenko looked alert to our dialogue for the first time. Gamaly smiled and said he was too busy with practical crises to have thought much about those "theoretical" questions.

His tone became friendly and confidential. I got the impression he was teasing Kvitchenko by continuing the line of discussion: "It's a shame that in our country, so rich in resources, we are poor because fools got into power, organized monopolies of the Party everywhere, and accept no criticism, no competition between ideas. I was in Denmark, so I know what is possible. We shouldn't be a nation unable to improve citizens' lives — our strange system of political monopolization stops good things from developing. Gorbachev doesn't understand everything." Kvitchenko cleared his throat and suggested continuing our tour.

Gamaly hardly wanted to take Russia private. He just wanted better supplies and regulations that would allow him to run his farm well. "I scorn people with no farm knowledge who come here and say collective farms should split into private farms.

Let's have all sorts of farms, but only farms without exploitation."

That standard phrase was the catch of liberal-sounding reform Communists. "Without exploitation" meant "without any owner profiting from any worker's labor." In other words, without private ownership or without autonomous management — without much change. I told him I thought reform ideas that didn't permit an owner to hire labor amounted to no real change. No, he said, he had seen Danish family farms, operated entirely by "owners," and they were, in his book, without exploitation. He was not dangerously Western, but he was heading west.

Just when I was getting wrong ideas about him, he complicated my estimate of how far west he'd traveled. "We had a leaseholder who failed. Why? Over the past sixty years, we've lost the sense of what an owner is. Our peasants are hardworking enough, responsible enough, but they are people who count working hours. We don't know how to aim where we need to go. Sure, if you had the right man, let him take as much land as he needs, he'd impress you, a Russian Man. But here we have eleven hundred workers, and not one of them *wants* to be an individual farmer. People know no other life. They don't have an individual psychology. The Russian Man would be afraid of so much personal responsibility. He doesn't know how to manage money. He's not sure what will happen to the country in five years. He knows if he sticks to the collective farm, he won't be hungry, and he'll have friends, fields — all the things he's used to. Workers get a lot here on this farm — twenty-six thousand rubles a year, free meals, free school, maternity leave of two years, nursery care after that. We take care of our pensioners in old age. No one wants to leave here."

It made sense, although he sounded a little like a kindly plantation owner in the American antebellum South. I told him that an Iowa farm town with eleven hundred workers in it is not a place with eleven hundred farmers. Perhaps ten residents have the right "individual psychology," and do not fear "so much personal responsibility," and run enterprises themselves. Other workers would be on wages — on factory lines, teaching, waitressing, policing, bartending, bar sweeping, working in fields as hands — and they'd be mostly people who lacked the "culture" to run a modern farm. Gamaly didn't contemplate this news of Iowa any more than he had the nature of family farms in Denmark. I wanted him to see that a very few talented local people — perhaps no more than were on his own executive staff — could farm his place privately. His argument about the defective "mentality" of Russian workers sounded heartfelt.

"Our workers are content here. But can we make our worker use his initiative? It hasn't happened, frankly. We still have Plan quotas — the *zakaz*. So someone just couldn't go and sell crops or meats anywhere." He was thinking about the mentality of workers in the context of the current Soviet system. I couldn't argue with that. "The *zakaz* ties up everything. I need metal pipe for irrigation and gasification of my villages. I've tried with the authorities for years but got only one carload. For it, I had to send back one carload of sugar. My work routine consists of handling such frustrations. We're putting up a school for three hundred children. At seven every morning, I go to a five-minute meeting at the construction site to resolve urgent problems. When I come back there are ten people waiting — not our residents but outsiders asking to join, because here we have enough of everything.

"Then I hunt for supplies, using my influence. Today I spoke to Kursk, Voronezh, Moscow. I need glass, marble, construction materials, sewage system materials. I confer with my agronomist, my bookkeeper. I delegate lots of power, so I have to spend much of the day convincing my managers to accept that power. I want them to be good assistants to the workers, not good bosses.

"As I talk to you," Gamaly said, "I wish I'd seen your world. We'd need billions of rubles to make individual farming work here, billions. I'm sixty years old. I have my job still because I have courage — I stay on to ensure that my point of view prevails: if the forces of the other side introduce family farms everywhere, absolute catastrophe will hit this country. Private farming should happen very, very gradually. The American farmer is a man of high culture; ours is still a peasant and most know little about soil and animals. The difference between our countries is the difference between earth and sky."

He was going on down his own track. "I'm an old man. Maybe we need *perestroika*, but not this *perestroika* with empty shelves and people scared of their futures and out for the blood of other nationalities. A man can be naked and hungry, but he can live well if he has a strong aim. I'm a Communist and a strong supporter of our Party. Yes, it was a mistake that we took command of everything, but things are getting more sensible. I don't receive commands about everything here from the Party anymore. And if I make a mistake I can admit it, because it no longer means that the Party made a mistake. We still have mostly Communists in the boss jobs on this farm, but every one of them is a pure, honest man, clean like a crystal, and when the people perceive that you work *for* them, and don't do bad things, they will be for you. That is not how the *nomenklatura* are perceived now, and that is our tragedy. How can some of those corrupt officials even sit next to our local Party bosses, who are such frank men?" Kvitchenko smiled as he led me away from this sincerity, heading ever deeper into the dream of reform Communism. Gamaly had reached an essential point that seemed right to me, too. Maybe saintly bosses could plan a just world for unselfish workers. I wondered if the Plan included a spare lantern.

◆

Several Belgorod officials picked us up early in the morning in a battered orange van owned by the regional office of Gosagro-prom, the national super-Ministry of Agriculture. We would go see the seed-corn plant. We passed a lime quarry and a cement plant on the edge of Belgorod. These industrial sites sent a foggy cowl of dust aloft. It bisected the sky at an absolute margin — half the heavens were sunny, half yellowed and dark. We drove in under the dust cloud. "Could our host drive closer to the factory over there for a moment?" I asked.

He couldn't. "It is military. On my own, I am the most honest and open man in this town," the chubbiest and apparently seniormost official said, putting his hand over my camera. Like the head of the sausage factory, who had claimed that his open plant was closed, this man said "It is not a residential area" at precisely the moment we drove by peasants' dusty cottages. We both saw residents, tots running around outside and an old man hoeing his garden. The ground was gray from limestone dust, and the old man's hoe scratched streaks of brown into it. His grandchildren stood behind a fence, heads pivoting to study our passing van. Behind them, a babushka swept her walkway, raising her own small dust cloud. I wondered this about the senior-most official in the van: was he on automatic, or did he feel it was slick or perhaps menacing to assert what was so obviously untrue? Did he intend to embarrass me by doing so and receiving no protest? Was he mouthing an obligatory claim that humiliated him? His expression gave no clue. He looked as somber as an undertaker's helper. He was someone in the profession of shouldering bad news.

Two gentlemen in the back seat were engineers, one with the Division for Technical Service of Animal Breeding Equipment and the other with the Station for Technical Service of High-Powered Tractors. Had they, I asked, seen meaningful advances under Gorbachev in the colossal task of updating Soviet agricultural manufacturing — which, from what I had seen, was often still mired in the 1930s? "According to our newspapers, future manufacturing will happen with computers and robots. Progress will help us solve our problems," one said.

I rephrased my question, and the other gentleman actually answered it: "I've worked here eight years. Little has changed. On TV, Gorbachev said workers now should feel like owners. But they don't. I spend my day as a guard of my own team of workers. I work from seven in the morning to seven at night. In the last year and a half, I never asked anyone for spare parts or materials. There are none. We find what we can by ourselves. We are preparing for the open market. Our new agreement with farms is that we'll fix a broken machine within twenty days."

I imagined telling some Iowa farmers I knew — who demand ambulance-speed service when their combines break, lest they suffer tens of thousands of dollars' worth of losses per day during the short time a crop is ripe — that a repair service in Belgorod, Russia, where the ground was gray from pollution, proudly said it would have broken combines up and running in just three weeks. I imagined trying to explain that this was a great achievement, that it pushed against the heavy weight of the system at a time when no Russian could even be sure of the real value of a hundred-ruble note, or a bushel of wheat, or an hour of working time. I imagined the Iowa farmers shaking their heads in wonder.

◆

The van full of officials stopped at a "tractor dealership." This place looked odd as soon as we pulled in, simply because in this nation of ceaseless disorder, it was orderly. Downright prim. We lined up and viewed the fifty new tractors, and the row of potato harvesters, the lines of new combine heads, and sugar-beet cultivators hitched to crawlers. The factory supervisor proudly showed us an assembly line that rebuilt fifteen hundred tractor engines a year, and took us into a warehouse where he'd racked up needed replacement parts — a rarity in most of Russia — for Don combines, then to a shop that conflated hulks of Niva combines into working machines, and finally to a shop that rebuilt pumps. "I'd like to go to America and visit a farm equipment show," said the supervisor. On his pump-shop wall hung an exhortation, in the sans-serif lettering of Party slogans. It offered sound advice:

REMEMBER SMALL DETAILS

Our keeper, Kvitchenko, nodded his agreement, shook his finger, and exclaimed, "Money — that's what counts!" That was once a heretical "Western" idea. As he relaxed, I liked him more and more. He laughed at his naughty thought.

◆

In fact, a piece of Iowa had already come to Belgorod. Viktor Lishchenko, the agricultural guru in Moscow who'd suggested my visit to the area, had, "because of Ponomarev," seen the region as the right place to situate a key showpiece of agri-modernization: a ten-million-dollar corn-seed sorting and storage plant. Corn seed, in high-speed Iowa agriculture, gets planted by laser-guided "air blow" planters, spidery machines that unfold and straddle sixteen or twenty crop rows at a time, spitting precisely spaced seed to a precise depth (and having it land root-end down) while moving along at ten miles an hour. The machine paints a field with seed. Alarms go off if it skips a row.

This level of planting speed and efficiency allows farmers to get crops on large acreage during short breaks in the spring weather, at just the right time. But the effort would be wasted were it unmatched by corn seed of uniform size and dependable quality. If even ten percent of seeds failed to sprout or grew up mangy, the tonnages of crop lost, and of pricey herbicide and fertilizer squandered, would be unacceptable. If the demonstration seed-corn plant succeeded and scores like it followed, Russians might get better yields from their nearly ocean-to-ocean swath of grain fields, and import less.

So Lishchenko, who knew several major Iowa farmers during his years as a Russian agricultural attaché in Washington, talked with the big boss Ponomarev and set Belgorod to building this plant. It would accept only hybrid corn grown just for seed on special "elite" farms, dry it to the right moisture content, store it protected from frost and rot through the penetrating winter (much Russian corn seed freezes). Come spring, it would deliver the right lot quickly to the right supply truck. After a year of haggling, the blueprints had finally arrived from Iowa — nearly complete. They showed acres of hoppers and conveyers and dryers and chutes and sluices, to be constructed under the supervision of an Iowa company owned by a man I'll call Block. An experienced engineer of specialized agricultural buildings at home, Block worked for a second year on building logistics. He'd loaded scores of cargo containers with a planned sequence of components and shipped them, along with a construction crew headed up by his son, "Chip," to the chosen site, on the grounds of a collective farm outside Belgorod.

Shipping containers of building materials had been lined up across a bare dirt field. In the bright sun, a few Russian laborers poked their shovels and picks at a trench. Stacks of steel and crates of bolts, pails of asphalt paint, boxes of spikes, showed at the open end of one container. Another had been made site headquarters. A drafting table stood inside the open end, and a big blond surfer in sunglasses, all amiable and full of smiles and a "Gee whiz" or two, an instantly likable man, leaned out and shook my hand. He was stubbornly, pronouncedly, surprisingly American. Not a hint of the ambiguous, apologetic body language travelers often take on while on alien soil — not a European whiff to him, not a gone-native haircut or shirt, just a smiling, hearty California presence. His surfboard might as well have been leaning against the drafting table.

Chip pored over page fifty-one of a fat book of plans, pointing with daps of a ballpoint pen. He looked as though he'd arrived straight from the set of *Conan the Barbarian*, six four, shirtless and broad, a bandanna tying back shoulder-length ash-blond hair. Nodding and tapping back with a blunt sausage-sized finger was an old construction supervisor, John Smith (or so he claimed), whom Central Casting must have shipped across from Hollywood with Conan — a wrinkled and silent gent in his fifties, with a feed-store hat and the knowing look and dignity of a town-taming Wild West movie sheriff. Smith had a face like the front of a locomotive, all square and steel and rust and a cow-catcher chin. They were discussing the placement of a pipe trench, finger-tapping at the blueprint and thumbing and chinning out toward the construction site.

The site looked Russian, not Iowan. It was a disorganized mess. The half-finished shell of one plant building rose far behind the field office. Work there had ceased. The steel was "still being fabricated" — the Russian inflection suggested completion of action in some distant moment. Meanwhile, Chip had moved on to the next step of construction. Nearby they were excavating two big cellar holes, although one had filled with muddy water and was collapsing. Rusty machinery lay about. A backhoe was partly unbolted from too small a tractor and looked like a fiddler crab. A large Kamaz dump truck slouched over with a front flat. Piles of scrap wood, metal, and cement block were strewn here and there on the torn ground. A battered steam shovel, with the boxy look of a 1920s design, stood by. A diesel engine swelled out of it, and a small internal-combustion engine — a "pony" — clung to one fender, its only purpose to kick over the big engine.

The Russian laborers left off digging and leaned on their shovels, lit up cigarettes, eyed the newcomers, and awaited word about their ditch. John Smith hustled out of the shed and shouted at the head laborer, as if volume might teach the fool English. A translator ran after them.

"That translator ain't much," said Smith, shaking his grizzled head. "He read books okay and passed tests, but after he got here, it came out that he never spoke a word of English 'til we come along. Well, he's working out great." Smith put his big hand on the slight translator's shoulder. "Tell 'em, Yuri," Smith yelled, "tell 'em there was a lil' misunderstandin' 'bout the ditch, and shove it out a little more, okay? Make it a meter point two deep, and have it start, oh, say here and run up to, oh, there."

The translator, amazingly, seemed to understand the vernacular and delivered these tidings. The workers smoked and discussed this turn of events for a while, nodded, and actually set to remeasuring, driving in a few wooden stakes along the far side of the ditch. Then they fussed with the steam shovel — cranking up the pony engine, coaxing the big engine as it wheezed and chuffed and quit and soon kicked in with a roar. The driver lurched the big rig astraddle the old ditch, and it clawed into rich black Russian earth.

Chip had brought in work crews — a Russian "union" crew of welders, another for the steam-shoveling, another of carpenters from Bulgaria. He complained about them: all were at odds. Some wouldn't even come to work. Corruption and meager infrastructure had slowed him as much as labor problems. Chip couldn't pour the "monolithic" slabs called for in the blueprints and specifications as necessary for the structural integrity of the plant: the concrete arrived in loads too small to fill the molds. Subsequent deliveries were never timely, or even certain, and often a half-poured slab had nearly dried before the next load arrived. The crew would pour more. Chip knew they'd gotten a weaker slab than they wanted, but he couldn't see any alternative. "Today are supposed to be seven loads of cement, and one went . . . well, somewhere we don't know, and only six came here. Couple of times I complained, but that got it even worse. Aside from the cement, there aren't enough threaded thirty-two-millimeter rods for double bolts. We're going to try thirty-millimeter rod."

They'd done better with metal than cement, met a man named Boris whom they considered a skilled metal-fabrication craftsman. Boris (said Chip) had worked his way up through the ranks and supervised an iron foundry across Belgorod. Chip called Boris a "can-do guy," and Boris turned part of his factory into a workshop that fabricated parts just for the seed-corn plant. The scheme was working — slowly — far behind what Block's contract called for, but at least they were moving ahead. And like the acceleration in combine-repair time, the seed-corn plant would move Belgorod further ahead of the rest of Russia — but still not up with the rest of the industrialized world.

All joint Russian-Western projects I'd encountered ran into such delays — often of half decades and decades. Delays put stress on shaky contracts and, in the absence of a rule of law, ignited personal disputes with local bosses. The flareups required measures to placate the proper officials, which kept things rolling — slowly. This seemed very close to the pre-*perestroika* style of Soviet business, except that now one of the players had hard currency, and placation was costlier. Block, said his son, was furious at all the holdups, while Ponomarev had apparently blamed Block for mismanagement. They'd had to "meet and iron things out."

The workers broke for lunch. Chip talked "ass" and slurped his soup. He was beaming. The lady in question was twenty and beautiful and lived in the village over there — thumb over the shoulder showed where — and she'd kissed him right in public as he was leaving the site the other day. What a blazing sun of a grin Chip flashed. Her husband didn't do anything — "He didn't know or he didn't care." Chip marveled at the imminence of her next arrival. She shows up in his room in the night, he said, and "teaches me Russian words. We joke a lot and fool around." He liked it when she said, "*Kak mekhanik*" — *kak* means "like" in Russian.

A few other good ol' boys from America worked on the crew too, mostly over at the foundry with Boris. They'd come in for lunch. To hear them talk, they were also meeting the young women of the village. We feasted — cold ham and chicken, *blini*, fried potatoes, and cakes; the surrounding collective farm was receiving hard-currency payments for feeding these galoots the best. I listened to that familiar boy talk in English on my left, and meanwhile carried on (between translations from Igor) a conversation to my right with the chairman of the collective farm on whose land the plant was being built.

He was short (and sturdy, and fiftyish) and utterly official. His name was "Dudnikov, Nikolai Semenovich" (he said it last name first, the bureaucratic way). He tumbled out those figures — 50,000 tons of sugar beets, 5,000 tons of meat, 7,000 tons of milk. And he said proudly that his farm would soon be the site of one of the largest seed plants in Russia. He charmed me with frank understatement: "Our collective farm could produce more goods than it now does." He simply had to remedy "a shortage of the machinery necessary for farming. Collective farms are the farms that can feed Russia — if and only if we turn our faces toward them." It was the reform Party line in compressed form — we do have the right organization; we lack the right equipment.

To my left, Chip was telling tales of his nocturnal activities; he lacked none of the right equipment. On my right, Dudnikov, Nikolai Semenovich's speech went on: "We think this factory for production of hybrid corn seeds is equipment necessary to our plan. Today we work together with Americans. We are reaching for the aim established by us . . ."

I asked — because he was old enough to have been there — about the famous and absurd order Khrushchev made in 1958 after visiting Iowa and catching sight of what Iowans call "wall-to-wall corn": Nikita Sergeievich went home and ordered wall-to-wall corn for the Soviet Union. Many farm chairmen had disagreed — they knew corn simply could not prosper in their drier, more northerly lands. Dudnikov agreed, and then again, he disagreed too. He said, in consecutive sentences: "It was a mistake for Khrushchev to order corn grown. Now local farms have a right to decide not to plant corn. My response to Mr. Khrushchev was very positive. He helped a lot and was right when he ordered corn production." I was impressed.

I asked if Dudnikov thought that high-quality corn seed from this plant would someday really boost regional production, given the many problems that also needed fixing. His answer should be in a primer on the arts of proper bureaucrats — his words sounded right, but his positions on the topics remained private, as in: "I'm against the command method of administration of farms. We have a planned economy. Our leaders should be careful to observe and adopt this plan, and have to take local farmers into consideration. Mr. Khrushchev brought us soybeans and corn. Corn has the highest energy of any feed — corn means meat. Nobody will replace corn as nobody will replace soybeans. That's why we have chosen the right direction in agriculture." You've got to hand it to a guy who can talk like that. And to Igor, who translated this substance with the delicacy of a poet.

Was Dudnikov also in charge of construction of the seed-corn plant being built on the land of his farm? He, of course, didn't quite say he was or wasn't: "It's contract work . . . We had to use what we call 'additional construction for our region — above plan.' Our organizations have fixed capacities and now have to do extra work. So we have delays. Now we have talks with everyone about everything — but little talk about real work. Yet, only work will solve our problems."

I think that meant "no one is really in charge," and seemed accurate. His discernment, expressed with candor, led him toward an antidote opposite the one a capitalist would seek: "In order to get all the work done, we have to keep discipline and order everywhere. We must find the forms of organizing people that will force them to work." A capitalist manager might have answered, "To get real work done, we have to relax regulation and pay salaries that will reward those who discipline themselves."

Dudnikov had even toured the United States, and had witnessed Western-style supervision of workers: "I saw a farm that grows grain on 3,750 acres and feeds it to 1,500 bulls — and three men do the whole job. Here? Multiply the labor by ten. I came back understanding market mechanisms." Could similar economics work for him? "A market system would lead to a new society. It is out of the question. The present command system has been built of many years' experience and will not change quickly." Dudnikov really knew how to put things. I felt the grim pleasure a news photographer might feel while shooting a close-up of mayhem. The showplace *oblast* of Belgorod — with priority above all others in Russia for receiving the scarce agricultural and industrial supplies that might make its reform-Communist "experiment" come out right — couldn't thrive with Dudnikov-style "talent" in force. Belgorod was not a lab showing the viability of *perestroika*. It was a lab showing, no doubt for the hundredth time, the best possible performance of the Soviet system when a well-connected Party boss of particularly forceful personality and legions of loyal functionaries happened to be in charge of a fertile region.

◆

Back in the orange van, my keeper, Kvitchenko, broke out a few apples. I started polishing one on my shirt. He plucked it back and trimmed both stem and bud ends off with a tiny pocketknife. "All the poison is at the apple's two ends," he said, returning it. "You cut them off and you're safe."

He continued to grow on me. He was the least obstructive and most human of the hosts who attended my Soviet-era rural wanderings. He had constant back troubles. He had surprised me a day or two earlier by lifting his shirt and tugging his pants down an inch or two, displaying a rat's-tooth-yellow wool scarf bound several times around his girth, like an Ace bandage around a swollen ankle. "Without this napkin, I have pain. My back aches as soon as there is wind on it, even with this cloth. Do you have the word *rheumatism?*" This aching, tumbledown man was put on last-stand guard duty, protecting idols about to topple.

He turned out not to be a shrewd official choice. On my last afternoon in Belgorod, he insisted on picking us up at the hotel a full two hours before train time. We drove off in the battered white Lada. His eyes gleamed and he had a hint of a mischievous smile — he had something in mind. The Lada bumped down a dirt road into a beautiful field by a stream. He broke out a picnic. Ceremoniously, he spread a white tablecloth on the car hood and laid out pickled fish, bread, sausage, and radishes (he'd noticed how much I liked fresh radishes). He snapped open a bottle of vodka and we drank a simple, unceremonious, and sincere toast, "To the pleasure of getting to know each other." When he had imbibed enough to speak freely, he unburdened himself of a tale he said he'd planned this occasion to tell:

"I want to describe to you my grandfather. He had thirteen daughters. He had cows and calves. He could build a house by any means. He was sent to Siberia by Stalin. But he was one of the miraculous ones whom the process chewed on but spat back out — perhaps by mistake. He was home again in thirteen days. They turned him loose with no explanations.

"He believed in God. That is my pain, too. My grandfather was a wonderful farmer — an owner, I dare to say. I buried him not so far from Belgorod, on the collective farm he'd been forced to move to. My grandmother lies next to him. I visit the two graves and I hurt. I visit and cry when I see them. He was a nice man, a lovely man — he had a long beard with narrow sides, and he had an open nature. He had a kind attitude toward himself.

"He taught me to treat farm animals well, and he taught me what hay means — which hay is rich, how to grow it. He used a wooden hayfork." The stream burbled and the wind blew lightly. Kvitchenko looked at me with sad eyes as we both contemplated this memory of a competent, affectionate, independent farmer. We stood tall in the weedy field of a collective farm and toasted his grandfather. Kvitchenko's eyes became teary. He clanked his glass smartly into mine, smiled, and said, "I tell you the truth."

◆

At the hotel, an ungainly band blasted out the lambada. It was two years since it had swept through European dance halls and gone out of style. Before *perestroika*, the dance would have bumped up against the Bulgarian border and keeled over. The fall of Communism meant Euro-fads crept into small towns in Siberia. Late in *perestroika*, that bane of outland tourism in Soviet Russia, the hotel band, was learning new tricks. Loudspeakers were standard government issue, and such bands had strummed and thunked along in small dining rooms at rock-concert volume. Every mill-city hotel had its own. Band members, regrettably, were among the few workers in any hotel who served diligently. From Riga to Vladivostok, no one chatted over borscht. Everyone had to shout.

A squad of Belgorod shopgirls, purple uniforms tied with apron sashes, bounded about, baggy, ungainly, and loosened by Georgian cognac. The big one in the corner darted a few steps and stood before a shy boy on the sidelines. She rolled her hips raunchily. He smiled back slyly and reddened. His friends teased him. Her friends scolded her and giggled. The two danced.

We sat, caged by the din of the awful band for an hour before food came — a breaded, deep-fried, skinlike sheet folded around a mucilaginous, eggy, barely warm oil slurry oozing chunks of ham-ish fat. "*Kotleta,*" Igor hollered brightly over the din. Hunger drove us onward, and vodka consoled us.

A waiter slammed down a bowl of whole cucumbers, field mud still on them. I peeled one with my pocketknife. And while I was doing so, the purple shopgirls discovered me. The girls must not have peeled muddy cukes. And like many people in the USSR, they seemed never before to have viewed a Westerner this side of a movie screen. They watched closely and silently as I picked at my food, and they were still watching when I paid the few rubles I was charged. Famished and with ears ringing, I strolled into the evening for a peek at the town. Belgorod spread across gentle hills, human-scale in a land of monoliths. It was kempt, less forbidding than many Russian cities, nearly picturesque. It looked homemade, with crooked walls and wavering lanes. It was full of low, old, pastel stucco apartment buildings, log huts, and a few prerevolutionary mansions.

A girl of perhaps fourteen found us at once outside the hotel and asked in formal school English, "Be kind for me seegrette." I gave her the only one I had. In Russia I smoke, although I haven't smoked at home in decades. I drop it without regret on the plane back. I can't explain why I do it. The girl scampered off to a few friends and displayed her trophy Marlboro. It was an amulet, conveying Westernness. We wandered down side streets and got disoriented amid the warren of hushed houses. Belgorod was an early town. A wild-eyed old man in a white tunic and golf cap squinted intently at us. Igor asked him for directions:

"Where is the ObKom building?" — that was both the Party office and civil government headquarters.

"Why do you want that? It's closed now," said the old man, who must have been a suspicious type.

"I don't want the ObKom building. It is my landmark on the way back to the hotel."

"So why didn't you ask me where the hotel is?"

"Where is the hotel?"

"Up to the right. You go past the ObKom building . . ."

We laughed, and he didn't seem to know why.

Up a lane, following his directions, we encountered a young father pushing his little girl in a stroller.

"Where is Frunze Street?" he asked.

"Up past the ObKom building," said Igor, laughing, and the fellow nodded knowingly and smiled as if he'd gotten the joke.

The stores stayed open late, although almost no one was inside shopping. A line of fresh chickens lay on parade down the center of a long, otherwise bare cooler. There was no crowd to grab up the chickens, and they were relatively cheap — a few rubles a kilogram. In the prior three years, whenever I'd seen fresh birds in a store in Russia, long, anxious lines had always led away from them.

Igor shook his head in disbelief at this abundance, but from my perspective the cupboard was nearly bare in this store. The entire rest of its inventory was: a few sacks of flour, plenty of bread, pickles and preserved mystery greens in big stained jars with rusting screw tops, a couple of stove-in cabbages, tanks of juice (bring your own jar), and a bin of loose macaroni. Maybe oil and flour and salt were available upon application. That was it. Not one more item.

"The difference between here and Moscow," Igor said, "is a big one. Here, in fifteen minutes I can buy everything I need to cook a supper — not interesting food, but supper, and not spending all afternoon shopping. In Moscow the shopper goes from store to store, searching and shoving for an hour and a half. Put it together. I would save six hours, seven hours — a workday every week — if I had such a store near my apartment."

The market he viewed was not the same one that I regarded

with my Western eyes. I saw a market to get depressed, not excited, about. Any poor shop in the poorest section of a poor city in the Third World — in Mexico City or Istanbul — had, at least in summer, more and better meat, fresher vegetables, and more spices and trimmings than did Belgorod's showplace shops. The city's markets stocked enough for people to get by, and not a bit more. But what Igor's reaction showed was that this shop had enough in it to win the hearts of the people for the *oblast* regime. Conditions all over were bad. A little reform went a long way.

"Are Belgorod officials doing a good job?" I asked Igor.

"Better than in Moscow, I see."

PART II

ACROSS THE USSR

1988

2

MY FASCINATION with Russia surfaced almost accidentally. In 1987 I'd been invited, along with my father, who was in the book business, to the International Book Exposition in Moscow. It was a new event, organized to show the world that *glasnost* had at last freed Soviet writers to write and Soviet readers to read.

That wasn't the message we got there. The big National Economic Achievement Exhibition Halls stood on parklike grounds. At the entrance, by the Cosmos hotel, an enormous cement and steel comma shot from a space rocket far aloft — a relic of the civic joy that had followed Yuri Gagarin's historic space flight. Russians jokingly called it "The Dream of the Impotent." Loudspeakers on posts blared slogans, news, and martial music along the ten-minute walk from the metro station. This was still a zone of propagandized recreation, a corny, alarming scene out of Orwell's *1984*. Riot militia in helmets ringed the exhibition buildings, shoulder to shoulder, shoving back a shouting crowd.

This was a mob hungry not to burn but to read books. Dozens of desperate ordinary citizens crowded in as I approached the hall, imploring me, some in pretty fair English, to say I knew them and to chat them past the police line. For me the line was trivial. I held up my exhibitor's badge, and with a chopped beckoning of the baton and a glance at my American shoes and suit, a guard motioned me in through the gate.

My wise old father and I were green there. We spent a few days scouring publishers' booths. They'd come from all over the socialist world, from Cuba and Czechoslovakia, Mozambique, Romania, East Germany, and from all the SSRs of the USSR itself. We found four or five children's books and some cookbooks that we wanted to buy rights to, and we admired the drawings of a few illustrators for whom we might easily have found further work with Western publishers. We wanted to offer the very thing everyone wanted — hard currency.

We were inexperienced enough to feel surprised when our straightforward offers (the very reason for trade fairs) led us through the looking glass. Successively higher officials in turn seemed surprised that we wanted to do business. We at last scaled the hierarchy and entered the elegant chambers of VAAP, the Party-controlled "copyright department" (its acronym translates as All-Union Agency for the Protection of Authors' Rights), which had to approve every foreign transaction and approved almost none. A Party honcho with courtly manners said he'd get back to us. And perhaps, the better part of a decade and several regimes and a fallen empire later, he will yet. Business proved impossible to conduct — we'd had a foretaste of the labyrinth into which many eager Western traders would soon wander.

We turned to tourism. In Leningrad I asked if our Intourist driver, Vladimir, might take me out to the country to visit a collective farm. It was not a sanctioned destination, said Vladimir, but he would do a drive-by. Out the window of the black Volga, I saw what I would see more of in years to come: poorly planted fields.

A farm, any Iowan can attest, places the industriousness of its owner on public display. American farmers are a high-minded bunch who generally keep their own counsel, even if they don't mind their own business. They peer into each other's fields as others peer into theirs. A respectable farmer's fields are green as early as climate permits, neat, thriftily and conservatively employed, and uniformly planted — no poor spots where the growing crop is skimpy and brown because herbicide or fertilizer missed or got doubled up, no rows skipped by the planter or

planted with seed that didn't take, no wet spots where the tractor rutted the ground, few converging or point rows to hamper
machine tillage and harvesting. Fields are business, serious business.

Russian fields weren't. Russian fields, I was to discover, were
for something else, something unbusinesslike: *fulfillment of the
Plan.* The Intourist driver drove between fields, and I invento-
ried skipped rows, wiggly rows, parched plants, pale patches,
fertilizer-burned brown patches, weeds everywhere — very un-
American. He drove past tumbledown greenhouses along a farm
road so muddy and potholed it slowed work.

That's all I saw in 1987. Unsuccessful in business, my father
and I remained regulation tourists for the rest of our stay. We
wandered through the Hermitage and visited the Leningrad Circus, where a gymnast ran into the ring in a long skirt that turned
out to be dozens of trained hamsters clinging to a metal framework.

From the moment I'd arrived for the book fair, I'd been phon-
ing the Writers' Union, trying to locate Yuri Dmitrievich Chernichenko. Finally a publisher slipped me his son's home number. I'd heard about Chernichenko from Dr. Mark Kuchment, a
historian of science trained in the Soviet Academy of Sciences
and at that time a researcher at Harvard University's Russian
Research Center (and now a political science professor at Em-
manuel College). Kuchment had read a book I'd written about
American agriculture and declared that Chernichenko and I had
similar interests.

Later, when I understood what Chernichenko had done, I
found that the comparison exaggerated. I'd written for comfortable readers about a farming system that has problems but
works. Our markets are full and our food is cheap. Chernichenko had described — candidly, when candor took courage —
a food system that worked so poorly that its empty food shops
later helped topple the Party and the government.

Chernichenko had risked his livelihood and freedom to publish his surprising, personal, literate essays, which meandered
acerbically from farming scenes to politics to autobiography.
He'd described a continuing national disaster in a nation whose
authorities didn't abide criticism. He knew the shoddy work of

collective farms, the lives of peasants in their huts, and the corridors of the agri-bureaucracy. While Party authority was still strong, he'd substituted allegory for forthright discussion — a literary technique as old as censorship itself. He'd walked carefully along the cliff of dissidence throughout a long career.

The book fair and my meeting Chernichenko were both byproducts of Gorbachev's information thaw. The thaw also enabled publication of Chernichenko's frankest essays, which had been blocked for years by censors. Their sharp points and colloquial style quickly had made him a national spokesman for farm reform. He was sixty, a veteran of the earlier "Khrushchev thaw" of the late fifties — as were most of the first wave of critics to attack (literally, in his case) the Party's sacred cows.

As a young reporter on the rise, he'd volunteered to live in Siberia. He'd written critically about Khrushchev's campaign to plow up millions of acres of virgin prairie in Kazakhstan and Siberia. He'd kept to the edge of society, making sense of it. Now he was riding high, in governmental good graces and back in Moscow with his own television show. His ideas — straightforward to us, but heresy in the dominions of Stalin, Brezhnev, and their heirs — were simply to peel the layers of bureaucrats away from farming, to let farmers farm, to establish real banks and crop markets and set competing firms to manufacturing combines (he'd been banned for life from the huge combine monopoly at Rostov-on-Don). In an internal struggle between reformers and old guard, he'd become an official at the USSR Writers' Union. His new rank hadn't stopped the old-guard foreign secretary from not delivering cables and letters I'd been steadily sending in my effort to meet him.

On my last day in Russia in 1987, Chernichenko had materialized at my hotel in his beat-up red Lada, freshly back from vacation on the Black Sea. The first thing we did together was push his car down the street to a gas station. It was running on empty, and so was he. His trip had left him pale green from a nasty flu, and only able to whisper.

Our translator was the foreign secretary who'd "misplaced" Chernichenko's mail. What a complicated country! At the Writers' Union restaurant, she was charming and helpful. She'd interpreted for John Steinbeck when he'd toured. She'd mothered

Steinbeck, she said, and she got right to work mothering Chernichenko in the grand oak-paneled dining room. She petted his feverish bald spot, eyed his slack face, and said, "Yurila, you've got to order the chicken soup." She leaned over and confided to me, "Here in Moscow, we call chicken soup Jewish penicillin."

Same as in Brooklyn, it worked. Yuri gathered strength with each spoonful. Soon it was a jolly luncheon. He thrust a copy of his newly republished exposé, *Russian Wheat*, toward me, tugged it back impulsively, and drew a bull on the flyleaf. It had been a classic when it was printed in *Novy mir* during the Khrushchev thaw, in 1959. I drew a spiral-faced pig on the flyleaf of my *Three Farms* for him. He said, "The shame of my nation is that it imports thirty million metric tons of grain a year." He called collectivization "tragic." Yuri stated what seems commonplace now, but his words were electrifying in 1987. In fact, the foreign secretary grew disapproving and distant, her translations elliptical. "He's known as highly opinionated," she tut-tutted, shaking her head. At the end of lunch, Yuri and I pledged to trade farm tours the following summer.

Over the winter we exchanged letters and then formal invitations. The plan I'd outlined shaped up easily. I'd rung Lee Totman in Conway, Massachusetts, Joe Weisshaar in Creston, Iowa, Chip Backlund in Peoria, Illinois, and Angelo Mazzei in Bakersfield, California; told them when we could make it; called a travel agent and booked flights; and I was done. Yuri held up his side of the bargain as best he could that early in Gorbachev's season.

Yuri wrote up a parallel plan for my return visit, but that was only the beginning for him. The following June (1988), when I touched down in Moscow again, I walked into an odd and revealing setup. Yuri met me at the airport gate and, smiling, handed me a tray on which he'd placed a loaf of bread and a pinch of salt — an old Russian welcome. At his *dacha* he had convened a picnic of a dozen agricultural-reform leaders. Nikolai Shmelev, a political economist (later briefly known in America for his book *The Turning Point: Revitalizing the Soviet Economy*, which was officially hopeful about *perestroika* reforms), held up his glass and ruefully said: "We struggled against private monopoly and got state monopoly. How can we organize competition in fertilizer and tractor manufacturing when we have three million professional supervisors? Their only real function is to enforce obligatory crop delivery."

Anatoly Streliany, an author and television producer, was there with his ten-year-old son. "Welcome to an absurd place" was Streliany's toast. And at this picnic I first met Viktor Lishchenko, the agricultural economist who would organize the seed-corn processing plant in Belgorod and also my visit there a few years later. These "agricultural intellectuals" hadn't sorted themselves out yet. They could hardly have known which way to turn, or even that such choices would soon be necessary. Yet in the next year or two some would prove to be anti-Communists, and some reformists hoping to save the Communist Party. But there at the start, at Yuri Chernichenko's picnic, all the guests were simply "pro-democracy," seemingly all in the same camp.

Yuri had bound a watermelon with twine and dropped it into his well to cool. We drank and ate and drank more. As the picnic waned, he unfolded the itinerary for our travels and we went through it. "It's not at all what we agreed to," I said. "It's not what I planned, either," he replied. It was one thing to meet in Moscow with social critics such as Shmelev (who later went off to teach economics in Sweden) and Streliany (who went off to write for television in Germany) and chat forthrightly. Out in the provinces, though, we would travel under tight Party discipline still.

The trip had been a stretch for the guardians of Soviet reputation. The foreign section of the new super-Ministry of Agriculture, Gosagroprom, controlled access to this turf. Yuri, a known adversary, had applied to the ministry. It had revised his plan.

I was traveling for the *New York Times Magazine*. My assignment was to report to American readers on why there were long food lines in Moscow if *perestroika* was the "good thing" readers supposed it was. Yuri thought that affiliation with the *Times* might have set off Gosagroprom's alarm. Had I been Gosagroprom's public relations adviser, I'd have suggested either cordiality or an outright travel ban. Instead they'd offered a take-it-or-leave-it itinerary. They'd had local Party officials suggest every event along the way. There was nothing casual about the chosen stops. The Party was far from extinct in 1988, and *perestroika* was a Party program.

For the next month, I was immersed in the "corporate culture" of Gosagroprom, my institutional host. Gorbachev had created this bureaucratic empire in 1985, lashing together formerly separate but already ponderous entities: the Ministry of Vegetable and Fruit Growing, the Ministry of the Meat and Dairy Industry, the Ministry of the Food Industry, the Ministry of Rural Construction, the USSR State Committee for Technical Supplies to Farming, the Ministry of Bread Products, the Ministry of Land Improvement and Water Economy, the Ministry of Fisheries, and the State Forestry Committee. Each huge entity had guarded its prerogatives. Gorbachev guessed that giantism was less paralyzing than rivalry — which turned out to be a moot point.

Gosagroprom essentially "owned" everything connected with food supply: all the farms and shops and trucking, the agri-research institutes, the industrial farm-supply system (factories that made tractors and combines and fertilizer, and processing factories), the higher agri-education schools, and even the village schools for children. It controlled domestic food production from bottom to top, and the lives of its producers, across a country that spanned eleven time zones.

Had its bureaucrats been innately noble and honest, with brains like fast computers and a commitment to miraculous economic models of citizens' desires that successfully expressed the perverse complexity of real life — that is, if planned economies were feasible and bureaucrats selfless risk takers — then Gosagroprom might have solved the USSR's food problems. What it actually did was to confound the already confounded. It worsened problems instantly.

A joke told to me across the nation by collective-farm chairmen went like this: Two former archrivals, Ivan and Joe, the one retired from the KGB, the other from the CIA, met in a bar to discuss old times. Ivan says, "Tell me the truth, Joe, you guys sabotaged Chernobyl, right?" And Joe answers, "No, Ivan, we did even better — we were responsible for thinking up Gosagroprom."

Yuri said that inside Gosagroprom were plenty of reformers

who knew the worth of managerial savvy, technical know-how, and investment. But the solutions that could revitalize agriculture endangered Gosagroprom. As long as organizational goals included maintaining an ideology that planned every enterprise's inputs, outputs, and relations with other organizations, Western solutions were simply inapplicable. They required reducing central control far below the levels at which Communist ideology and administrative fiefdoms could be enforced. If, for example, instead of ministries determining enterprise budgets, banks could have loaned money directly, based on their own estimates of the merit of projects, the rule of Gosagroprom planners would have faded away. If farms and factories could have freely dealt with each other, instead of having to apply, deal by deal, for approval by Gosagroprom, planners' rule would have faded. If hiring and firing could have been based on merit, Gosagroprom labor regulators' authority would have faded away. But the need to plan was a given, and nothing faded away, although everything would soon crumble.

In retrospect, I'm surprised Gosagroprom received me. There was little for them to flaunt, save the enduring spirits of so many individuals. But official reformers in 1988 probably didn't know how far behind they were. And they still seemed to hope that Westerners might point them toward an economic vigor that left room for a reformist, technocratic Communist Party. In the end, Western ideas would merely prove to be as pernicious as the stodgiest Communist ideologue ever feared.

◆

Traces of Yuri's original itinerary did survive the final trip plan. Yuri consolingly reassured me that we'd meet a few of his favorite rural souls, but no activity remained for which some bureaucrat might face blame. Controversial places and persons were gone. My visits were to showplace farms and factories and proper leaders. John Steinbeck had been one of only a few previous Western writers granted extensive rural treks. In 1946 he'd tippled his way around the Soviet outback with Robert Capa as photographer. His description of his trip's planners, in *A Russian Journal*, reminded me of mine four decades later: "No one is willing to go out on a limb. No one is willing to say yes or no to any proposition. He must always go to someone higher. In this way he protects himself from criticism. Anyone who has had dealings with armies, or with governments, will recognize this story."

I'd asked to visit a few farms and to spend several days at each. I wanted to wander, meet people at random and chat. The Gosagroprom itinerary Yuri apologetically handed me scheduled three farms a day. I'd meet the bosses; discussion would be followed by feasts; there'd be little time to look around. Seeing my reaction, Yuri had teased me: "Don't forget that there'll also be some bright-eyed young policeman out of uniform listening to everyone and making reports. Less has changed than you'd imagine."

I understand better now than I did while discussing the itinerary with Yuri that it was not a world that was much at ease with candid inspection. It was a sad and awesome time for a Westerner to be there, one of those moments when cataclysm is fated and poised, the keystone dislodged, pebbles skittering down, some stones starting to tumble and some just holding — a quiet time overpowered by the imminence of utter change. Dispirited Soviet citizens were, while hardly realizing such a process was possible much less under way, already shouldering a colossal, intricate undertaking, not one that would naturally follow from their reluctant turn of conviction. Before the transformation was done, it would cost all the political and financial and human pains that go along with rearranging basic beliefs, habits, alliances, and institutions. But for the moment, the structures of central control were still mostly in place.

Yuri did negotiate for a genial translator, Pavel Pavlovich Sorokin, a brawny professional soccer player turned professor of farm maintenance economics (and since the fall of the Party in 1991, dean of foreign students at Moscow Technical College, then an administrator at the Academy of the National Economy's international business school, and then agricultural counsel at his nation's Washington embassy). And the next morning, after I'd slept for a dozen hours, shaking off jet lag and the reformers' welcoming picnic, Sorokin and I flew off on Aeroflot to Lithuania, to start at the USSR's western border. Yuri would join us in a few days. It was June of 1988, and he had been elected a delegate to the Nineteenth Party Conference. The day after I arrived, the historic gathering had more or less voted a parliament into existence. Yuri would soon campaign hard and end up an elected people's deputy in it. The final efforts to rejuvenate or to topple the regime were at full intensity.

The initial candor of Sorokin's translations surprised me — he even quoted people making rude comments about me. They'd spoken with good reason: I'd gone about my first visits untactfully, jousting with Gosagroprom and collective-farm officials who orated pieties. Sorokin enjoyed my sparring and probably my naiveté — guffawing in our private conversation the first evening, adding his two kopeks' worth about the personalities we'd met.

However, at breakfast on our third day of travel, my field notes record, Sorokin gravely declared, as if delivering a formal announcement, "Henceforth, I may not translate overheard conversations. I will translate the words of the people you are scheduled to speak with — only the words said intentionally and directly to you."

"Why, Pavel Pavlovich?"

"To do otherwise would be like reading you someone else's mail."

A few days after we'd left Lithuania, Yuri joined us, elated after the Party Conference, full of smiles, greeting everyone in the hotel lobby, a celebrity reveling in being recognized. Sorokin said, "I am so relieved. Now whatever happens is Yuri's fault." Yuri could handle a lot of fault. He glowed with anticipation about the changes afoot and where they'd lead. From the podium, Gorbachev had called agriculture "the nation's most painful, most acute problem." He'd consulted privately with Yuri, but followed far more conservative advice.

◆

Peasants, and many of their bosses, hugged Yuri Chernichenko delightedly. He was clever and charismatic. His television show, *Perestroika Spotlight: Agriculture Hour,* had brought his face and ideas and sense of fun to the troubled farms. The show had taken viewers to an Iowa farm — the cameras had panned across the fields and then gone right through the farmer's home into the kitchen, with adoring, covetous close-ups of dishwasher, toaster, trash compactor.

Burly, ebullient, genial on good days, Yuri sparked with energy that belied his sixty years. He was quick, with full, wide-armed gestures and a broad smile. He was a compulsive, constant communicator; he clowned and mocked and bullied everyone around, his expression always in motion, his clear gray eyes taking in everything, reading everyone's reactions to his running performance. In the midst of restless silences, he blurted proclamations to me. He'd shouted in the car after a particularly officious encounter, "Secrecy has been bureaucracy's medium. Bureaucratic power requires it."

Chernichenko wrote in a warm, humorous voice but explored a serious subject: the connection between shoddy farming and bureaucratic control. His key essay, "Two Mysteries," had recently come out in *Literaturnaya gazeta*, the leading literary newsweekly at the time, spelling out a major fact of national history that citizens had previously discussed mostly in whispers: while collectivizing private farms by force between 1929 and 1933, Stalin and his cohorts had slaughtered ten to twenty million peasants (there are several, inexact, ways to count) by enforced starvation, execution, and exile to cold places. Add four or five million people lost during another "artificial famine" a decade earlier, and fourteen or so million casualties of Stalin's prewar purges, and the result is a looming, nationally shared heritage of family loss, of awful, grisly events that happened when today's grandparents were children, and that had gone undiscussed for half a century, not set to rest by public acknowledgment, outrage, reconciliation, mourning, memorialization.

Yuri's own desire to write "Two Mysteries" had evolved from strong personal memories of the traumatic time of mass collectivization and mass death. He had been a young child but remembered days with no food, and his mother weeping. She'd kept Yuri indoors during the worst of the desperate months in the early 1930s because in his native Krasnodar region, as in other areas of starvation, wandering children sometimes got eaten.

"Two Mysteries" reminded readers that before the Revolution, Russia had been a major exporter of grain to Europe. But now Russia was importing the grain for every other loaf of bread baked there. Yuri's two mysteries were questions: Why hadn't the public yet been officially told about the slaughter that had accompanied collectivization? And why, following the universal establishment of collective farming, did the country still depend on imported wheat? Cheap American wheat was what had long stabilized Party rule and allowed the government to cover up the inefficiency of collective farming.

Sorokin gradually loosened his ban on interpreting side comments as we wandered with Yuri through the 1988 harvest, the worst in three years. Everywhere, drought followed disorganization, and as ever, imported grain took up the slack. In the end, Sorokin's translation restrictions hardly mattered. He interpreted Yuri's conversation freely. The disorder and inefficiency of Soviet collective farms and food factories showed anyhow — even along our blue-ribbon route. There was little to admire, and that was the more damning because we were visiting the best places.

◆

We region-hopped on fearsome Aeroflot and drove across endless plains and low hills in a series of black (the color of official cars) Gosagroprom limousines and orange vans, stopping at farms now and then. Dodging fuming trucks on choked rural roads, we inscribed a long arc from Lithuania on south of Moscow, through the Ukraine, eastward into the Caucasus. We jogged south to Georgia, then flew northeast into Siberia.

Watching from car windows, I often felt haunted by an absence. Houses were missing from nearly all the pleasant sites where houses sat in most other countries. People milled everywhere: old babushkas sat on boxes by roads and hawked melons and red roses, and boys on bicycles herded calves along muddy footpaths. Men and women dabbed at the rich dirt with hoes, clowned and gossiped, waited for diesel-belching country buses. But their cottages did not sit by the ponds nor face the beautiful broad prospects.

We'd emerge from deep country suddenly, into some rural community that always looked like an industrial slum, not a farm village. Apartment blocks, one crammed hard upon the next, each with flats for twelve or eighteen families, rose above multifamily houses and a few ancient, slouching log *izbas*, eaves and windowframes trimmed with pale blue scrollwork. It was always like that.

On schedule day after day, we arrived at collective farm after farm. We always pulled up before some large cement administration building (which wasn't surprising, because most were built at about the same time, from master plans) and shook hands vigorously with yet another cluster of bulky officials. We sat in similar paneled offices thousands of miles apart, at long T-shaped conference tables. Lenin's picture scowled down behind each farm chairman. Just one progressive-minded chairman, in 1988 on that first cross-country trek, had added the portrait of a smiling Gorbachev, birthmark airbrushed out.

"We have five hundred field workers and one hundred office workers" was always the sort of introductory remark the directors intoned. The ratios stayed at about five to one, workers to bureaucrats. "And we farm forty thousand acres." Or sixty thousand acres. The size always was ungainly — an order of magnitude larger than that of efficient large farms in the West.

In the courtyards beyond the office windows, large block-lettered billboards always exhorted the right glad spirit:

> **TEND THE LAND NOT FOR TODAY,**
> **NOT FOR NEXT WEEK,**
> **BUT FOREVER**

> **YOU MUST IMPLEMENT THE**
> **DECREE OF THE PARTY CONGRESS**
> **INTO LIFE**

> **PROSPERITY OF PEOPLE IS THE**
> **HIGHEST AIM OF THE PARTY**

Many farms had been vested with rousing names during the forced collectivization of 1929–33: "Spark" (after Lenin's news-

paper), "Bolshevik," "Bountiful," "Victory of Communism."
Yuri whispered dramatically, "Their names could have been
written in the blood of the grandparents of peasants who labor
there still." Only in the USSR's last decade were country dwellers (who peeked shyly at our "delegation" by the hundreds every
moment we were out in the open) free to leave farms for city
life. As soon as they were equipped with passports, which happened in the late 1970s and early 1980s, the younger generation
left in droves.

A motorcade of black cars inevitably loaded up before the office building. What chairmen called "farm inspection" followed
the stiff office interviews. We wound out along sultry field roads
raising dust clouds. Distinguished *apparatchiks* of the regional
Party and Gosagroprom, wearing heavy suits at high noon,
clambered out to audit my questions and some hapless field
hand's answers.

Pressed by me under those inconsiderate conditions, many
souls said the right things. And some spoke with courage and
abandon. In a peasant's cottage near Poltava, the august secretary of the district Communist Party committee saw me admiring an icon. "We don't encourage religion, but it is now permitted," he said. The old man of the house yelled at him, an ancient
genie newly rubbed the wrong way, loose from the lamp for the
first time in nearly a century: "Well, I'm religious, especially
when someone's sick," the peasant spat, "and I don't care what
anybody says about it!" His name was Sasha. He was a wiry,
restless man, and he proudly poured me a shot glass of honey as
if it were vodka. He beamed while I sampled it and smacked my
lips. He patted my back and before he let me leave, handed me
two thin fish he had caught and smoked himself and wrapped in
old newspaper. As it happened, we traveled all evening, and arrived at a guesthouse too late for food, although the night clerk
did miraculously produce thin beer and a loaf of bread. At midnight in Kharkov, the fish sustained us.

All along the trail, farm directors sighed about the nation's
long-repeated mistakes. Many spoke with tentative frankness,
as if trying a new, daring fashion. Some wished ideology and
regulation hindered work less. "Every month or so I received a

package from Moscow, pages of rules to add to the rule book we already have," said one director of a research farm. He shook a sheaf of papers and said, "These are something new — a list of rules to *remove* from the rule book."

Many higher officials clearly didn't want much reform, and with good reason. They especially feared the social autonomy that would accompany freeing up farms to act independently. In Georgia, my Gosagroprom hosts substituted smothering, ritualized hospitality for candor, and wouldn't even let me (or possibly Yuri) near a farm. We sat through three days of ceremonial feasting. In marble halls presided over by Tbilisi's agri-business princes — in the House of Tea, the Soda Factory Hall, the House of Champagne — we supped regally from the regional cornucopia. At a time when good food was rare, the tables of the Georgian elite groaned with *piti* soup, curried eggplant with walnuts, charred *shashlik*, tangy green-plum sauce, brown walnut sauce, sturgeon, rice, cucumbers and tomatoes, spiced chicken, nut pastries, apricots, cherries, raspberries, nuts.

And fine champagne. The *tamada*, or toastmaster, invariably called for bottoms-up salutes to motherlands and mothers, missions and milestones, from each diner. Florid but barbed orations preceded each gulp, while a tribe of officials with hollow legs took measure of the increasingly woozy stranger. The Georgian banquets were only apparently cordial; they were rough and profound rituals, bullfights of sorts, with heartburn replacing the final sword thrust. On the evening of the third day I rebelled, bolting on my own for a glimpse of a city market before I departed. Except for that hour, my hosts succeeded in showing me only what they wished.

We pressed on, fatted, to the Kuban, the Soviet big-sky country east of the Ukraine, a place of fertile soil, temperate summers, and vast fields. Here I especially felt as though I were traveling from factory to factory, not farm to farm. Under close guard, and by special last-minute intercession that Yuri had won at long distance from a friend high in the Party, we hurried through Mikhail Gorbachev's home farm near Stavropol (Gorbachev's grandfather was on the nonfatal side of the collectivization — he was the farm's founding director). We'd come to meet

Aleksander Yakovenko, a weathered old combine operator who had taught a teenage Gorbachev to reap grain in the lean postwar summers of 1947 and 1948.

"Slept on haystacks, could never get clean," Yakovenko said, recalling their long days. Both had received the Order of the Red Banner, a rare distinction that had helped Gorbachev's admittance to Moscow University and his slide along the fast track through Komsomol, the Communist youth organization, and on to higher Party education.

"Did you have any inkling Gorbachev would be a leader?" I asked the shy old man.

"If only I knew . . ." Yakovenko trailed off, his gap-toothed smile full of joy.

"Is your life good?"

"I'm in the fields," he said, shrugging with sweet acceptance.

That was it. Nothing more. We left the farm. We'd never entered a building there. I'd been shown that the general secretary of the Communist Party and chairman of the Supreme Soviet had come from the soil. The Gosagroprom van driver sped right past Gorbachev's village, Provolnoye. "It is not permitted to stop here," the police guard who had climbed into our van especially for this outing had said.

As we drove away, I was afflicted with traveler's troubled stomach. I asked the driver to stop by a roadside corn field. Our attending officer, a young blood with karate-hardened hands, had previously muttered to me, in shy school English, just one phrase, "Rambo moofies, gooooot," while whacking his hand against his own throat. He perked up when he heard my request to the van driver, and attempted to assume command. "Ve must drive on. Ve may not stop on zees road," he shouted at me in English. He shouted in Russian at the driver, who, fortunately, had the good sense to ignore him. I headed into the cornrows.

He scurried right after me, yelling, "Halt, it is forbidden to go there!" I glared at him over my shoulder and he backed off, leaving me to plunge onward through the cornstalks. Out of spite, I did what any inquiring journalist would do upon finding himself with a bad stomachache in a forbidden corn field: I inspected the crop that grew all around me. I counted just one ear of corn for every fifty pale green stems — evidence of prior chronic misapplication of fertilizer.

At the time, Yuri still was more or less compelled to go through the motions of being loyal opposition. A year later, he'd be one of the first people's deputies to resign from the Party, reject Gorbachev, tilt toward Yeltsin, and join with the pro-democracy opposition faction called the Interregional Group. And a year and a few months after that, in 1991, months before the abortive coup, Yuri would go still further and form one of the first independent political parties, the Peasants' Party, and start (not very successfully) building a rural constituency openly favoring land privatization. All that would come soon enough. For the moment, he said his line in support of Gorbachev: "What other major leader has that background?" he asked me in front of local functionaries.

After weeks of hard traveling, after so many top farms, model food factories, "elite" machinery- and seed-testing stations, numbed and glad of an afternoon's relaxation, we picnicked in a birch grove, lazing about and joking with some congenial and funny Siberian farm-reform leaders. We ate milky fish stew and drank vodka and bottles of *kumys* — fermented mare's-milk beer that looks like skim milk and tastes like ripe Brie and tobacco. Talking quietly in the eternal twilight of a subarctic summer evening, this group of buddies gazed across a broad lake at golden grain fields.

Their upside-down world had its own logic, in which the absurdity of the detailed supervision of each boss, and the unaccountability and absolute power of higher-ups, created a contradictory mission for each farm chairman: avoid responsibility for punishable mistakes and at the same time somehow skirt regulations and get things done. It is the basic credo of the successful bureaucrat. Full of fish and vodka, Yuri meandered into melancholy. "Even if a farm earns money in the Soviet Union with honest labor," he said, "to spend the rubles to build a barn, you still have to have a thousand signatures. The person who gives orders isn't responsible for the results."

3

IN 1988, DURING MY TRIP across the USSR with Yuri Chernichenko, the disorder of Soviet farms was new to me. I'd written about the kempt fields of America and had visited European
farms. The bedraggled fields, scrawny animals, and rusty equipment of Soviet farms amazed me. Afterward I experimented
with what I called a *Catalog of Faulty Practices.* There was material in my notes from everywhere along the route. I attempted
a straightforward outline, a few fragments of which looked like
this:

I. Troubles with the selection and use of INPUTS
  [followed by A's, B's, and C's, and a's, b's, and c's]

II. Troubles with choice and execution of METHODS
  A. tillage
  B. substance application
  C. planting
  D. cultivation
  E. harvesting
  F. handling output
  G. coordinating operations
  H. managing people

  [and so on]

III. Troubles handling OUTPUTS
[followed by A's, B's, and C's]

IV. FARM-INFRASTRUCTURE troubles
  A. banking and finance
  B. subsidies
  C. transport
    a. roads
    b. trains
  D. communications
    a. phones
    b. journals
    c. education

The alphabet stretched onward. I'd hoped that such an outline would sort memories of the jumble, the way a surgeon organizes a mangled wound. But the relations among the broken and missing parts of the Soviet food system were so multiple and incalculable that the outline soon became a way (a playful way, by the time I was done) of asserting how far beyond the capacities of an outline the problems reached. The connections joining a given moment of work in an American farmer's day to the greater national good are so commonplace, so built in and habitual, that legendary "invisible hands" of economics might have drawn them.

Imagine an impossible experiment, a thought experiment, that brings out the meanings of the institutions and conventions joining particular jobs to the general economy. Imagine Iowa without banks, and without hard currency, and with the individual's right to buy and sell removed, and the freedom revoked to work, hire and fire, communicate, contract with, set prices for goods and labor, and pay for goods and labor. Until then, these meanings remain transparent and pervasive, unperceived, like water for a fish.

The farm situation in the USSR replicated the thought experiment. With that in mind, I continued my outline as a way to get my bearings in the midst of complicated disorder. It was even hard to limit the outline to events inside the farm fences. The problems on farms came from the society, and flowed back into it.

At the start, in Lithuania, then, at the western edge of the Soviet Union, I recorded this entry: *Apple Farm named after Michurin renewing orchard by planting stock for full-sized apple trees. Commercial apple growers back home, by the 1960s, shifted to semidwarf and dwarf trees, which can be picked more quickly, cheaply, and efficiently, grow more densely, yield more per unit of land, labor, investment.*

At a ceremonial lunch in the gym of the farm, administrators sat me down next to a young, dark-haired, fast-blinking engineer. To my surprise, between formal toasts to international friendship, and exchanges of gifts and photographs, he whispered to me that he'd spent two years at MIT studying plasma-field engineering. He'd come home, he said, and been shipped at once to this farm. He'd had to organize a small factory for etching little fleurs-de-lis on wine glasses, which were then sold in northern Europe, bringing the bosses hard currency. The engineer was furious at this misuse of his training. He hated doing this assigned work. And he despised his bosses. He'd been invited and seated next to me because he spoke English. But throughout lunch he whispered to me contemptuously about his bosses' mismanagement, about mishandled harvests and epidemic mastitis in the milking herd. He beseeched me to visit his apartment in Vilnius that evening after my farm tour. I was especially interested because my great-grandparents had fled from there a century earlier.

After lunch, a jeep drove me to an obviously prepared spot, a patch of newly mown grass in a green orchard thick with red apples. I gazed as required, nodded appropriate appreciation, and then lit out cross-lots, striding briskly away from my hosts as fast as I could. I hadn't covered twenty yards before I heard alarmed yelling. I figured they were upset at what I'd see outside the scripted area, which is what I wanted to see. I kept going. So when the chief field supervisor of the orchard caught up to me, I gestured — heartily and nonchalantly — for him to walk along with me, and I crossed yet another row of trees. He darted past me, planted himself, put his hands on my shoulders, and stopped me dead. He was shouting.

Sorokin, my interpreter, huffed up to us. I was finding it awfully hard to get an unscheduled glimpse at anything. I surveyed the trees. The yield was in fact pretty good here, too, ten rows off the designated viewing spot, and the pruning no worse. The field supervisor was still yelling and pointing.

"*Ostorozhno! Sobaki!*" Beware! Dogs!

Far off, two German shepherds bounded up the row toward us. At the top of his lungs, the supervisor commanded them to stop. They kept barking as they ran. He commanded them again, and finally they lay down, close by, watching carefully. He escorted me back to the jeep.

"You could have been attacked!" he barked. "I was shouting because we have dogs patrolling the orchard."

"Do you have a problem with deer?"

"No, with people."

"Why?"

"People are people."

My hosts had a sauna fired up. They'd laid out fragrant birch switches for stimulating the circulation. My engineer friend showed up as I sat in there with the officials. He sweated and switched and waited, obviously suffering, until all his chubby bosses had left the sauna, and quickly panted out a plan: he'd offer me a ride back to town in his car, just when everyone else had entered the Gosagroprom van.

It didn't work. After supper I found myself climbing into the van. He was not in sight. Just as I sat down, through the rear window I saw the engineer's car pull up. I saw a boss lean in the window and say something to the engineer. The van pulled away; the engineer's car stayed behind. I never saw the engineer again.

Back in my room, I turned to the *Catalog of Faulty Practices* section of my notes, and after the part about the dwarf trees, wrote: *Engineer's skills mismanaged, misused. Social conditions lead toward theft by farm residents; dogs needed.*

I looked up Ivan Vladimirovich Michurin's history. He was a useful hero, a Soviet Russian from the Ryazan region, a few hundred miles southeast of Moscow, not from Lithuania at all — heroes had been imported into Lithuania along with the regime. He'd been an industrious amateur, a peasant puttering at fruit breeding, backed by no stringent science, a benign crank. He bred a few hardy apple varieties. Because of this work he was selected as an exemplar of a new social truth: agri-wisdom "rises from the earth under socialism." Soviet home-grown talent beats fancy Western science. He was systematically mythologized. His village was renamed Michurinsk in 1932, a few years before he died. His name was transfigured into a praiseful adjective — used in such phrases as "Michurinist agriculture" — to signal the grassrootedness of the anti-Western pseudoscience of Trofim Lysenko, the academic tyrant who dominated biological and agricultural research from late in Stalin's reign through Khrushchev's. I added the *deification of Michurin* to my *Catalog.*

◆

At the other end of the trip notebook, in Siberia, I found more *Catalog* entries — many about run-down grain fields. Out the windows of many cars, Yuri and I saw sorry, ill-plowed, depleted fields pushing out scrawny wheat stalks — to my eyes, a sign of *effort squandered on ground too infertile to merit man-hours and tractor-hours and the price of seed and fertilizer and pesticide and management* (I wrote). By means of crop rotations developed and proved out over a century in the grain-growing areas of the Dakotas and Saskatchewan, and in central Sweden, rundown fields always got fallow time. They'd even been a mandatory part of Soviet agriculture, especially a "seven-field rotation" developed by a naturalized ex-American named Williams in the 1920s. A collective-farm chairman near Novosibirsk said dolefully that he did indeed know better and it pained him to supervise some of his fields, but that his *"big bosses" in the region and back in Moscow had ordered him not to fallow* because "they need the grain for the quota."

"They need the grain," the chairman said. But (my *Catalog of Faulty Practices* records) we'd *crossed the nation during winter-wheat harvest and saw workers building grain mountains, truckload by truckload, in many open-air storage yards.* An urban tourist might view this as the sight of bountiful harvest. Anyone from Iowa would have been surprised that the grain lay unsheltered from rain. There were far too few on-farm grain sheds, grain bins, grain elevators. And to Yuri, the outdoor grain mountains symbolized the Soviet Union's agricultural paralysis. The grain crop loss was officially estimated at about thirty percent a year.

Viktor Lishchenko, the agricultural economist, later recalled the history of the outdoor grain piles, in a conversation back in Moscow: "Officials for decades insisted that centralized grain drying and storage were more efficient, so the grain must be taken away. They never allowed farms to build grain dryers and storage bins, which exist in your Midwest on every farm." These policies were designed to prevent peasants from gaining power by holding back grain. But (I wrote in the *Catalog*): *Low storage capacity leads to spoiled grain.* "Grain that stays on farms often gets wet," said Lishchenko. "Multiply this by many farms and many years — it is a big error, a huge error. Sometimes we have thirty or forty million tons of grain a year lying on the ground. The agricultural bureaucracy's secrecy has been not only from the people but from the leaders." Lishchenko spoke as if Gorbachev (who had in fact risen first through the agricultural bureaucracy) might yet save the system, now that the secrecy was gone.

◆

In the Kuban region, the day we drove the dirt roads through Gorbachev's home farm, ripe wheat had waved teasingly in a sunny field soaked by rain. The farm had the privilege of possessing a few lightweight Finnish combines. Beside us, they skittered through the muck, harvesting in the sodden fields. The farm's fleet of older, Soviet-built Niva combines stood in a storage yard, too heavy to get on the fields, as were its Don 1500s. These were the latest from the combine monopoly that had banned Yuri. *Heavy combines* went into the *Catalog*.

◆

One afternoon we'd visited the Kuban Machine Testing Institute, where combine prototypes from the monopoly were evaluated "five or six years before they are on the farm," Director Aleksander Korobeinikov said. "This is a very *long advance design time* [I wrote in the *Catalog*] by Western standards." He also boasted to us that "our testing institute was the only one that didn't recommend passing the Don for mass production."

It had gone into production anyhow. The official Canadian farm-machine-rating organization ranked its performance far below all Western combines. The older Niva, many Russian operators told us, was hard to reset for harvesting tall grain, and missed wheat if the stalks were "lodged" — bowed over by heavy yields. *Bad feedback between testing organization and combine manufacturer,* I wrote.

◆

Near Pyatigorsk, on the crowded airport road at Mineralnye Vody (Mineral Waters), we'd dodged past a rickety red dump truck heading from a farm field to the central grain-storage yard. The truck's tarpaulin flapped above a smashed tailgate. A thick flume of grain poured from the truck as it drove, splashing onto the road. Yuri shouted at our driver and made him pass the truck. Yuri flagged it down. He flashed his Party ID — he was still the loyal opposition at the time — and dressed down the driver for ten minutes. I wrote up the infraction: *Demoralized driver with no stake in careful work.*

◆

"The Soviet Union doesn't even grow high-protein wheat," Yuri said when he climbed back into the van. New wheat varieties had lower protein content than older ones. "The bureaucrats for decades demanded higher yields in each successive Five Year Plan, at any cost. Now drivers who don't care spill this inferior grain on the road — grain that would spoil in uncovered piles anyhow. That is the cost of Five Year Plans!"

The tyrant Trofim Lysenko had played a part. He was an anti-geneticist of sorts who'd believed in the heritability of acquired traits and the glorification of Soviet research. The political utility of these convictions helped Lysenko muscle his way to the head of the agri-science establishment under Stalin. He'd destroyed it, and engineered the executions of true scientists. Yuri especially remembered Nikolai Ivanovich Vavilov, founder of the Institute of Genetics of the Academy of Sciences, who had developed disease-resistant grain varieties and revamped the seed array chosen by Soviet farmers, while also cataloging 150,000 cultivated plants he'd gathered in expeditions all over the world. Yuri spoke with fury. Early in his career, Vavilov had helped "discover" Lysenko. Lysenko had had Vavilov killed. *Lysenko did bad science. Bad wheat resulted.*

Later, I looked up Vavilov. During the brutality of Stalin's purges, he had been mocked by Lysenkoites as "anti-Michurinist," which meant reactionary and, ironically, unscientific. One of his denouncers wrote: "Vavilov . . . and the organization . . . give refuge at the institute's experimental stations to men who cannot be politically trusted." In August 1940 Vavilov was arrested by the NKVD.* After a perfunctory trial, judges found him guilty of belonging to a rightist conspiracy, of spying for England, of leading a fictive "Labor Peasant Party," of sabotaging agriculture, and of having links with "anti-revolutionists" abroad. The tribunal sentenced him to death. He spent months of uncertainty, then his sentence was commuted to ten years' imprisonment. But he died in a windowless cell in 1942, of malnutrition. *Lysenko killed Vavilov.*

Shortly before his death, he'd been elected to the Royal Society of London. But inside the USSR, it wasn't until long after Stalin had died, and Khruschev and Lysenko both were ousted, that Vavilov could be rehabilitated. Lysenko was toppled in 1964. Nowadays there are a few collective farms and research centers named after Vavilov, right alongside those named after Michurin. An entourage of officials took me to a statue of Vavilov beside an agricultural college in Poltava. Once the long-suppressed criticism by real scientists had broken free, an investigation of Lysenko revealed wholesale research fraud. Even his nationally glorified dairy herd of Jersey crosses, which Lysenko had kept on a show farm, turned out to be a sham. Lysenko had secretly had all but the best animals culled. *Catalog* entry: *Dairy-breeding efforts sidetracked by Lysenko.*

The damage Lysenko did long outlived him, because of the nature of the Soviet system. Saying he represented true science, Lysenko had *installed loyal drones throughout the network of research farms, labs, and colleges, and their administrative*

*My recounting draws heavily on material in Zhores Medvedev's *Rise and Fall of T. D. Lysenko,* Columbia University Press, 1969.

influence spread. In 1965, after Lysenko's downfall, authorities suspended instruction in biology all over the country for a school year so teachers could be retrained and textbooks rewritten. So that no student would miss out, the course was moved the following year from ninth to tenth grade. Although Lysenko's damaging regime came under public scorn in the Soviet Union decades ago, his academic appointees often kept their jobs and kept advancing. They are just now retiring from the shambles of a system they shared in creating.

◆

Half a continent away, Dr. Pyotr Goncharov, a post-Lysenko genuine scientist and the director of the Siberian Research Institute of Plant Breeding and Selection, told Yuri and me about another problem concerning wheat. "We use vast amounts of grain inefficiently in feeding animals," he said. "Half our grain, including much wheat, is fed raw, unprocessed, so its nutrition is largely unavailable to the animals. This is not done in the West. And, the animals we feed it to aren't genetically efficient by world standards. We feed animals one hundred fifty million metric tons of grain annually — twice what we'd need if we did it right."

◆

The year 1988 was an apogee for *perestroika,* and often farmers didn't bother pretending things were great. In many places, frankness was in. And in some places where it wasn't, there was still no point in pretending while, within view, milkmaids kneeled at their work in muddy wooden summer sheds. Yuri's presence as a knowing insider also helped us avoid the outright charades that Western journalists often suffered on brief, guarded tours of top farms. But on one farm in the central Ukraine, we walked into a barn and "Aha!" exclaimed the chairman, as if making a discovery. "Over here, they happen to be milking!" "Technicians" were, by chance, milking six unusually good-looking cows, just after noon, in a high-tech milking parlor that wasn't hooked up to the barn's plumbing yet. No cows were coming in, no cows going out, and the milk drained into a barrel. *Catalog* entry: *Potemkin cow milking. Old administrative habits endure.*

◆

At State Breeding Plant Red Giant, outside Kharkov, I finally had a chance to ask an accompanying Gosagroprom official why (I wrote in the *Catalog*) *they chose Simmentals — a dual-purpose, milk-and-meat cow breed — although Western farmers have long known Holsteins have superior genes for milking, and that beef breeds such as Angus and Charolais have better genes for growing meaty haunches and shoulders.*

He said he'd had the same thought, but that in reality, "our hay and ensilage won't be protein-rich enough to make use of a Holstein's genetic potential for quite a while." A hay quality-improvement program would have been one of the simplest advances to try — one within the grasp of an ambitious farm chairman. But there was no point in throwing that into the conversation.

Out of curiosity, after returning from that trip I'd called Steve McGuire, records manager of the American Simmental Association, and asked for his assessment of Simmentals as a main dairy — or meat — breed. He'd replied, "Simmentals don't do either job as well as dedicated breeds." In U.S. farming, the Simmental breed is often used to contribute an especially aggressive mothering instinct useful in cross-bred range cattle.

On the Red Giant farm, we were surprised to find one of the nation's few dairy cow ova-transplant labs. Ova transplantation is at the leading edge of Western dairy technology, and is transforming the industry. Using new methods, a technician harvests dozens of fertilized eggs from one of the nation's rare few supermilkers — cows that yield three or four times what normal cows do. The technician then plants the eggs in "host" mothers. In a year, a barnful of average cows will all drop borrowed world-class calves. And the next generation of calves starts with those world-class mothers. Ova transplantation across the United States and Europe has shot dairy productivity upward in the past decade.

"The usefulness of this technology is not so clear now," said the Ukrainian farm's embryologist, Viacheslav Kartashov, in his tiny lab. He and I had both dusted off our college French and were able to chat unmonitored by officials. *"Mais malheureusement,* we haven't enough equipment, reagents, special mediums. The best are from West Germany — they cost hard currency, which leads to many paper steps. I write to my department authority. He writes the proper authority in Kiev. Kiev approves or not, and passes the application up to Moscow. Moscow waits, collecting similar requests, judges their relative value, and maybe approves. The supplies might arrive — in about two years. I am working as my main project on getting twin calves by manipulating embryos. But it's hard to be in touch with the international scientific community. We have no money even for the international journals." *Catalog* entry: *Rigid infrastructure blocks access to Western information about easy high-tech solutions. Wheels being reinvented here. Low funding and isolation lasting heritage of Stalin's policies favoring industry over agriculture.*

A year later Kartashov wrote me, asking to be put in touch with ova-transplant researchers in the United States. I passed along his note but don't know if he got the mail written back to him.

◆

Soviet agri-researchers shared his dilemma, right through *perestroika* and into the present. A mere border away from solutions that they were struggling to rediscover independently, they were so underfunded that they lacked the small budgets of hard currency that could have brought them into the flow of world science. They were standing still while Western researchers ran exuberantly ahead toward biotech farming. As technical development accelerated in world agriculture, the cost of each decade's nonparticipation by the former Soviet Union mounted.

And yet, so fundamentally irrational was the Soviet system that during those decades when the USSR was falling behind the West, it had spent billions of dollars of hard currency importing grain. Had the Soviet Union created even one "island" of West-

ern-level efficiency, Yuri said — one collective farm or one region — it would have been a beacon of the possible, and therefore a mockery of Soviet accomplishment. It would have driven
the system to wild reactions. Thus the few researchers permitted contact with the West dealt with Western suppliers only
through Vneshekonombank, the state bank with a monopoly on
international transactions. This structure concentrated transac-
tion-by-transaction decision-making on the subject of the dangerous but vital Western interface in the hands of central government ideologues in Moscow, who surely considered politics
ahead of productivity. *Catalog entry: Structures walling out
Western technology not naive. Needed for protecting stable
Party control of possible entrepreneurship.*

◆

At the time of my Soviet traverse with Yuri, many European
and American investors were optimistic that joint ventures
with the West held the promise of bypassing state bureaucrats
and really bringing Western solutions to Soviet problems — and
Soviet profits to Western companies. Such ventures did have
the potential to "de-state" business problems, to make the usual
activities of enterprises — buying, producing, selling — also
normal behind Soviet frontiers. That potential, though, was exactly why *regulators and taxers and suppliers and licensers all
made sure joint ventures got snarled by rules, taxes, shortages,
and delimited operations,* I wrote in the *Catalog,* having met
many Western investors who weren't getting anywhere. Joint
ventures were disabled by a system whose reformist spokesper-
sons were calling them a key to reform.

Had joint ventures developed freely, they would have transformed old patterns of work, distribution, and transacting business. Unrestricted, they would have challenged the purpose of
central ministries. The actual terms of investment were almost
always commercially absurd, made profit repatriation difficult
and, ironically, made planning impossible. Few joint ventures
attracted major investment. Most business people who did get
in soon enough regretted plunging. With a few exceptions
(McDonald's is the best known), only large international compa-

nies endured, and what they did was start "beachhead operations" — small offices and token enterprises run at losses, for the purpose of keeping contacts warm against the day when government would open to substantial development.

Model schemes abounded — "agro-industrial associations" that linked farms and processors, quota planning from lower down on high, demand-based ordering of supplies, and a hundred other adjustments that left the basic scheme of things intact. The sum of them all was that *perestroika*-era collective farms and their suppliers and markets slogged toward the uncertain future, adjusted but not essentially changed. Hardly a day passed during my travels with Yuri when local officials didn't casually suggest that I find Western investors for their farm or milk plant or cloth mill, and when local officials didn't casually wonder how their particular job in the scheme of things was handled in the West. But when I pressed officials with questions about how they imagined a Western investment might work out under law, none turned out to have a real business plan — they just had longings. When I described how jobs got done, sadness was often their reply. So after a while, I tried not to have those conversations.

◆

Soviet farms did things so primitively that sweeping technical improvements were just waiting in the West — not even in laboratories but right on the dusty shelves of feed stores and in the garages of equipment dealers in any Iowa town. Soviet farm bosses and chairmen told me, enviously, how eager they were for the West's high-quality technology. However, good technology without good "economic relations" (they called it that) seemed the less essential part of a solution. Soviet regulations forbade the demander and supplier of whatever — funds, services, or technology — from simply getting together and dealing directly with each other as needed. They all had to go through their respective ministries' planners.

Even the rudimentary banking and credit mechanisms that funded technology were restricted by arcane rules to suppress autonomous entrepreneurship. No matter how rich it was, a farm couldn't legally buy what it needed with its profits. Each purchase had to be made from the right sort of bank account, and accompanied by the right stack of permissions, which didn't happen until all the account supervisors and permission-givers had been propitiated. In the absence of hard currency, there wasn't much choice. But even chairmen who longed for better technology often found the prospect of changes to long-set patterns of "economic relations" abstract and unsettling.

There was another element missing too, one even tougher to remedy than bad technology and bad business structures and bad entrenched bureaucracy. *The very infrastructure that enables modern agriculture is woefully underdeveloped — the phones, railways and rolling stock, highways and trucks, trade colleges, animal- and plant-breeding networks, input supply industries, the advisers of how to do things and the timely fixers of what breaks, the processing plants, the storers, the wholesale distributors, the retail shops, the banks to fund the development and operation of every strand of this intricate web of commerce, the currency and laws and even the customs that guide the interactions of all these parts — all are stunted.*

On-farm problems started off-farm with this poor infrastructure. I passed an hour standing in a shower of sparks and watching a virtuosic and very funny machinist near Krasnodar grinding burrs off a homemade stainless-steel tractor gear that he'd spent the day crafting because the part wasn't available and they needed the machine to keep harvesting. Ivan Ropovka, chairman of Collective Farm Lenin, near Poltava, had summed up his situation frankly: "You have an infrastructure. We have to build one. There is nothing to argue about. My workers spend a lot of time looking for a carburetor, or two extra sacks of fertilizer. When there are enough supplies, I can put responsibility on men. But if a brigade chief can't get spares, he'll say it's not his fault he can't fulfill his quota."

◆

All the *Faulty Practices* I'd recorded, the transcontinental display of poor farming Yuri and I witnessed in hundreds of fields and barns on dozens of farms across that dying, stuck-together empire, convinced me that the best of the Soviet Union's collective-farm chairmen were remarkable. They farmed with Soviet bureaucrats rumbling and threatening overhead, and Soviet infrastructure leading to and from the farms, Soviet regulations restricting all work, and Soviet warehouses receiving nearly all of whatever a farm grew. Their business context was so illogical and prohibitive of rational procedure that a transplanted Western go-getting executive would have made even less headway. Chairmen worked with whoever remained at hand — they'd lost the best workers to cities (rural population fell forty percent in the twenty years before Gorbachev). The jobs of remaining workers had grown specific — scribed in rule books, assured by unionlike regulations that also assured salaries. The rules forbade extra pay for good hard work, and strangled initiative.

The large remaining farm population (about twenty percent of Soviet citizens, ten times our farm population) worked, often casually, to fulfill specified quotas. Those workers had every encouragement to just hunker down. Even in a chaotic and hungry nation, few collective-farm residents had to worry about food, clothes, and shelter. No wonder farm workers later favored forces resisting change. Under Khrushchev, peasants had departed from a long period of drudgery. Gorbachev's reforms threatened to restore uncertainty — and Yeltsin's later ones did so.

Intertwined bureaucracies permeated farm chairmen's authority. There were technical advisers (local, regional, all-Union). There were civil, or soviet, officials (local, regional, and all-Union). There were Party functionaries (local, regional, all-Union). The whole lot of them arrived with rule books in hand, offices to defend, and pockets open. An odd accounting system called *khozrashchet*, or "self-accounting," had lately given farms glimpses of their inefficiency, but didn't remedy what it revealed.

For millennia, good farmers of every nation had learned from their own mistakes as a matter of common sense. Frustrated Soviet farm chairmen couldn't even freely react to changes in the weather. Many daily farming decisions simply never got made — no chairman could reliably preempt decisions taken off-farm in ministry or Party offices, months and years beforehand. Crucial decisions — short-term ones like when to plant (when the soil was warm and wet enough) and when to spray (when bugs threatened), and longer-term ones (what machines to order, buildings to build, animals to rear, crops to grow, where to market) — all this farm business happened off-farm. Farm chairmen toiled in that strange context, and the best managed with grace and humor, if with imperfect results. They had to be smart and tough and daring to pull it off.

◆

Yuri and I flew back to Moscow from Siberia, having wandered six thousand miles. We'd done some hard traveling and staggered off the airplane (after the Aeroflot journey from Novosibirsk, on which a family of eleven occupied seats for six across from us). Within an hour, Yuri said his goodbyes and disappeared back into the hubbub of the new political life. I spent a day dozing, stubbornly dreaming private dreams in idiomatic English. I strolled the streets with no mission at all. Moscow was still, in 1988, a challenging city for Western visitors. Except for a three-hour line snaking away from McDonald's and half-hour lines outside every food store, the city presented almost no commercial face. The handful of state restaurants were for official sorts. It often took connections to get in to them. The handful of newly opened cooperative restaurants — they'd been authorized only in 1987 — were too dear for all but gray marketeers and foreigners. The workers' cafés served thin soup and gritty porridge, frequently eaten standing up. The few bars in town served the *nomenklatura*, or, deep in the best hotels, served tourists for dollars.

For those who put in their time in the long lines, the food stores were as drab as the imagination of the state and the vengeance of the clerks could make them, and were nearly innocent of merchandise. Out on the street, peasant vendors, many of them defying anti-market regulations, hawked dried mushrooms, a box or two of garden vegetables, *kvas* by the tankload, gulped from shared glasses. On New Arbat, the walking street that angles through the center of town, *matryoshka* dolls within dolls now included not just cutesy peasant girls within girls, but a Stalin doll with a mustache inside a Khrushchev doll with a bald pate inside a Brezhnev doll with bushy eyebrows inside a Gorbachev doll with a birthmark, serial succubi haunting their ill-fated heir. When it later became semilegal to buy and sell for private gain, the commercial landscape of Moscow metamorphosed in months, and the gangs moved in to control it, but all that hadn't happened yet.

I chatted with a tall young poster merchant who stood bravely by his table on New Arbat. He had a scout down the street, and he was ready to flee at the first whistle. He'd designed his own corny rock-star posters. He'd skimmed paper from the office where he worked days. A buddy in a printshop had "used the machinery at midnight." He offered the posters to eager passing teens, and a knot of customers inspected his wares. He was lighthearted and having fun making money on his own account. I felt that nothing short of a new reign of terror could stop what had started. He'd descended from a lineage of commercial sensibility that reached through centuries of black marketeers and horse traders, under-the-table dealmakers, fixers, skimmers, opportunists, survivors, capitalists all.

Compared to this city life, the farms were still, and would long remain, controlled territory, unventilated by new commercial winds of the possible. A communal conservatism built on a long history of serfdom, restricted activity, and regulation had bred bitterness and futility. Jealousy was still a patriotic emotion out there. In sloppily farmed grain fields, I'd asked ordinary workers why things were no better. They'd said: Wrong equipment, no chance to use personal knowledge of how to do things right, no permission to do jobs well, therefore no enthusiasm for trying.

Walking down New Arbat, where artists sketched portraits, babushkas sold sweet wafers, and folksingers strummed guitars and sang love songs, these farm memories led me to realize something about America that is obvious in the reciting but that I hadn't bothered seeing as remarkable before wandering through the Soviet Union during *perestroika:* our pervasive marketplace calls into being, sharpens, renews, and coordinates wanting with getting, desire with satisfaction. To my chagrin, I caught myself reflecting — no, marveling — that the lineup of shops on a Main Street, or in a mall for that matter, reflects the bountiful, even playful concentration of hundreds of thousands of private ambitions, strategies, skills, and moments of tenacity.

I was stuck, there on the walking street in Moscow, celebrating the connection between greed and many corny human virtues, even if Rotary Clubs and Chambers of Commerce celebrate the same thing.

For many proud people living under Soviet rules that made it difficult to get anything done properly, integrity had often meant resisting or sidestepping usual workday activities rather than engaging in them wholeheartedly. Back in the USA, private desire inspires others to effort; thoughtful service and good work do come up for hire. The marketplace, however clumsily, usually urges folks to do jobs right. Having come of age as an anti-war activist in the late sixties, I found this an alarmingly flag-waving line of thinking on my part. But standing by the rock-poster merchant in the middle of New Arbat, I held it to be self-evident.

4

ON PAPER at least, and in Moscow at least, the state monopoly of commerce was starting to loosen. You could read such assertions by both Soviet and American politicians in the *International Herald Tribune,* if you were quick enough to find a copy on sale at the lobby newsstand of one of the international hotels, which were still off-limits to ordinary Muscovites. On the first afternoon back from my trip with Yuri Chernichenko, my writer friend, I'd had a decent lunch served politely and quickly at one of the new cooperative restaurants. The experience was not normal at all, but downright wondrous for Moscow.

Lenin wrote, "The system of civilized cooperators is the system of socialism." Under that license, the Supreme Soviet passed new laws on cooperatives in May 1988. On casual reading, the new laws seemed, for the first time in half a century, to invite people longing to do private business to jump in. A few adventurous citizens tested the waters, often well-placed young folk with the right connections for cornering private access to public commercial space and for keeping gangs and inspectors at bay. The new laws even stipulated that cooperatives had the same rights as state-sector enterprises, and were exempt from state economic planning. But as cautious Muscovites had anticipated, in Moscow, nothing works out straightforwardly: the old guard immediately applied new local laws that taxed co-ops up to ninety percent.* Still, a cooperative sector had launched it-self. Taxis in Moscow went almost entirely cooperative. The malnourished service sector followed; by mid-1989 co-ops em-ployed about three million people.

Ordinary citizens didn't celebrate. They didn't feel liberated. Many people I would have thought pro-reform, it turned out, hated the idea of cooperatives, and despised the sort of people who went into business. When the new entrepreneurs were Caucasians (from the Caucasus, and especially from Georgia), the muttering got vituperative.

One new "company" whose reported activity had provoked public outrage bought up government-produced T-shirts at gov-ernment-set prices, silkscreened designs on the shirts, and re-sold them at what the market would bear. That infuriated the man in the street, who hadn't found T-shirts in shops in a year and needed a few. He identified with the poor stiffs getting forty rubles a week in the state T-shirt factory. He found it immoral that a few guys were getting rich merely by dabbing a little ink on shirts that they'd probably bribed officials to acquire and to sell. Those guys were getting rich from the labor and property of others. The moral themes that had long been worked to stir popular opinion against private enterprise ran deep in this fourth generation born to socialism. Every high school student had read these lines from Lenin's 1920 essay *"Left-Wing Com-munism — An Infantile Disorder"*:

> Unfortunately, small-scale production is still widespread in the world, and small-scale production *engenders* capitalism and the bourgeoisie, continuously, daily, hourly, spontaneously, and on a mass scale. All these reasons make the dictatorship of the proletariat necessary and victory over the bourgeoisie is impossible without a long, stubborn and desperate life-and-death struggle which calls for tenacity, discipline, and a single and inflexible will.

Perestroika hadn't erased generations of public training. To the contrary, it was a Party-preserving movement and implied a re-inforcement of such doctrinal convictions. But at the same

*This paragraph follows pages 292 and 293 of Richard Sakwa's 1990 book, *Gor-bachev and His Reforms*.

time, there were plenty of comrades in the street with plenty of rubles in their mattresses who were aching for jazzy T-shirts and for beer in the new cafés and a hundred other amenities. The market instantly showed itself ravenous for novelty. For the year or so that the new laws on cooperatives were interpreted liberally, entrepreneurs set forth as best they could to experiment in the turbulent zone between public and private interest. The few cooperative restaurants that had managed to open found ways around the prohibition against buying scarce supplies at state shops. City inspectors could collect their bribes every time they found butter in restaurant refrigerators. Profits were sudden and enormous for T-shirt makers, vendors, restaurateurs, and for inspectors.

The boundary between public fairness and private advantage had always been a major theme of socialist ideology, and seventy years of public training had tilted the popular morality that most parents taught their children far toward fairness and away from private advantage. All-Union, regional, and city officials (of both Party and soviet) fiddled with contending turf-saving and face-saving ways to crack down on cooperatives even while nominally supporting Gorbachev's reform laws permitting them. It was a very complicated time. The precise location of this margin whipsawed mysteriously, but public opinion remained grumblingly, steadfastly against overt commercial assertions of personal advantage.

Nevertheless, the poster and T-shirt salesmen and likeminded entrepreneurs had flooded onto New Arbat quickly, like swamp water that had found a hill to flow down. Virtually moments after they could do so while risking only police harassment but not their necks, the street salesmen defined desires for which passersby would pay cash, found paper or blank shirts, ways to print, and showed up on the street aiming to sell desired things. Laws, as much as any fatal dimension of "Russian character," shaped action.

My thoughts cautiously drifted toward intercultural comparison. It wasn't mistaking Soviet behavior for American to consider the mystery of why we differed so. The salesmen brought to mind what had seemed fresh about *perestroika:* the prospect that the state was opening itself to the mighty economic force of individual initiative. It was a good time to think about individual initiative in Soviet life.

Opportunities for exercising individual initiative mostly weren't there. It had been officially excluded. It had always been suspect. It threatened to put some people above others, and selected innovators over ideologues. It was incompatible with planned development, because innovation by its nature leads in unplanned directions. It upset hierarchs with all the threats to established order that accompany conspicuous merit.

And yet the challenges of growing food and getting it to everyone, throughout a century of rapidly evolving technology, have required of scientists, funders, farmers, distributors and administrators in every other nation on earth, constant and decisive innovation at all levels. In the aftermath of my transits of the USSR and the USA with Yuri Chernichenko, these were the sorts of things I was thinking about. Across the nation, just as I'd found houses missing from all the most beautiful house sites, I found innovators missing from all the likely sites for innovation.

It would be wrong, however, to say I did not encounter individual initiative on my trips. I found plenty of it, and not just in the accomplishments of the best collective-farm chairmen and in the daring of a few heroic big shots who muscled the system forward in spite of itself and in the irony-free efforts of those model *Stakhanovite* citizens — the workers who got deified on posters for their hyperactive feats on behalf of the system. Innovation blazed outside the system, in the brilliant farming of tiny private plots all across the country, in the ambitions of a few new lease-brigade leaders, in the deeds and tales of renegade reformers who had suffered for their audacity.

◆

I spent an afternoon in a borrowed office in Moscow, interviewing a grand old man of Soviet agriculture, Fyodor Trofimovich Morgun. Out on the collective farms, Morgun was well known, venerated as a crusader, a rare insider who had succeeded in doing his job effectively. One of several books Morgun had written, *Field Without Plow,* sat on the shelves of nearly every collective-farm chairman I'd visited. More than one chairman told me, in maudlin voice, that in the 1960s Morgun became known as "the Father of Minimum Tillage." And, at least by his own account, Morgun's earlier history included several decisive moments when he'd taken innovative stands against higher Party authority, his career at risk, and imprisonment threatened.

Morgun was a wiry man in his mid-sixties. He moved slowly. His health was poor. He had retired just weeks earlier and said he was keen to reflect on his career. It was a sad time for him. He'd just come from the hospital and his wife's health was failing. My conversation with him complicated my vision of Party obduracy. As self-serving as such an autobiographical recollection surely is, the sense came through of a man who had acted with courage in a perverse system. He'd fought that absurdity, winning respect as an *apparatchik* who worked from the inside. He described a losing battle and a few others he'd won. Wistful reformer was a role he'd often played. His private good sense and his drive to innovate made him singular — if only because, as his tale shows, the application of common sense was itself innovative and required courage. He'd fought for a straightforward technological reform and never quibbled with the need for Party micromanagement of the food system — nor with state-fixed prices, state-planned production goals and methods, and state ownership of land. Ironically, his anti-system heroics led to his elevation to the highest ranks of the authority he'd fought. He'd ended up as Party chief of eastern Ukrainian agriculture.

"Bread from overseas is bitter," Morgun began. He was a speechmaker. I listened. "Over here we have discovered the reverse of the alchemist's philosophers' stone — we buy foreign grain and feed it to cattle; we've found a way to turn gold into manure. From my childhood, when I ran around our village before World War Two, or plowed or harvested, I looked at the fields. I always walked with open eyes, attentively — back when the people were crazy with Stalin. It sounds strange, but even before the war — from the fifth grade on, from age eleven or twelve — I believed Stalin was a con man. Our radios screamed his praise, as did newspapers and movies. I knew already these were all lies. In our hut hung a peasant calendar.

One day, we turned the page and there was Stalin's portrait. I wasn't brave, but I socked my fist against his face. I gave him the finger. My family and my whole village had suffered from collectivization — working day and night while mass repression went on and you couldn't even get bread.

"My sister is four years older, born in 1920, and my brother two years older. They are peasants who work hard — honest people. An honest person is like a saint. Had I dared say to my own sister, especially after the war, the things I say now about Stalin, she would have denounced me and led the KGB officer to me. My father-in-law, an honest Communist, joined the Party before the war. During the war he'd commanded a heavy tank at Stalingrad, Berlin. He was wounded many times, and marched in the victory parade in Moscow. A legendary man. If he had known what I was thinking, he would have killed me himself. The fact that honest people believed such things demonstrates the power of propaganda.

"Even as a child, I noticed our soil was in trouble. If you sow the land every year and plow deeply, you lose a lot. I saw it on collective-farm fields. At Petrovsk Agricultural College, Professor Berkovich, who taught us soil science, described Manitoba and Saskatchewan, which he had visited during the dust bowl. I thought about tillage that worked to prevent such problems. Later, I became chairman of State Farm Tolbukhin in Kokchetav, Kazakhstan, the Virgin Lands. An event there shaped my career.

"It was 1955. There was a big plenum of the entire regional Party. Every chairman of a collective farm, director of a machine tractor station, and the like participated. We were led toward making a decision to double the quota for tilling virgin soil. We'd already planned to till forty-five thousand acres. Suddenly, the new plan from above was for seventy thousand — and of course it specified exactly which ground would be added. Every speaker got up and said, 'Yes, I am for it, I agree with it.' I asked for the floor. Surprisingly, I was given it.

"There, I revolted. I objected to this plan. I said we're being driven to plow salty soil, sandy soil, the banks of a lake, and tight around the villages where we lived. 'We'll lose pastures for our cattle, and will end with fields of weeds, and have our own dust bowl,' I said. 'We'll have the disasters of Canada and America.' I started to explain the lectures of my professors, but people were shouting, pulling me from the lectern, trying to prevent me from finishing. I was scared and sweating, but kept going. I said I absolutely support the Party's decision to develop the Virgin Lands, but we must carry out the decision wisely.

"The next man up was the first secretary of the regional Party committee, a man named Pazhits. His whole speech hit against me, trying to refute — no, not just refute — trying to smash me. Among other things, he said, 'What we can smell is a lot of stink, and the rot is this anti-Party speech by Morgun. The country needs bread. We must till more land.' I still recall the date, it was such an important one for me: June 5, 1955, over thirty years ago.

"I had been scheduled to go from this plenum back south to Poltava. I'd spent the winter in the Virgin Lands, in a tent, because there was no housing yet. I'd finally gotten a new apartment and was going to get my kids and wife, reunite our family. But as soon as the plenum ended, they called a meeting of the executive committee of the Party. The first secretary of the regional Party committee moved to expel me from the Party and fire me from my job.

"It was the second secretary, Sergei Ivanov, from Leningrad, along with a guy named Smirnov — he managed the regional trust of farms — who saved me. They didn't defend me for my being right. They simply said he's a nice guy, and he's young, and he lost control of himself. That's all.

"The plowing went on. After five to seven years it was a disaster, one more severe than I could have envisioned. A dust bowl, weeds, erosion of land — it all happened.

"In 1963 Comrade Reganets, by then minister of agriculture in Kazakhstan, ran into me and recalled the meeting. He liked me. I'd gotten back in the Party's good graces by then, and had become minister of all state farms of the Virgin Lands. 'Fyodor, Fyodor,' he said to me, 'could anyone have imagined you would turn out so right?' Reganets sat in Alma-Ata — my office was in Tselinograd, in the middle — and we both had tried to put things back in order.

"That year, I was second secretary of Pavlodar. And I was

ordered to go to Canada for a month. I went and studied Canadian methods, farming without plowing, with minimum tillage. To my amazement at the time, the Canadians received us with open hearts, concealing nothing from us. There's a chapter in my book describing this trip. It had a big effect on me.

"Ten years later, in 1973, back at last in the Ukraine, I became first secretary of the Poltava regional Party committee. It was the moment I'd been waiting for. The first thing I did was introduce the 'flat cutter' instead of the plow — ten years after I'd seen it. Eighteen years after the plenum in Kazakhstan.

"Poltava had been devastated by World War Two. The Germans, defeated near Kursk and Belgorod, had retreated through Poltava. Hitler had ordered a strong defensive line set up there. Advancing Red and retreating German forces had confronted each other; the battles ruined everything, and the economy stayed wrecked long after the war. So in 1973 the Poltava region had the lowest grain yields in the Ukraine and their cattle had the worst statistics. I knew they'd have to be solved from the grassroots upward. I chose two directions: rebuilding villages and tilling the earth without plows.

"We needed better crops so we could make enough money to pay people for their labor. Because I was the first Party secretary, I could publish certain orders. One was interesting: if a peasant starts building himself a house, the procurator has no business setting foot on this land or looking into where the peasant managed to get the building materials — I ordered these people, 'Don't bother him except to help him.'

"You see, when a peasant built a house, there was no legitimate place he could buy bricks, cement, paint. If he had them, of course it meant he was stealing them. Here is a forest, and there is a tree, perhaps fallen in a storm. A peasant will come pick it up. It's a crime. He could be put on trial. On the other hand, he needed it. I shouldered this responsibility and protected them.

"You know, this is still true of our system. Suppose a collective-farm chairman needs a big quantity of some building materials for a project. If he's a wheeler-dealer type he goes to the city, taking enormous amounts of good food, and bribes the right people with presents. It's a crime. He's got to glance over his shoulder for the procurator. But still he takes the risk. There were always movements against such people. Can you imagine how many times every strong farm chairman was denounced — how often the procurator got letters denouncing them? I got reports from the head of the regional police. I really saved a few from jail.

"Another report: One fall, two tractor drivers from a village near Kobiliaki stole three sacks of oat seed. The police had arrested them. Their trial was near, and I was just hearing about it. Each could have gotten seven or eight years in jail. I asked questions: 'Why were they stealing those things? Who are those people?'

"I made a habit of telling the whole region over the radio whatever I found out in such cases, from the office of the regional Party committee, in clubs, offices — people came together in the evening and listened around the radio set. I was able to reach the whole Poltava *oblast*, and I described the case of the tractor drivers. Each could have suffered in jail for years. But they weren't that guilty. They had taken the barley from a stack of animal-feed sacks. But they had done it because they knew the seeds were excellent, and they'd wanted to sow them at their private plots. It would have made more food for everyone. So I gave an order not to punish them. I said the case shows that the people know what seeds are good; we leaders are the guilty ones — especially the leaders of that farm who hadn't planted the seeds, nor offered them to the farm members either, for free or for token payment.

"During the forced collectivization peasants had to steal for survival; they got no pay for farm work. So I was lenient. As first secretary, when I punished somebody, it was for a bad attitude toward the people. That was one side of my life work, the social-reform side.

"There is the technical side: the flat cutter versus the plow. Everybody was against me — the more supposedly scientifically sophisticated, the more against me. Can you guess why? Only because the idea came from the West! The big Party bosses already thought I was soft because I was reasonable with peasants. Then I introduced this foreign technology, and they thought I was an utter adventurist. They accused me of trying to destroy the region that I was actually helping rebuild. Official scientists reviewed my work badly. Some made anonymous complaints to the Central Committee in Moscow, to the first Party secretary in Kiev, to *Pravda*, to *Izvestia*. I was cornered, the complaints were everywhere. The seven years between '73 and '80 were very difficult for me."

Some background: "Minimum tillage" had been common practice in the American Midwest for fifty years. Farmers stir the soil and incorporate crop residue with chisel-shaped plows or big discs. Older-fashioned "moldboard plows" knife under and fold over a continuous strip of soil. Sod from the surface then sits underground in a thin sheet at the depth of plowing. A zealot, E. H. Faulkner, wrote a book called *Plowman's Folly* in 1943. Agri-scientists have verified his finding that soil stays more fertile when stirred, not flipped. In America, the selection of tillage methods never became politicized; farmers did what worked best.

Morgun's screed, *Field Without Plow*, preached the gospel that improved production was within reach through minimum tillage. It suggested something that Party authorities later actually came to like: a mere technical fix could make the food problem go away. Switch to minimum tillage and farms would get efficient. No need to cleanse the Party of that stodgy old guard of central planners and quota enforcers. Party regulars hadn't liked minimum tillage when it first came up for discussion in the fifties. The transformation didn't take hold until the late seventies.

A farmer in Iowa first hearing about minimum tillage, or any other innovation, might just up and try it. Most basic innovations in Iowa started that way. A few farmers here and there fool with a new piece of equipment, or a new crop or a new barn design, often one proffered by a private company based on its own research. Then academic experimenters study field tests, and then farm magazines write up the news. I once interviewed Adolph Oien, a farmer from George Washington, in Washington State. He'd noticed that one of his cows was always clean, observed why, imagined a barn filled with little fences that guided cows to walk head-forward into patches of clean bedding, but didn't allow them to turn around and foul it. Within a few years, without divine guidance of Party or government, his vision had spread all over the country and became the "climax" version of dairy housing. That wasn't how innovation worked in Morgun's Ukraine.

"From '81 onward, my Poltava's yields were invariably the highest of all neighboring regions, so my way worked best. We had the best statistics in tillage improvement and in cattle production in the entire Ukraine. But there are agricultural scientists in Kiev and in Kharkov who, to this day, long after *perestroika* has started, still feel my method was adventurist and irresponsible.

"I believe *perestroika* will improve farming. Of course years will pass; we'll move through a complicated period — collective and state farms, lease brigades, individual farmers; I'm supporting all of it. I am even for some private ownership of land. You'd start with the property a peasant has next to his house, with his little orchard, his vegetable garden — but the agricultural land base should remain state-owned, supporting state and collective farms. Leadership should be by bright managers, democratically chosen."

Morgun was a high bureaucrat in a path of command that led from the Communist Party Central Committee straight down through the system to the peasant who reluctantly (and as minimally as he could) tilled the assigned crops in a collective farm's fields. Morgun's special concerns encompassed technical reform and a certain appreciation of local peasant life. Markets and private initiative remained anathema to him. Morgun was what a bold official innovator looked like, fighting for limited change, risking rank and freedom to institute a reform as basic and restricted as allowing Soviet dirt to be plowed the same sensible way that the rest of the world had plowed for decades.

◆

The average collective-farm cow gave forty percent as much milk as an American cow. A collective pig ate the same weight of feed every month as an American pig, but because it had inferior feed and breeding, the collective pig took twice as long to fatten to one hundred kilograms. Soviet farms ran a third more combines than American farms, but harvested half the grain. And the Soviet Union's farms, according to a 1988 article in *The Economist*, were a tenth as productive as Western farms in yield per work-hour, a measure of labor efficiency. That sort of disparity has been true for decades.

There was a place along that great chain of absolute authority where I'd regularly witnessed a Protestant-level work ethic and widespread innovation — right at the bottom of the chain, in the private plots peasants were allowed to maintain behind their apartments and cottages. Those gardens were always pretty, adjacent tiny flags of green land, all neat, industriously weeded, with pampered plants and jury-rigged cold frames, the subject of lavish and constant hand labor. Produce poured forth — a third of the nation's milk, meat, eggs and vegetables, and sixty percent of potatoes and fruit came from the two percent of farmland in private plots. Peasants' evening labors on these private plots yielded far better crops than did their day labors in planned fields. And in adjoining sheds, peasants' private cows milked more, and their private pigs fattened faster. The privately tended vegetable gardens grew as gloriously as any behind a cottage in rural England or Italy. These gardens were glaring but unacknowledged advertisements against collective enterprise. Even before Leninism, they had been a much regulated embarrassment and a necessary source of sustenance.

Zhores Medvedev's 1988 book, *Soviet Agriculture*, argues convincingly that those in charge, whether local aristocrats or local Party bosses, had adjusted the size of these tiny proprietorships as the economic needs of the era demanded. Sometimes so little land was granted that peasants fell into malnourished peonage and ceased producing surplus for sale in the cities. Sometimes plot grants grew so large that peasants resisted work in the bosses' fields or factories. The Bolsheviks promised "land for people" in 1917, and after taking over that November, encouraged smallholding. By 1927 Stalin and the Central Committee considered support of smallholding "right-wing deviation." The deadly period of forced collectivization started. Squads of Party organizers appeared in every rural district and made peasants aggregate their small farms into collective farms, turning over land, crops, animals, and houses. Amid widespread resistance, the organizers confiscated villagers' food, which of course led to widespread starvation. Soldiers stormed the huts of any peasants holding normal household supplies, charged the families with the crime of hoarding the people's grain, executing many, confiscating and collectivizing their land. Peasants retaliated by slaughtering their own private chickens and workhorses.

Fifteen or twenty million deaths later, the forces of revolutionary cooperation had won out. Zhores Medvedev observed that at that point "the crisis became permanent." During the six ensuing decades of collective farming, private plots were sometimes officially considered shameful and sometimes as wholesome as victory gardens — depending on the intent of the latest propaganda campaign. As the Second World War approached and Stalin squeezed farm workers' salaries in order to fund rapid industrialization, he also allowed private garden allotments to increase so farm workers could feed themselves. In the early sixties Khrushchev called private garden plots relics of capitalism and trimmed them back, complaining that peasants spent too little time at collective-farming duties. The shift back didn't solve the problem. Gorbachev again allowed plot size to expand, to fight food shortages.

The private plots Yuri and I had seen averaged about three quarters of an acre. Peasants mostly grew cabbages and cucumbers, tomatoes and turnips, berries and fruits, which they ate, canned, or swapped. They sold a quarter of what they grew, often at market prices.

A peasant could not legally hire another to work in his garden, nor legally use motorized equipment or horses. Still, enforcement was lax. I'd spotted decadent traces of innovative personal ambition: one homemade "doodlebug" tractor and a few ramshackle greenhouses large enough to grow hothouse crops for market. And we'd heard gossip about the occasional private hiring of neighbors or transient labor. Such enterprise inspired fierce envy and righteous vandalism. Neighbors were known to burn down such greenhouses. Peasants told a self-mocking joke: When Boris got a cow, his neighbor Pavel's ambition wasn't to get a cow too, but to kill Boris's cow. Keeping down the Ivanovs was to the Soviet regime what keeping up with the Joneses was in America. The national mission of ensuring fair ownership of all wealth elevated envy to an inevitable, and even patriotic, emotion.

◆

As peasants walked from their own soil to communal fields, their zeal diminished and their labors slowed. It wasn't surprising. Soviet farm management assigned work crews daily quotas for exactly specified chores — plow fifty hectares, pick fifty crates of apples. Workers rushed the plowing, bruised the apples, punched out after eight hours, and scurried back to their plots. With pay guaranteed, few workers relished a widespread *perestroika* management innovation — shifting field workers to piecework payment. And, it didn't work very well. Total wages were low relative to city wages, but with little to buy and rent, and with social services provided by the sheltering communal farms, workers across the nation had accumulated a huge "overhang" of private savings. Higher pay linked to greater effort in public fields just didn't inspire many workers. A feed-mill operator on a farm near Kharkov had shrugged and said to Yuri, "I'm not interested in working harder or longer. We have enough." Reform economists came up with a scheme to counter that attitude: they'd import billions of dollars' worth of Western kitchen appliances to excite peasants and coax savings out from under the mattresses. What really happened to all their hard-earned savings was sadder: they never got to spend it. Between 1990 and 1992, inflation melted it. Stacks of rubles turned into piles of paper in a few months, leaving no more motivation to work for low wages, paid piecework or monthly, than there'd been before.

Back in Khrushchev's time, a Ukrainian named Ivan Khudenko, assigned to head a collective farm in Kazakhstan, had tried the piecework-pay solution that *perestroika* reformers revived. But in Khudenko's era it was an innovative and heretical social experiment, perhaps in part because it reiterated a management technique exploitive Western mill owners had used since the first steam engine cranked over the first spinning jenny. Khudenko offered a crack "link" work crew high piecework rates — at a time when a ruble was still a ruble and money could motivate workers. The workers responded, and Khudenko's crews reached high levels of productivity that shamed regional administrators.

Yuri Chernichenko had known the man. "Khudenko was a husky man — acute, clever, and his plan worked wonders. Productivity doubled, tripled, and kept climbing. High production shames supervisors of lesser crews. Prospering workers gall neighbors. It is harder to tame the envy of a babushka than the greed of a Georgian profiteer. After a season or two, Kazakh leaders fired him. He wrote a few more payment vouchers to finish business, and that gave authorities an excuse. They trumped up criminal charges and sent him to prison for writing the vouchers. He died there. His was a new movement they knew they must kill. Now we have a nice documentary film about him."

◆

Khudenko had been on the right track in identifying and solving a chronic problem of the dictatorship of the proletariat. His sin was that he'd been too effective. Around the same time, a milder, ineffective innovator, Vladimir Pervitsky, became a Hero of Socialist Labor, winning the Order of the Red Banner for "inventing" an ideologically acceptable scheme to pay workers more. His particular genius seems to be that he provided administrators a tool with which they could appear to be addressing the problem of worker motivation without rocking the boat. Yuri had met him, and rediscovered him during our travels together, still heading a "brigade of intensive labor" on a collective farm in Novokubansk.

Pervitsky was a short, rectangular man with a granite handshake and tattooed forearms. I recognized his sort from back home, a stolid, can-do, nuts-and-bolts type, eager for specifics, allergic to fuss or ornament; he was the genuine article, and would farm enthusiastically in any country. His mild version of a work-related payment scheme simply spread piecework bonuses among entire work crews — often ten or twenty workers — and kept the bonuses small enough so they didn't change much. They even required idealistic behavior, in theory amplifying the social responsibility of labor: presumably, a brigade's zealots would urge its slackards along so all might benefit. Reality just didn't work that way, and by much informal testimony it seems the scheme fell flat. A bonus for exceeding the work quota became a minor pay feature of brigade accountancy all over the country, a gesture that hardly knocked the dent out of productivity figures.

It had meant more to Pervitsky. He'd been on television a thousand times, held up as the voice of the people, beaming, explaining his plan. In his almost British cottage parlor, we'd sat on plump couches, admiring the bric-a-brac in his glass breakfront, drinking tea from cups with saucers and eating biscuits.

The tacky finery of the room brought to mind the notion that the Soviets had imposed a prison-style economy on the entire nation — in prison a few cigarettes, or the right to an extra blanket or pillow, or the right to take a trip "out" to the world beyond the wall magnified into great wealth and status. Pervitsky must have been granted permission to visit a special store with decent furniture. We thought his parlor looked dowdy and dated. But in Novokubansk it was a room that inspired envy — that emotion tied up with patriotism again — a reward for a life of sincere dedication, and for allowing himself to be used to represent a useless idea in a meaningless campaign. No one else in town sat as comfortably.

Pervitsky himself sat straight as an I-beam, smiling with pride in his celebrated accomplishment. He believed. He was a Pygmalion, one of those statues of workers, kissed and brought to life by the authorities. He must have started out in a simple cottage, and must have been a nice guy who could work. He'd ended up, ironically, as a phony professional object lesson, often seen from a distance, flickering on TV screens across the nation, doubted, resented, his image serving more to remind viewers of what was broken than of what was fixed. He delivered a practiced reminiscence to us — he was permanently scripted. His voice was mellow and lifeless, and he was humorless, wholesome, humble, sweet, innocent — at least of the workings of economics: "In 1961 my brigade technique yielded twice what an adjacent field did. It was not a dangerous idea, but one ahead of its time. No one could understand it. My work crew was being paid at the normal job rate, not quality-related. A tractor driver plowed just deeply enough to paint the soil behind black. A field might have had fifteen operations done, and no one working had any interest in the outcome. At the time, I got thirty rubles daily to harvest corn, because that was the rate for combine drivers. My companion got five rubles daily to haul the ears away. That was the rate for his work.

"My companion said, 'I want to run the harvester, to get the better rate.' I let him. But next day the machine was damaged. I simply said, 'Let's each do what we know best, but share our wages.' However, our chief said, 'I can't do that. It's against regulations. Divide it all up yourselves, off the record.' So we did. Next time, I was paid fifteen hundred rubles, and my companion five hundred. I gave him his extra part. But the time after that, *he* got the higher salary. 'It's a pity to divide it,' the guy said, and he didn't divide it. I wasn't angry. The idea was mine, and the guy got more only twice. The followers of my system understand that every operation is equally important. Still, some ministers didn't approve."

Pervitsky's plan had become the norm. It combined low fixed wages; small, shared quality and quantity bonuses to whet ambition; *and* a wage cap to tame sharpened ambition. Brigades didn't improve workers' motivation or pay much, but Pervitsky remained proud. "Brigades came from lower farmers, from us," he told me. "I have been in Khrushchev's home. I have known Gorbachev since 1961. I knew that *idea as idea* couldn't be stopped. Now we come to leasing!" The legions were on the march, in circles.

◆

Lease brigades were the new *perestroika*-era heir to Pervitsky's brigade scheme. On paper, lease brigades went further. They did offer workers substantial pay hikes for hard work, and the autonomy to do jobs well. Lease brigades came close to the scheme Khudenko had tried. Similarly, they had the potential for being so effective that they would constitute a social disturbance. In October 1988 Gorbachev proclaimed lease brigades the socialist cure for labor malaise, "the highest form" of labor. He said that "the entire agricultural sector should follow this path."

It couldn't, wouldn't, and didn't. At its inception, local officials warmed to the new form a bit, insofar as it helped their own schemes. In every region, on just a few of the scores of collective farms, one or two lease brigades got started — and the lessors often turned out to be friends or in-laws of the farm's ruling family. Leasing land that families and small work teams could farm their own ways indeed upped productivity. But such teams didn't need chairmen and layers of bureaucrats and planners. If "the entire agricultural sector" had followed that path, it would have ended the power of those in charge of implementing the new scheme. Unsurprisingly, they weren't interested.

Yuri and I had visited three early lease brigades. None resembled a Western farm. Like the show farms of the Belgorod district I'd visited two years later, they were hothouse creatures, dependent on special conditions. The lease brigades we'd visited had been carefully contained on parent collective farms that subsidized and supplied them. Outside experts still commanded them to grow their crops, still set their sowing and harvesting dates, and still established their marketing plans — all standard collective-farm practices. All were show farms, run by selected proletarian heroes and supplied with rare good equipment.

Parts of the approved innovation did survive the misexecution of Gorbachev's idea: each brigade planned its own daily work schedule — the lowest bosses were gone, and workers had more scope for doing what needed doing. The promise of renewed leases raised workers' ambitions. A father could think of his child farming the same land. And every day, lease-brigade workers could cross job descriptions. A milkmaid could plow. A carpenter could feed hay. This amounted to a retreat from Soviet socialism's industrial model of agricultural work. Also, Pervitsky's salary cap was gone. The five or ten workers in a lease brigade often earned three or five times what other workers on collective farms earned. This upset the sense of enforced social equality at the core of socialist morality, and may have been the main reason the chairmen set up so few lease brigades.

"We started a free-will collective," Leonid Kozhukov had told me. What a wonderful, oxymoronic name they had chosen for it. The two long, dark brothers Kozhukov had slouched, like open and close parentheses, on a steel cot in a tiny sleeping hut on their Siberian leasehold, talking shyly and quietly. "Professor Krasnoshchekov here made our plan," a brother said, gesturing toward their smiling gray-haired maestro of free will.

Next to the brothers, beaming, sat Professor Nikolai V. Krasnoshchekov, Academy Member of the V. I. Lenin All-Union Academy of Agricultural Sciences and First Vice-Chairman of the Siberian Department of the All-Union Academy of Agricultural Sciences (so his business card read). He had lectured me for the entire afternoon in his office in Novosibirsk, waving his carved birchwood pointer over colored flow charts on an easel. He was presenting his worker-satisfaction theories. They amounted to ways of framing justifications for "autonomous" work units in terms that proved that these occasions for profitable private innovation were still really "socialist." He was preparing me for the farm visit. With an amiable farm chairman named Yuri F. Bugakov (who sat on the adjacent cot, also smiling pleasantly), Krasnoshchekov had selected the brothers Kozhukov to test his innovation: an array of labor and machinery that they would run on Collective Farm Bolshevik, near Novosibirsk. The experiment parodied the scientific method.

Hypothesis: if we handpick three proven ambitious workers, give them a few thousand acres of fine grain land and a healthy start-up budget, supply them (with atypical promptness) with atypically well-designed equipment, with the usually unavailable best seed and best chemicals and best technical advice, and if we permit a usually impermissible profit incentive to help motivate them, and if we provide them with daily advisory oversight, then the resulting farm production will exceed that of the surrounding collective farm.

Result: Yes, that's what happened.

Said the elder brother, "We were given a bank account, twenty-five hundred acres, four tractors, three combines. We've got a work chart from the professor for every crop — budget, fuel consumption, timing. We're happy about the prices our grain brings. We earned nine hundred rubles a month this year — four times average. Neighbors complain — let them!" He was well protected by Soviet science and in the right position to enjoy the deliciousness of being the object of envy.

Farm Chairman Bugakov said, "Their leased field exceeds the

parent farm's yield by about thirty-three percent and its labor productivity by five hundred percent. Thirty percent of the five hundred farm chairmen in Novosibirsk district agree that this labor form is the promising way to go, and the percentage will increase." I didn't believe him, because I didn't believe that regional authorities would favor a system that got good results at the cost of their power and that disrupted the fiction of their moral advantage. Ultimately, the emergence of productive farming was not a technical but a political problem.

◆

In spite of demonstrations such as Professor Krasnoshchekov's, no one was surprised that regional authorities soon sharply cut back on the few lease brigades they'd started. They often went so far as to impose harsh income taxes, sabotage allocations of equipment, and manipulate neighbors' envy, fanning it into anger.

Years later, just one result of the lease-brigade fashion of 1988 and 1989 proved oddly satisfactory. During the first flush of official compliance and enthusiasm following Gorbachev's recommendation of lease brigades, many chairmen set up one or two per farm and supplied them well with combines, tractors, and hundreds of acres of land. They would be the best-equipped survivors in the lean times to come for private farming. There may have been just thousands in the whole nation, but they were about the only private farms with adequate land and equipment right after the August 1991 attempted coup.

Lease brigades founded in the final year of *perestroika* were another story. They were mostly established by the fierce wills of little groups of workers fighting against local authorities, and most failed, frozen out by the collective-farm establishment. And in Russia, after the fall of the Party, local officials and farm chairmen openly obstructed the many new small farms later adventurers tried to start. Most were effectively limited to a few acres and little equipment.

Perestroika's late exponents went back to urging "decentralization" and "intensification" — "within the framework of collective and state farms," as the conservative Party agriculture chief, Yegor Ligachev, had insisted from the start. *Pravda* complained about sloppy farming, but kept on publishing long interviews with well-known farm chairmen who were dubious about lease brigades' promise and urged instead "less control from Moscow" — increased regionalization — but, of course, no decrease in centrally supplied farm subsidies.

The lines drawn on the farm question between a tiny faction that favored privatization, the market, and democratic reform, on the one hand, and the more popular clean-the-system, pro-planned-economy, pro-Party reform on the other, mirrored struggles in every aspect of late Soviet life.

As I came to understand the complex social coordination that enabled Western farming, the position of the Party conservatives became clearer to me. However efficient, family-farm, land-privatization reforms required transformations that went far beyond farming and encompassed the whole economy. They'd involve changing everything.

The most parsimonious apparent road toward getting chickens back into stores, for example, was indeed to tinker with the existing structure — to strengthen, not destroy, vertically integrated chicken monopolies. In Stavropol, I'd visited a single "enterprise," reformed during *perestroika,* that did a better than usual job supplying the region with eggs and chicken meat. The well-connected boss had taken control of the region's chicken farms, poultry slaughterhouses and processing plants, trucking fleets, and even urban shops. He ran it all like a general, and kept chaos at bay.

Private farming made sense to me, but could private farmers get started when every official for a thousand miles around and from dozens of authorities opposed each farmer? How could farmers go it alone when even the heritage of knowing how to run a farm had been destroyed by the execution of their grandparents? How could anyone run a modern farm — which assembles complex biological and technical components and then markets crops for further complex processing and distribution — without banks, dealerships, parts stores, willing technical advisers, marketplaces? How could such farmers find the supplies they'd need when all resources were kept from them? How could crops even get to plants and shops when truckers and processing plants were creatures of the collective-farming bu-

reaucracy? Family farms in the West, I realized as I'd never realized before, exist in a thick web of coordinated enterprises that
set them up to innovate, as farmers must.

◆

In the aftermath of my travels with Yuri, I spent days walking
around Moscow. Outside a neighborhood food shop, a young,
scowling truck driver lazed about watching a store clerk. From a
slanting pile of cabbages that had rolled around the battered
truckbed, the clerk pawed a few dozen into a crate. He dragged
the crate inside, nudging the door with his hip. Then he did it all
again, many times.

I had my own innovative moment, redesigning the scene in
my mind: I rewrote job rules and put the driver to work unload-
ing beside the clerk, and got them one of those conveyers with
roller bearings, and packed the truckload of loose cabbages into
lugs, and conjured up a loading bay for the back of the shop. Just
those changes might have reduced cabbage-unloading time from
an hour to six minutes, multiplying the driver's productivity
tenfold. I quadrupled the truck's size, so there'd be cabbages
enough to occupy his new time, and remapped his route to reach
more shops, probably doubling efficiency again.

While I was at it, I repaved the bad road from the new loading
bay clear back to the cabbage farm. I instituted similar changes
to all the cabbage shops, trucks, and routes in Moscow. That
made things pretty complicated, so I materialized a few competing cabbage brokers and found them working telephones
and fast computers equipped with programs that juggled cabbage bids. I delivered unto them sound and wise bankers who'd
loan hard currency to smooth the funding of the various parties.
I threw in a contract, and made it enforceable under a reliable
code of contract law. I was just getting around to the consequences of adding some boiled beef to eat with the cabbage
when the kid drove away.

I stood there imagining this tall tower of improvements and
thinking about Gorbachev's presiding over a glum but equal empire of poverty and isolation. The Party had long invested only
in state monopolies, and stifled foreign news that made it look
bad. Few citizens knew how much better factories and farms

elsewhere ran. Gorbachev had slackened press control and enterprise management in a doomed final attempt to resuscitate
Party control. Instead, he had triggered the inevitable, gradual
toppling of Lenin's grand experiment. Dispirited Soviet citizens,
mostly unknowingly, were shouldering a colossal, intricate undertaking, not one that would simply follow from their reluctant turn of conviction. The transformation would cost all the
political and financial and human pains that go along with rearranging basic beliefs, habits, and alliances. Little of the political
structure of the Soviet Union had altered yet, but the restrictions on our observing it were lifting.

◆

On my final evening in Moscow in 1988, Yuri and I again sat
over a meal at the Writers' Union, together with the political
economist Nikolai Shmelev, who did know Soviet citizens were
shouldering a colossal, intricate undertaking. We recounted
our journey for him. "It will take time," Shmelev said, after
listening. It was perhaps the last year of public cautiousness,
and Shmelev may have still been minding his words, and later
would join anti-collective-farm reformers: "Our collective
farms can be livable, even competitive, if freed from the administrative pyramid. In the Baltic states, Belorussia, much of the
Ukraine, the North Caucasus, they can survive — with lease
brigades. But in non-black-soil regions, where they didn't take
you, collective farms are completely ruined and quite hopeless.
Here, only family businesses — farms leased long term, for life
and longer — and small co-ops, five or seven families, can help.
There are still two hundred thousand orders, decrees, official
instructions, ministerial instructions. Our economy is tied by
all those like a bound child. I believe in general mess, general
chaos, nothing strictly regulated. Let some forms survive, some
perish. A creative mess."

PART III

IN THE
CORNUCOPIA

1989

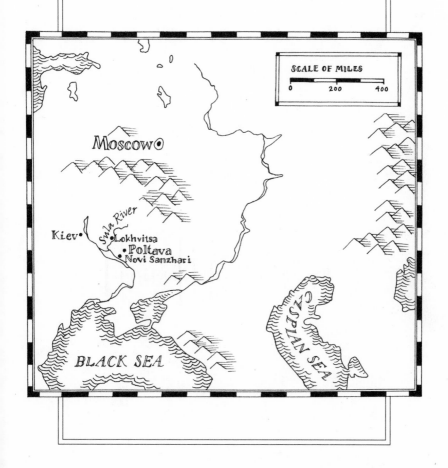

5

ON A MIDSUMMER midnight in 1989, railway stations remained in ceaseless rush hour, what the economist Shmelev had termed, back a year earlier in the Writers' Union dining room, "general mess, general chaos, nothing strictly regulated." We squeezed across the Kursk station waiting room. The station connects Moscow and the southern cornucopia — the tastiest, most sinful direction, the direction of gluttony, of bread and wine, of Ukrainian grain fields in the midst of harvest, of the Georgian farms and vineyards and orchards spilling out tea and grapes and apricots.

It was the summer after my cross-USSR journey with Yuri Chernichenko and the reciprocal trip we'd taken across the USA. Another year of *perestroika* had gone by. The increased candor of the newspapers at the kiosks held steady, and food stores were as empty as the year before. I'd landed at Sheremetyevo Airport and friends greeted me. For the first time Muscovites were experiencing combative politics in the Western sense — street-corner orators, newspapers disputing each other, a working parliament with factions and alliances. Even so, central authorities remained firmly in charge.

This time the authorities had accepted two requests of mine that would change the character of my journey. I was to stay on far fewer farms, for long enough to look around, and I was able to bring along a friend from America. So I came with another Mark, a native of Odessa with a doctorate from the Soviet Academy of Sciences, who had immigrated fourteen years before to Boston.

We shouldered past a family hugging a tearful, boyish soldier. Teenagers huddled in the center of the wide, dingy waiting room, their teacher circling like a sheepdog who smelled wolf. Three wiry Tajik men squatted silently by battered cartons, eyes glazed, innocent of the pandemonium. Kite-tail lines of tired travelers streamed across the floor from a kiosk selling bread and another selling *Pravda*.

In stations like this, no matter the city, the big overhead notice boards posted arrivals and departures in Moscow Central Time. It was a metaphor for centralized management. Moscow still ran the railway — and the country — in its own good time, and, as ever, damn the consumer.

Our train creaked slowly out of the station on schedule, headed for Poltava in the Ukraine. Yuri had helped me arrange this trip too, although he'd been elected a people's deputy and had to stay in Moscow. I opened the corridor window and looked out at the crowd on the platform, saluting us with big, slow, stiff-armed waves like the cast of a happy musical taking a curtain call.

The train swayed as it picked up speed. Western economists had called the railways as outmoded as the rest of Soviet infrastructure, but the trains I took were more reliable than, say, Soviet telephones. For that matter, they ran better than Amtrak's, which Western economists also called outmoded. The Soviet Union's nearly universal inefficiency relented for trains. They ran better than almost everything else in the country; they'd long been a priority. In an empire that stretched across six thousand miles, the intercity trains bound all the ground between Europe and Korea across a barren of bad roads and bad weather. Our train pulled some unreserved hard-class cars, musty and sociable and cheap; they'd piled up with peasants, a few of whom lugged piglets and chickens. A dormitory car and several cars of four-berth compartments led the train, the berths booked up weeks in advance. Our soft-class car rode in the middle of the train, behind a dining car of sorts and beyond the reach of most Soviet citizens. Influential friends had performed a feat that would get tougher a year later and that never happened after 1991 when Communist authority withered: they booked a private train compartment for two foreigners at the last minute.

Every booking made for me doubtless displaced someone — probably someone official, but vouched for by an organization with lesser clout. The Soviet Union ran by reenacting, millions of times a day, a mythic battle: You want meat? Your factory needs steel? You need a train seat? At the moment of every allocation decision on every level, clout-wielders on one side duked it out with access-deniers on the other. A travel clerk at my official host's research institute — "a Jew, waiting to emigrate," my host had said — knew special phone numbers that had reached the right railway bosses who had bumped those whose travel benefited the state less than ours.

On an earlier trip northward, I'd ended up sharing a four-berth compartment with two Latvian schoolgirls, probably after having displaced their parents. A slight, wide-eyed student nurse had chatted with her sister in shy near-whispers and giggled stiffly whenever I looked over. They'd turned in early. After midnight, I'd climbed up past the tiny nurse, who'd snorted like a horse.

This time we'd been granted a cushy two-berth compartment. My traveling companion was giddy because he was headed back to his native Ukraine for the first time in years. At seven in the morning the train would reach Poltava. Someone named Tanya would meet us, "on behalf of the Academy of Sciences," their Moscow representative had told us.

Travel by foreigners still required approval and a sponsoring organization. Some cities and some routes were closed. We were "the American delegation" and were never on our own. The Academy of Sciences had a Tanya or two to greet and track its foreign guests in every open region. With Tanya would be one "Vitaly, an agricultural executive." We were institutional objects and would be passed along from the Academy of Sciences' kind supervision to that of the super-Ministry of Agriculture, Gosagroprom. "Vitaly knows farm chairmen. He will discuss what Ukrainian farms you will see," our Moscow sponsor had said. For whom did he work? Who'd requisitioned and paid for his excursion with us? The nation's business proceeded in spite of the official economy and laws, and because of personal contacts. "Arrangements were made," our host had said proudly, smiling genially, his reach so obviously mysterious and vast.

Mark toasted the prospect of this Tanya with French brandy we'd brought along. The cotton window curtains in our little cabin had been cross-stitched with an edging of hammers and sickles and ornamental silhouettes of a famous Poltava battle monument, and Mark recognized it at once from his boyhood. I felt sure I'd all too soon encounter the real thing — it was the nature of foreign delegations to view monuments, a liability of this kind of travel. The curtain trim matched the orange of the velvet seats.

In this land of hierarchic elaboration, some intercity routes had their own assigned color schemes, applied variously on its crack, or trademark, trains and its rank-and-file trains. The fanciest coaches featured finer decor — the embroidered curtains hung above tablecloths in coordinated colors, and senior staff wore uniforms with matching detail. Trademark trains had priority at sidings. Their passengers would likely be the heaviest-weight bureaucrats. Ordinary coaches had plainer curtains, no tablecloths, junior crews, and the passengers might be plodding pen-pushers. The dormitory cars would be full of workers and peasants without clout and lowly clerks out of favor at the office. It seemed like the protocol of Peter the Great's reign, not of a classless society in the making.

Officially, even directors of enterprises and movie stars made just a few times the pay of factory workers. Indeed, wealth or fame alone bought no privilege here, as they do in market economies. Nobility of service to the state — or what passed for it — was the only quality that did add privilege. War heroes and workers who had been awarded the right badges got it. They could cut to the front of lines and shop in better-supplied stores. And by the same logic, senior bureaucrats got it too, in their capacities as self-sacrificing administrators of the revolutionary will of the people. In that nation of nearly uniform poverty, the perks of privilege seemed far greater than in American corporations, where it won pile carpets and corner offices. A Soviet perk was always access to something — a nice rib roast, a thousand tons of steel, our train seats. But it was often access to things the lowliest American burger flipper or warehouse clerk back home could buy as needed.

Soviet society, purportedly still thrusting toward classlessness in its final years, embodied the strictest, most elaborated taxonomy of privilege I'd encountered anywhere. The ins and outs of British protocol were weak tea by comparison — although they had mattered mightily when aristocracy was the only legitimate source of distinction. Sports, the arts, scholarship, and business all distinguish English folk now, and the right to do well at these things has moved beyond the purview of lords and ladies, so that the entitlements of rank now seem more quaint than enviable. In Soviet Russia, there was still only one game to play in, right up until the attempted coup of 1991.

I found it comfortable but awkward to be a guest of a ruling clique I didn't much care for, and to have a bit of influence by proxy. We didn't have much choice; foreigners traveled only where and how officials sent them. Our rural trip was still a rarity. Steinbeck's *Russian Journal* had described the same sheltered style of travel through the rural provinces: "Being the guests of VOKS, we walked through the public waiting-room and into a side room where there was a dining table, some couches, and comfortable chairs. And there, under the stern eye of a painted Stalin, we drank strong tea until our plane was called." In our posh train compartment I felt isolated from normal Soviet life, and I was. But it was an isolation shared with the Soviet *nomenklatura*, the ruling elite, my fellow travelers to Poltava.

It was hard to discern privilege in the faces of the big men in suits lounging stiff-legged in the soft-class corridor, or in the demeanor an Uzbek family of six who had levered themselves and a dozen crates and suitcases into the tiny two-bunk chamber next to us. Three kids with gleaming black eyes and ringlets clambered over all surfaces from floor to luggage rack. Several wives, cowled in muslin, watched their mayhem placidly. In the cabin on our other side two stolid engineers sat immersed in two newspapers and a shared bottle of vodka. The car rattled into the next day.

It was an old car; our cabin had been repaneled in wood-grain

Formica. At the end of the corridor, a samovar glowed comfortingly in a special niche. The coals in its cast-iron firebox might have been burning since tsarist times. Half an hour out of the station our porter appeared, a sturdy woman in her fifties with a face as bright a red as the samovar fire. She spoke rapidly, one pointing finger and one word for each of us: *"Chai?"* Point. *Da.* *"Chai?"* Point. *Da.* She returned with tea in beautiful glasses, dime thin, to take on boiling water without cracking. She'd set them inside ornate tin holders that shielded one's hand from the heat, a comfort in a place with little comfort. But she did even better. With each cup of tea she delivered four wrapped sugar lumps as big as fingers. It was a summer of rationing. The stores rarely had sugar, even for those presenting coupons — part of a national anti-moonshine campaign. But the officials who ran soft class had access to sugar. We drank the tea straight up. Everyone's pockets bulged with sugar fingers.

I recalled that my grandmother had told a Russian sugar-shortage tale. She'd been born on the Polish-Russian border, and as a toddler had come by steamer to America. "My family was so poor we'd hang a lump of sugar over the table on a string," she'd said. "We'd look at it as we sipped. That made the tea taste sweet, and the sugar lasted all winter."

I told the story to Mark. "It works, too," I said. "I've tried it."

"In Boston, it works," he answered. "In this country, nothing works."

Mark sized up the tea lady. "Such people have business buying things in Moscow to sell in Poltava and vice versa. That's how the country gets by in spite of itself. Such trade has long been their capitalism."

On a train to Latvia once, a porter had asked if I would like supper brought. I'd worked all day without food — when one moved between organizations at mealtime in the USSR, one starved, because food was served in workplace cafeterias — the few restaurants cost hours and battles with waiters. The train porter delivered imitation airline food. I was ravenous, but couldn't manage that mucoid *kotleta*, nor the beans glued with rancid fat. I ate the bread and watched jealously as Latvians, who'd carried food aboard, gnawed on garlicky hard sausage and big chunks of black bread.

On this train, too, sausage scent intertwined with scents of vodka, sweat, tobacco, smoke from the samovar, and drift from the W.C. — this was the consistent perfume of Soviet railroading. We broke out our own black bread and sausage; I'd wised up. I placed a portable shortwave radio in the compartment window and tuned in the BBC World Service — government jamming of BBC radio signals had stopped only a year before. Mark produced the French brandy. We listened to a program about dahlia gardening in Yorkshire, then to anecdotes of a Shakespearean troupe playing to full houses of Pakistani elementary school students in Liverpool, who were thereby bettered. In the dim compartment, I pictured millions of ears cocked to this relic of Empire Britain. I wondered what Uzbek schoolkids, honing their classroom English, made of dahlias and Shakespeare for the new masses. Up the dial, Voice of America programming reflected demographic studies of audience. A calm woman read, at half speed, in e-nun-cee-ay-ted English, an amiable tale about children on holiday. This was the once-banned firewater of Western propaganda. It went down as smoothly as an airline movie.

In our fancy train car, even in the midst of *perestroikan* turmoil, we privileged travelers lay down to sleep on clean white sheets. I dozed as we crept out of conquering Russia and into the submerged Ukraine. The train hooted and clanked. All night, sunk in fitful naps, I gazed up through the glassy surface of wakefulness. In the sudden stillness of some minor station, I squinted out past the embroidered curtains at bleary peasant couples hovering over cloth bundles and rope-bound valises. We clacked onward, and then it was dawn and on a far platform yet another queue awaited the opening of a tiny kiosk that might sell a shipment of something rare. Across the USSR, people awaited access to anything, as they had for seventy years, because whatever might come — a seldom-found food, pants a few sizes too big or small — would be tradable for something else. In every town, citizens somehow knew when to arise in the middle of the night and queue up. Rumor motivated shoppers far more than advertising did back home. I dropped back to sleep. The clatter wove into my dreams, into thumping, imperious pounding.

The tea lady leaned into my face, hollering. She'd put on a

baggy white smock, also trimmed in the train's orange theme color, I blearily noticed. This morning she was cleanup lady with a harsh voice, not tea lady with sugar. She was all business. Her new outfit brought out new aspects of her personality. She knew her duties, and like all Soviet workers, she also knew her rights. When we hit Poltava, she had as much right to be off the train as any citizen (this was the same philosophy that granted restaurant workers the right to close for lunch at lunchtime). Two hours before arrival was the time for her to collect bed-sheets and roll up mattresses. She thumped on my bunk with the broad red heel of her hand, right by my one open eye. I got the idea, and scowled.

I soon discovered that in the morning she also stepped up her execution of the duty of locking washrooms before the train entered stations — she'd interpreted broadly the mandate of limiting access and simply kept them locked. She'd cleaned in there and turned the key. My pantomime of desperation did not interest her. Mercifully, the porter in the next car ran a slacker principality.

Cleanup lady, her pillows counted and mattresses rerolled, watched from the platform with hands on hips as we all de-barked. She wore civvies now — a baggy brown dress and a ban-danna around her hair — so that only her proprietary posture distinguished her from a hundred other babushkas on the plat-form.

True to plan, a smiling woman in her mid-forties soon emerged from the hubbub of melodious Ukrainian greetings, grabbed my hand, and shook it.

"American?" she asked. I nodded.

"Tanya," this Tanya said, welcoming the newest American delegation on behalf of the Poltava office of the Academy of Sciences. She pointed to a slight, balding man in a big brown rumpled suit limping toward us from far up the platform, squinting into bright sunlight. She introduced Vitaly Karpovich Chuiko, our new keeper, the gentleman from Gosagroprom, dean of an agricultural college. Vitaly Karpovich inspected his new charges. We sized him up, too. It was obvious right away that he was a personage and no mere tour guide. Nearing sixty, he had a bit of fair hair remaining, framing tired blue eyes. His brow was permanently knit. He carried himself with martial erectness and gestured with economical, miniaturized, courtly flourishes. His smile came slowly. He issued it, first holding back, then relenting. It was warm when it did arrive, which threw off any assumptions one might have been developing about his demeanor. A considerable smile.

Gosagroprom gazed at Academy of Sciences. The two bowed and then shook hands. *Exeunt* this Tanya, and her institution. We had been signed over from one bureaucratic dominion to another, soft-class prisoners in transit.

◆

Vitaly Karpovich's directions to the driver of his car were hardly suggestions from comrade to comrade. Vitaly had the habit of command. For decades, he informed us as we drove away, he had been the ruling don of Poltava's college of agricultural research — recently renamed after Vavilov, the plant geneticist killed by Trofim Lysenko. Vitaly was clearly used to handling people, to screening casual chats for political correctness, to encouraging good attitude with his faint smile and slight gestures, to scrutinizing projects for aptness in the proper scheme of things. His presence spoke to the wisdom of whatever cautious authority had selected him as our Ukrainian Virgil. He was all business, and so he remained, sixteen hours a day for the next week.

We drove for a long while nearly in silence. I looked out at bountiful farm country, which until recently had been the fiefdom of Fyodor Morgun, the minimum-tillage innovator. The Sula valley is open, with flat fields stretching along the river and rolling fields far behind them. The valley was farmed, horizon to horizon. Trees marked distant fencerows and filled a few hillside copses. This was the extraordinary Ukrainian *chernozem* — black soil — that had tempted armies of Swedes, Tartars, Germans, and Russians. The land has lured for millennia. The patchwork of fields faded into far-off hues of green (suggesting growing crops), of tan, and of dark brown (suggesting grain ready to harvest, and newly harvested, and newly plowed ground).

Vitaly Karpovich broke the silence to discuss itinerary. He cut us no slack. It was done, approved by local, district, *oblast,* and republic levels of the Writers' Union and Gosagroprom and

Party officialdom. It was nonnegotiable. We were en route to Collective Farm Victory of Communism, in Poltava *oblast*, east of Kiev. We would stay there.

For the form of it, I grumbled at the lack of promised choice, but I was pleased we'd be on another show farm, one of the top in the Ukraine, a place to which visitors were shipped for dazzling. By the same process, I had also been sent there the year before for a day on my journey with Yuri Chernichenko. I would hunt for changes wrought by *perestroika*. I'd been there just long enough the year before to have realized its chief was a four-square symbol of the old guard at its finest, staunch faithful Communist, charismatic horse trader, a prototypically successful chairman, and, I recalled from my conversation in Moscow, a long-time comrade and ally of Fyodor Morgun's. Farm Victory of Communism would therefore be a good place to see the next link down from Morgun along the great chain of command that stretched from Party Central Committee to peasant.

I was glad at the prospect of visiting with this paradigm. There would be time enough to hunt up reformers. We were going to the real thing dressed in its Sunday best.

◆

Nikolai Timofeyevich Yurchenko met us in front of his drab yellow cement office building. He nodded familiarly to Vitaly Karpovich, squinted and jerked his chin in a curter nod that seemed to say he'd placed me in his memory from my earlier visit — that Chernichenko's American friend.

A kidney-shaped pond before the office reflected zigzagging propaganda billboards (at this late hour of *glasnost* when they'd come down elsewhere) urging hard work (zig), safe work (zag), Party loyalty (zig), and world peace (zag). The homilies shattered into ripples as geese, and then two heavy swans, skidded down from the sky. Yurchenko walked us past the pond to a stucco guesthouse in a birch grove. He leafed elaborately through a jailer's hoop of keys, each the size of a carrot. With grand deliberation, he clicked open a series of padlocks, admitting us to a big farmhouse parlor furnished with overstuffed couches, a large TV, and a string of episodic revolutionary murals. Four bedrooms ringed the parlor. Every collective farm had such a facility, most far humbler, for the convenience of the visiting inspectors, planners, expediters, and advisers the government constantly paraded through. This guesthouse even had an indoor toilet, which had been stocked with translucent blue toilet paper sheets the consistency of Saran Wrap.

I unpacked under a poster of a full-rigged ship sailing up a sea lane of moonlight. This could have been a farmer's house back in Iowa, right down to the shelves of knickknacks. The place felt quaint, as if I had stepped into the American past. Of course (I know from a decade of residence in a scenic New England farm village) no place on earth is quaint to insiders.

The other Mark, deep in Ukrainian countryside after a long time away, had a more knowing and no doubt accurate reaction. He eyed the fixtures, the plastic drop ceiling, the elaborate desk, the plump chairs. His postwar Odessa hadn't included such things. He touched furniture and asked, "How can they get such a lacquered desk? How can they get this fancy new desk on a collective farm? Such items can be bought by the privileged only, in the largest cities only! There must be something going on here. When we listen to this Nikolai Timofeyevich Yurchenko, let us not worry much about ideology but about how he gets lacquered desks."

Yurchenko sat us in the parlor and gave us something to listen to: his farm facts seemed invested with the sort of totemic wonder that tour guides lend to the height of the Washington Monument or the weight of the stones of the Tower of London. He'd performed the same show the year before, according to the notes I'd just checked on my laptop computer; he'd offered up all the same numbers. "Farm Victory of Communism was established 12 April 1930 (yes, certainly in the middle of the period of collectivization, isn't that when all our farms were established?) and like many of those other farms took its name from Lenin's writings. The farm had 1,200 hectares of cropland. In 1958 (yes, certainly during the Khrushchev reforms — which included combining farms into large management units) we added two farms. The area of that part of the farm is now about 10,000 acres. In 1971 (yes, during Brezhnev reforms — which also combined farms into still bigger units) we added another two farms. Today Farm Victory of Communism totals 27,500 acres. About 20,000 acres are plowed or pastured." It was, in other words, a farm so big that even in America, careful management would be difficult. For that reason, few farms in the West approach this size, and those that do usually specialize in a very few crops, and don't run as efficiently as smaller farms.

With the ritual slowness of a boss at a staff meeting, our host consulted a fat gold pocketwatch. The stained, skinny tail of his brown tie hung longer than the fat forepiece. His skull had been dented in at the left temple (a war wound, perhaps — he'd have been of soldiering age in the 1940s). He maintained a constant bemused smile, displaying gleaming golden front teeth.

For thirty years Yurchenko had run one of the top farms in the Ukraine. Authorities sent the younger generation of farm managers to the guesthouse at Victory of Communism for spiritual guidance and to see evidence that collective farms can be firmly managed. He grew the most wheat and fattest cattle in the *oblast*. And some of the nation's fastest racehorses lived in his Olympic training stable, his pride and hobby, a plum permitted to honor his success. He'd gathered in the best horses and the best riders and trainers — the ones sent by the state to international competitions — built them a beautiful training ring and proper housing. I'd toured this part of the farm the year before and remembered it well.

In a system thirsty to display its validity, he'd become an institutional icon, a vindication for the ministries resting on his broad shoulders. His horse facility was a bold emblem of official success. Indeed, few farm chairmen in the nation had done as well. Yurchenko had the technical competence expected of him — he liked to talk crops and cows and combines. But agricultural know-how was the least part of his success, and financial intuition surely counted even less. Unlike American farm executives, he'd mainly needed political instincts. He'd had the stamina and toughness to deal with the mess beyond the fences, to haggle with authorities for subsidies, exemptions, permissions, supplies, fulfillable quotas. His achievement had come from guarding his flanks, from decreasing his vulnerability, finally from gathering in the privilege of managing sensibly. He had been a delegate to the district soviet. He'd gone to Moscow (as had Yuri Chernichenko, his political opposite) as a delegate to the historic Nineteenth Party Conference, which had advanced *perestroika* in ways that would later prove fatal to the Party. He was a major figure in an organization of farm chairmen.

He pulled off his shoes and rubbed the ball of one stockinged foot with thick thumbs. "The secret of this farm is that I pay attention to everything — *everything!*" He sighed. "One may keep extra administrators and pay them high salaries. But I don't. One may neglect machinery, take it from new to banged up in a year. But I don't. We're highly mechanized, although our machines require investment. The machines save us on labor. This has proved a good program."

He hiked his other leg onto his knee and dug into the ball of the other foot. "I have four hundred sixteen contented workers, not counting husbands, wives, kids, grandparents. I am in charge of their villages. Every worker knows clearly how much he will get if his work brigade exceeds its quota. That is uncommon. Most farm workers do not understand such things." This atavism — Pervitsky's brigade system — had hardly raised production anywhere. It was ideologically useful. It set up a handy paradox, a fiction that nevertheless worked administrative magic — a way of appearing to address a systemic problem by offering workers achievement-based pay incentives, while at the same time keeping their paychecks nearly equal.

Yurchenko had the unusual combination of political and technical savvy that it took to make the old system work; he wasn't enthusiastic about even Gorbachev's limited reforms. "Do I believe in *glasnost?* I listened closely to Gorbachev's talk just yesterday. What he sketches, if implementable, will be great for our people — less bureaucracy. But there is another side of the picture — discipline. Order. Not everyone understands *glasnost,* so it leads to demagoguery. People more on their own aren't good citizens. *Glasnost* can bring harm. Yesterday I caught a drunken tractor driver. 'I can work like this! That is my freedom,' he shouted. But I didn't let him. I fined him."

We went prowling around the farm. Vitaly Karpovich, my keeper, rode in the passenger seat of the jeep. On the dashboard, a two-way radio hissed out chatter between field supervisors and command central. The other Mark and I rode in back. Yurchenko came along for the ride — for all our rides, in fact. Whenever we got out, Yurchenko got out, moving incessantly, stiff-gaited, grave, the thick ring of keys clanking in his suit coat.

Yurchenko pointed to a Belarus tractor stirring (as per Morgun's teachings) the aftermath of a spring-wheat crop into the black earth. "Work at the Victory of Communism farm is performed by sober drivers, all specially trained, mounted on 113 tractors, 57 trucks and pickups, 28 combines, 6 sets of forage combines, and much other machinery. Our farmers raise feed for 10,000 cattle . . ." He loved to recite those numbers.

Here and there, knots of workers dabbed and dawdled through some post-harvest raking. Others sat on the ground by old parked trucks waiting out the workday. We passed through fair fields of grain and a scraggly field of sugar beets — "a special mission of this farm," Yurchenko said. He said beet byproducts provided his 10,000 cows scarce high-protein feed. He had made "technical changes" that had doubled sugar-beet production in the past ten years. He had pulled off an agricultural triumph. I was delighted with this dull news. The idea of a Western farmer's doubling the yield of any commodity crop in a decade was far-fetched — any Western farmer who hadn't done things nearly perfectly to begin with would have been out of business.

By the time we headed back, work was over, and we rode in the midst of a rush-hour convoy of trucks carrying the field-workers and their hoes and rakes through the farm's villages in early evening. Workers climbed off before their cottages. Others walked in with rakes and shovels on their shoulders, past neighbors already tending their own rich cottage gardens and feeding their own fat cows.

◆

Our excursion among sugar-beet fields led me to ruminate on crop deployment. With each year of *perestroika,* regional Party authorities had further relaxed their once-obedient enforcement of farming plans made in Moscow. As cynicism grew and fear faded, the center's grip on them had weakened. They'd begun concocting their own plans. The same locals ran the show wearing new hats — often non-Party, soviet hats. Crop quotas became more negotiable.

Western observers who had predicted that a decline of central planning would lead to a rise of normal market relations were surprised that the change was merely taking farms deeper into barter. Regions were on their own. The decay of national crop quota enforcement had left each area's bosses worrying about famine, and maneuvering for their region's advantage. Bosses turned collective farms back toward basics — growing grain and meat, withholding crops from national distribution for local use. They withdrew from supplying the nation with crops that best suited their particular climates and soils. This was a retreat from the sorting-out, or "rationalizing," process that the West was completing a century before. Even in Georgia, where over ninety percent of the USSR's tea grew, regional officials had started plowing tea plantations back into grain fields.

The West has rationalized its crop array — crops are planted where they grow best. The unfathomably complex and kinetic problem of assigning each field in a nation its most appropriate crop solves itself in the West year after year (granted some persuasion by government subsidy) without much help from planners. The invisible hand does indeed do it. Hardly anyone loses money by unknowingly sowing wheat on land that would more profitably grow apricots. Riding with Yurchenko, I imagined a Washington office building — a very big one even for Washington — full of officials anticipating apricot demand, setting prices, selecting apricot farms and then fields (after regarding climate, soil, managerial competence, workers' cultural traditions, budgets, markets, technical and industrial capacities, etc.), and wielding police power that enforced the apricot order with jail terms and shattered careers.

It would be a big job. I was glimpsing what central planners attempted. I multiplied the apricot problem by hundreds of crops and many thousands of fields, each requiring its own large

Washington office building, and wondered that the Soviet system had lasted three quarters of a century. The idea refreshed mundane memories of the motley precision of capitalistic disorder: potato fields in Idaho, corn fields in Iowa, and spearmint patches in the muck soils of Indiana grew where each crop grew best — with only selfishness and the harsh consequence of folly guiding farmers.

6

AS RUSSIAN OVERLORDS have for centuries, Yurchenko of the Victory of Communism farm ran a few thousand rural lives. He was elected (unopposed — that Soviet tradition continued even late in *perestroika*) by peasants whom he ruled with the force of judge and jury. He described himself as "a peasant at heart," but was no one local's peer. He backed his lordly authority (another Soviet tradition) by keeping up his many alliances at the top of agriculture-related ministries and Party offices. Thirty years of favor-trading and perspective-sharing had made him useful to the right friends all over. His show farm demonstrated his friends' legitimacy, too. Besides, with shop shelves nearly bare, his farm sent regular food packages to the apartments of allies in Kiev, and maybe even in Moscow, who helped procure privileges, goods, and services. A guidebook for the perfect rural Soviet courtier might have described Yurchenko. He was a model low man. He'd thrived amid palace intrigue, doing a pretty good job of running an extensive industrialized island of enterprise in Third World prairie country, commanding a sluggish work force whose culture had been confounded by a thousand years of similar noblemen. And the text might also describe Yurchenko's ally and friend Fyodor Morgun, who'd finished up a few rungs higher — both stylish courtiers.

Their style was the one that worked. Any farm that more or

less functioned had a Yurchenko astraddle it. That's what suf-
ficed. Nice guys got mashed. His own court of under-princes
convened at the breakfast table. His hushed, hurried conferences with these supervisors (in Ukrainian, not Russian) guided
work crews and production priorities all day. His ornate conversations with visiting inspectors and officials and dignitaries
from other regions (occasionally in Russian, mostly in Ukrainian), and with a decades-long string of visitors from abroad, sustained the farm. The table itself groaned with Ukrainian riches,
morning and night: roast chicken, *pirogi*, herring, squares of
smoked backfat impressed with peeled garlic cloves, sour pickles, scallions, and, best of all, buttery buckwheat groats baked in
a crock, the way my own grandmothers made it.

◆

After breakfast, the third morning, Yurchenko, big keys jan-
gling, trotted us over to the farm library. He never chatted. He
orated. It was animal day. "We have a beef-breeding section, but
we must sell the cattle just before they are fully grown. They are
finished at a centralized feedlot, where they eat the byproducts
from the local sugar-beet plant. Let me tell you frankly that the
district authorities invented that oversized facility. If I could
keep my animals home, and wasn't compelled to send them
away there, my good management would bring us much better
profits. But if I say no to sending away the beef cattle, local
leaders will withdraw my allocation of the sugar-beet meal,
which also gives my dairy cows much milk. Most farm chairmen in the area also wish they could fatten beef animals themselves." It was the only complaint about Yurchenko's superiors
that he permitted himself all week.

I asked about the relationship between state-assigned crop
quotas — the infamous *zakaz* — and his tools for inspiring his
workers. Through Brezhnev's time, chairmen ignoring these
mandates, or even trying but falling short of them, sometimes
went to jail. Quotas, in 1989, were set near but not quite at
the productive capacity of each field. A brigade that harvested
above quota shared a bonus. The prospect supposedly motivated
members to exhort shirkers onward to harder work for the peo-

ple — Yurchenko was discussing Pervitsky's brigade method in action.

The brigades "hadn't much altered" the way most work got done, Yurchenko agreed — which might have been precisely why the idea of brigades had been universally applied for decades after everyone knew they didn't solve the problem of motivating farm workers. Bonuses for over-quota efforts were diffused among such large groups, and were so small and so routine, that no one gained much by working hard. Real access to opportunities for working thoughtfully or innovatively or directly for one's own advantage were still, as ever, systematically limited.

Had Yurchenko tried to negotiate lower quotas with his superiors, so his workers could get more substantial bonuses? "That wouldn't excite them," he answered. "Productivity is increasing anyhow. In '86 a day of labor was valued at 41 rubles. In '87 it was up to 54 rubles." Had he considered inflation? His answer took him elsewhere: "A milkmaid earns 380 rubles for a certain quota from each cow. She gets 70 kopeks more for each hundred kilos over quota. Many milkmaids own cars here! But she doesn't care about the quota, and doesn't know if she's fulfilled it. She just works. Last year, we paid labor a million rubles for planned production, and the routine bonus premiums came to another 300,000 rubles."

The master manager did not seem tantalized by the possibilities of motivating workers with higher pay. He surely did not say, "Oh, if only I could pay the hard workers directly and well for their work, how much they would produce!" Like his ally and former boss, Morgun, Yurchenko spoke of efficiency only in the context of the Party's system. He, too, worked with the possible and didn't fiddle with the rest.

Standing at the head of the library table he proclaimed, "You will learn more about the farm by meeting our zootechnologist. With him you will study our cattle." I'd spent much of my twenties and early thirties milking cows, making hay, and writing about dairy farming. The fluorescent lights in the long library buzzed. *Pravda, Izvestia, Kommunist,* some local and agricultural newspapers had been fussily fanned out on the table in elaborate piles by an unseen librarian with decorative instincts and little to do.

The "zootechnician" was thin and alert. He stood and peered at the American through thick horn-rimmed glasses, smiling shyly, speaking eagerly, with ostentatious precision. Yurchenko leaned over, put his hand on my shoulder, and attempted to negate whatever harm might arise from an unsupervised exchange with the veterinarian: "This man has many ideas. He may voice them. But it's up to me to go along with them or not." He stalked away. The vet, the other Mark, our keeper Vitaly Karpovich, and I strolled back into the big barns.

Were these barns the standard, Moscow-issue design? I asked. Had he, the vet, had a chance to modify the plans? Vitaly started his own answer, and I reminded him that he'd pledged to let me interview others without his leading them. But the vet's answer was tame: "When you design something, why do you have to deviate from it?" He spread his hands in the international give-me-a-break gesture. "Our complex here," he said, "was planned by the agricultural institute nearby in Poltava. We built it and scrupulously followed all strictures. Until two years ago, it was illegal to deviate. In *perestroika*, there has been some decentralization."

I told the vet that on my trip to Siberia a year earlier, farmers had complained that even recently they'd had to follow standard, all-Union plans, and as a consequence had built dairy barns that trapped far too much moisture for their extreme weather. The Ukrainian vet got competitive about winter storms. "We also have snow on the ground. We have barn insulation. Our winters get to minus thirty degrees Celsius. Body heat of cows is not enough. Our barns have proper vents." An American dairy farmer working in a program that advised Russian specialists had commented to me that every Soviet dairy calf he'd seen had lung disease from the overinsulated, underventilated standard barn designs. He'd thought this was one of the principal reasons that Soviet cows yielded less than half as much as Western cows.

I asked if there were other herd health problems. Perhaps the vet couldn't order medicines for the thousands of cows? Modern dairy cows are victims of domestication, fragile inventions of breeders striving for yield. High producers regularly contract mastitis and hoof rot and a dozen other barn-induced ailments that Western farmers medicate routinely. "We order medicines from a state allocation system, Zoological Veterinarian Supply. Brucellosis and tuberculosis vaccines we must order a year in advance. We must predict. It is not bad, and it is efficient for them." Vitaly Karpovich must have decided the vet was about to complain. "The supposedly inflexible organs of state will supply you in days," he interjected. "We can stop any epidemic from spreading."

The big barns were long, low, trim, and in reasonable paint. They filled a large field. While far from state of the art (which, in the USA, reaches absurd levels of high-tech automation with double-sixteen, rear-in, automatic-udder-washing, crowd-gated, self-metering, electronic takeoff, super-deluxe milking parlors), they were the sort of tie-stall barns that still housed many of the best dairy herds in the United States and Europe — except for the possible ventilation problem. Farm Victory of Communism's barn included automatic manure disposal with chain scrapers (standard in American barns since the 1950s) and wide aisles for offloading feed and fresh greenchop from a horse cart.

In these barns, cows got far more attention than any in Wisconsin did. Two shifts of dairymaids fussed over the cows from eight A.M. to ten P.M., and each woman cared for only ten animals — five per dairymaid. An efficient Wisconsin farm might average one hand for each fifty cows, and unlike Yurchenko's dairymaids, who were specialists, the Wisconsin hands would plow and plant and harvest between milkings. The women dumped the fresh milk from stainless-steel buckets at sanitary intake stations around the barn, whence it traveled through sterilized pipelines to a central cooler — a businesslike Wisconsin-style setup. There was no want of mechanization.

At the far end of the spotless barn, a few milkmaids clanked and murmured to each other in the dim light, just finishing a morning milking. Mooing and shuffling, the cows swayed out into a barnyard. They didn't look like dairy cows or like beef cows; they were short, scraggly, and gave nearly four tons apiece less per year than the average Wisconsin Holstein. They stood two-thirds Holstein height. They were generic dual-purpose animals, with neither the high lactation of Holsteins or Jerseys nor the fuller haunch of meat breeds.

In scores of barns in which I viewed cows, such indifferent genetic stock was probably the main obstacle to world-standard dairy (or meat) production. It takes decades of nationwide orderliness to isolate good dairy genes — widespread recordkeeping and coordinating and checking and honest sorting for many years to separate out the best few producers and collect the semen of their best sons. Then it takes hygienic supercooling of the semen, and perfect timing in delivering the semen to each cow in heat. It's a process involving persistent meticulousness. Holland and Denmark do it especially well. In Wisconsin, the plainest dirt farmer inseminates his milking mothers from the few bulls whose genetic potential tops national competitions.

The scarcity and sloppy handling of feed also inhibited high production. Relatively little soy was grown, even in the Ukraine, and hay was often harvested so late it lost feed value. The vet and I peered into several hay storage sheds. Even this show farm didn't get its hay in on time. Yurchenko's hay would have been barn bedding in Wisconsin. It had been harvested a month late (when most of its feed value had gone). It was tough and stemmy, and had been rained on (which leaches out protein). The vet knew this. The problem wasn't any lack of knowledge. He said, "The feed plant here could produce high enough quality feed for top dairy cows, but its staff doesn't care about quality. It wants only to fulfill its annual plan, and it is permitted to deliver by weight, not content. Our government shouldn't allow this deficiency of the system."

The vet understood the wisdom of breeding separate dairy and beef cattle. "We were afraid for a long time of dairy or beef specialization," the vet said. Soviet breeds remained dual purpose — black-and-whites, striped *cherna pyostia*, Ukrainian reds, and Simmental crosses dwelled on farms of every climate and topography, from Europe to the distant Pacific. The rationalization that profit-making imposed on American farmers put beef cattle on Texas dryland ranges, where they could graze economically, and dairy cows on the Wisconsin grass and corn lands.

Officially, a few million pure beef animals were in the census of Soviet farms, but that wasn't many. Campaigns to breed separate beef and milk herds had failed. Khrushchev had ordered beef animals milked, so urgently had he wanted more food. Old-timers remember holding ornery beef animals with long poles so dairymaids could approach. The poet Mayakovsky wrote about the campaign: "If your name is cow / You must give me milk . . ."

The vet, suddenly daring, said, "Our people are wonderful, industrious, modest, hardworking, more precious than gold." He turned a bit red. He was mocking Vitaly Karpovich, and our keeper's scowl deepened. The vet went on. "We did try to specialize in dairy breeding, until it went out of fashion. Now our system demands certain structures . . . I'll tell you a story . . ." The vet warmed, and Vitaly Karpovich scowled profoundly.

"I read it in the newspaper *Zaria — Dawn*. In a research institute, they designed a cow robot. They sent it to a collective farm for testing. It was shy by nature, demanded no feed, was sturdy and survived cold winds, in fact was completely indifferent to poor weather. At the same time, it behaved like a real cow — butted you with her horns, said moo, knocked her feet against the floor, swished her tail. And she was no trouble at all. Never got sick. She was immortal, so if you had a herd of these, you always had the same number for the account books. It was wonderful technology, perfectly suited to the role for which she was designed. She was the pride of the farm. But, she produced neither milk nor meat." Performance, the vet's story signaled, wasn't what had mattered in his world. Still, low productivity had real-life consequences for his nation's citizens. The Soviet national dairy herd was three times as large as America's but produced about the same amount of milk. And Soviet citizens, even before late-*perestroika* hard times, ate (perhaps for the better) only half as much meat as Americans did.

Said the vet, looking right at Vitaly Karpovich with a smile, "The U.S. exists for how long? Two hundred years? We've also got an agricultural tradition. Farming here started in the thirteenth century. Traditionally each American owner tried for self-sufficiency, right? Perhaps our collective farms do too.

We're moving. This is a good farm." Vitaly Karpovich, enforcer of piety, nodded agreement.

◆

After a big Yurchenko lunch I slept in the guesthouse, trying to shake a traveler's cold. I nested, dozing through a fever, snuggling into that strange place. The noise of a passing tractor awakened me. I wasn't much refreshed, but somehow had softened to the surroundings, reminded by my sleep that plain old fragile real life, beyond issues and history, happened here, too.

The other Mark and Vitaly sat together in bright sunlight on a log bench under a birch tree — the kind of scene that belonged on a calendar of beloved Ukrainian vistas. I had asked to visit the collective farms directly adjacent to ours, hoping by this specification to short-circuit some hidden Party boss's impulse to send us to yet another show farm. Vitaly had said, "Of course. We have no secrets."

But "No outing" is what he said now, under the birches. Party officials had told him to stick to the approved schedule. I shuffled back to bed, relieved not to be traveling about. But Vitaly Karpovich's response set me brooding.

A rule I already knew and should have remembered: regarding negotiations with Soviet officialdom, "no" meant "no"; "yes" also meant "no." He'd spoken without apparent embarrassment or regret, although he'd favored the idea hours before. "You are registered now for travel to and from the Victory of Communism farm on a set itinerary, and according to our regulations that's what you must keep doing," he'd said. "We'll see other farms soon."

He'd shrugged, unmortified, dutiful. In fact, he'd seemed to be enjoying himself telling what I could not do. He'd given no private gesture or signal that this prohibition surprised or frustrated him, no sense that he felt separate from the state that had just restricted his own forthright inclination, which he'd mentioned. He'd always lived in an orderly world. Authority routinely arrived from elsewhere, no matter where in the system one dwelled. "Most of my career took place under Stalin and Brezhnev," he had said. "I know my duty."

I supposed that a good monk's spirit soars from the discipline of accepting arbitrary regulation. Even obviously wrongheaded directives by proper authority should not shake a good monk's faith, nor leave him chagrined about his obedience. Perhaps this ten-thousandth chance to react mildly to a dictum reinforced Vitaly Karpovich's facility for enjoying the perverse nobility of the routinely obedient, the disciplined abdication of personal responsibility. This trained accession seemed one of the most fearsome accomplishments of totalitarianism, more dismaying than control won by beatings or intimidation. It was installed eventlessly in the young by calls to patriotism and loyalty and faith and fellowship with other decent citizens doing their moral best. The commonness of it, in so many societies East and West, ought to deromanticize what it means to be human. In the USSR it lingered in the gentlemanly likes of Vitaly Karpovich, in his resistance to reform.

Vitaly Karpovich Chuiko was a big shot. Scientists researched at his college and farm leaders trained there — and followed his orders. I imagined the chain of command, the authority at each level seeing itself as merely transmitting higher authority, with those on high impelled toward orthodoxy by duty and creed and ambition and real-enough political danger. Vitaly was the ghost of management past, alive and holy and influential in a tricky present. To the long list of crucial Soviet problems affecting dairy yield, I added docile, compliant decision-making.

Yet if a society's operating rules determine how character expresses itself, seeing oneself as a conduit for authority was only a paradoxical half of the picture. Morgun, Vitaly Karpovich, and Yurchenko, who demanded order in the name of the People, the Party, the Plan, themselves often had disobeyed in the service of the People, Party, and Plan. Not to disobey would have been elementally disloyal. They'd had to pick their spots. Those in positions of responsibility who followed all regulations couldn't get good results.

Their disobediences created the shadow economy, and the shadow economy *had* worked, just well enough. That's why the regime had endured for so long in the face of its structured-in inefficiencies. And it was leaders in the middle of the chain of command who made it work. They lived dual lives, of obedience and of subterfuge. Yurchenko couldn't have risen without facility at patriotic two-facedness, because market reality — he'd had to scrounge what the Victory of Communism farm needed — drove him in one direction, and the vested ideology that backed his command drove him in another.

I guessed that these rules of the game had become second nature to him. Yurchenko and Vitaly Karpovich must often have adjusted commands from on high, especially because they tended living creatures and plants, and because Yurchenko ruled several rural villages of real people. They'd learned how to satisfy their bosses and be satisfied as bosses. Their own lieutenants must have learned the same lessons, creating a great chain of deceit.

They were all very good hosts when higher-ups visited. They all backed their bosses with the necessary paperwork. They had everything right on paper. Yes, the May 20 planting deadline had been met on all fields, the forms would have said, while Yurchenko actually would have awaited dry weather or spare parts or poky labor brigades. That necessary duplicity would have traveled up and down the lines of authority of all administrators.

Every second of all of their lives they'd have been vulnerable to punishment for not fulfilling the plan, and for lying. To sleep well anyhow, they'd all have developed networks of allies in high places and fall guys in low places, done full shares of favors and accumulated knowledge about the similar sins of those who might cause them harm.

In this way, Party discipline had accumulated into an overriding, widespread, action-stifling style of doing business — a result of the ironic structure of pious central command as much as of the personalities of particular tyrants. The Yurchenkos and Vitaly Karpoviches were local powers, low in the command chain. When the system was fully intact, collective-farm chairmen were vulnerable to scores of governmental agencies. Yurchenko had a bathhouse, kept a good kitchen and the fine guesthouse. He danced in an eternal quadrille between cautious deceivers and the knowingly deceived. Following out this notion from my sickbed, I felt awe, and despaired of comprehending the soul shaped by such demands. I sneezed and got up and took a walk through the countryside.

◆

Other callers came to stay in the guesthouse. A young farm chairman from Kaluga, a grain-growing district a few hours southwest of Moscow, had driven a thousand kilometers with his assistant. They'd pulled in noisily late in the night, stamping their feet and laughing in the middle of a rain squall. Sniffling out of a deep sleep, I'd squinted at them. Both were Goliaths — a pair of barrels would have clothed them skin-tight. Both were mustached and smiled and performed darting little bull-necked bows next morning when introduced to Vitaly Karpovich.

One of them, Boris Petrovich Tagalai, said, very seriously, "We have come to study Nikolai Timofeyevich's management." They had mostly come to talk him into selling them some quality seed grain — just the sort of semi-illicit outside-the-plan barter that made the creaky system work in spite of itself. I chatted with Boris in the guesthouse after lunch. He was half Nikolai Timofeyevich's age and spoke eagerly and boldly. It was my first conversation with a collective-farm chairman unplanned by authorities. His commentary was less official, too.

He was part of a new wave of younger, more independent operators. He'd recently graduated from agricultural college (post–Lysenko's influence), recalled nothing of the time of starvation, and seemed not to have fought and good-ol'-boyed his way up through the Party bureaucracy. He was more nearly just a businessman on the make, hunting deals and supplies. He'd really been elected in a *contested* election — something that had occasionally happened in the first enthusiasm of *perestroika*.

Unlike Yurchenko, Boris was full of questions about America — farming questions about yields and machinery costs and planting strategies and herd milking averages. Questions about commerce, too — how a midwestern farmer orders a tractor, who fixes it and how does the fixer get paid, and how the farmer sells what he grows. And questions a country dweller might ask even if he lived not in Kaluga but in Kentucky: why is the U.S. president cutting down on handguns — isn't this limiting freedom? And a contradictory follow-on: why is TV so violent? And does it influence people? And by the way, how much does a car cost, and how long to get one once it's ordered?

Boris was thirty and had taken charge recently. His was the first competitive election on his farm. He'd outpolled the old-line candidate. I could imagine why he attracted votes. He smiled easily, spoke humbly, walked with a sportsman's musclebound, balls-of-the-feet gait. He was genial, knowable, low-key, logical, not flashy smart, the sort of straight-ahead soul one meets again and again running rich farms in Iowa. He was a rarer sighting in the Soviet Union.

"Actually," he said, "I defeated the older candidate, but came in second to another, who then declined the responsibility. I was already district chief agronomist. I'd graduated from our Far East Institute of Agriculture, on the Chinese border. I met a girl there from Kaluga and we married; she was on vacation in the Far East. My own father managed a farm in the Far East for thirty years. Farm management runs in the family, so the idea wasn't new to me.

"This business is changing. Managing is becoming more complicated. As a *perestroika* reform they just merged two smaller farms, to strengthen management. So we have 4,000 hectares [10,000 acres] of tillable land — a big size, hard to manage well. If I farmed privately, my cows would milk 16,000 pounds [the American average!] a year. My wheat crop could top 50 centners [a centner equals 100 kilograms] an acre. I could do every task myself! I'd need small machinery. I'd like that."

He was not quite sounding like a would-be Western-style family farmer, because his dream was about five cows, not fifty, forty acres of grain, not four hundred. It was a nostalgic daydream of "repeasantization" that Soviet farm executives often came up with when they talked privatization. This had been the size of their grandparents' holdings, not the size of modern, high-tech European family farms.

He wasn't heading toward that daydream, however. "On my state farm, we don't grow as much food as we could. We could produce far more efficiently if we were a bunch of private farmers on the same land. So I'm interested in the new lease-brigade farms Gorbachev now allows. I allowed one such cooperative to organize itself — five ordinary guys formed it. Without so-

phisticated technology, without the agri-scientists who supervise every other activity on our farm, they just started working
hard. In the fields they doubled what our farm workers got for
hay, sunflowers, beet root for cow feed — routine crops. It's a
dairy. The results show what I am talking about. It's simple.
Sixty milk cows, and just two or three people serving them. A
quarter the usual staff. What kills us even with their good milk
production is the low price Moscow bureaucrats set for their
production . . ."

Vitaly Karpovich had been sitting in the corner of the guesthouse parlor, gazing sourly at Boris and quietly monitoring our
chat. Then he was shouting, enunciating his words one by one:
*"Listen to me, sir: the low price represents the voice of the peo-
ple!"* Vitaly had stifled many conversations during our travels,
but the temper of the time was rising beyond his reach. Threats,
backed by Party power, would have strengthened his word even
a year earlier. He settled deep into his chair.

". . . while milk and other crop prices stay fixed." Boris had
gone right on, making a show of being unperturbed, and denouncing the system that hemmed in his ambition. "Farm
equipment costs shoot up. Can we survive when there's no gain
for harder work? How can I even ask people to work harder?

"I started a new enterprise, growing virus-free seed potatoes. I
let it set up as a lease brigade; it manages itself. A state enterprise in Moscow has a monopoly on all stages of potato growth
— distribution and storage, too — the Moscow Research Institute of Potatoes under the Academy of Agricultural Sciences
granted us this contract. We have a laboratory building, research
fellows, and product. Wearing white coats, under sterile conditions, we grow virus-free seed and test new varieties. We sell
seed potatoes to Moscow-region collective farms. It's a very
good business. It helps us turn a profit on our farm. We also have
the usual enterprises you'd expect — a thousand pigs, a thousand sheep, fifteen hundred milk cows.

"I'd like to start more family lease-brigade farms, except that
almost all our tractors are huge — the K-700s, 310 horsepower.
The group at the potato lab, fifteen or twenty people, and the
lease-brigade farmers, another ten people, do feel like owners.
My hundreds of regular fieldworkers just do not have that feel-

ing, and they don't like work. They don't make money. The cooperative guys made a lot." As he described money, his big hands gesticulated precisely, sketching a rising stack of bills. Then he turned his hands palms-up, shrugged, and smiled. The ruble pile disappeared. "I know how many rubles I advanced on the cow farm, and crops were very good. Seems their salary will be about seven hundred rubles a month — twice regular pay, and the farm makes more too.

"But here's a problem. When they show good results and high wages, envy develops in the farm villages. Other workers came to me complaining because I'd given the lease brigade a written guarantee that they would be first in line for getting equipment and calf feed. But that is the best use of such equipment! They work hard with it, using equipment and feed well. Let me tell you, lease brigades are very good business — worth pursuing. These peasants are the only ones on my farm who feel the land is under their control. I hear American businessmen are ruthless. Is that true? I wasn't when I negotiated a contract with these guys. I wanted their lease brigade on my farm, so I yielded them a lot of ground."

Boris left for his meeting with Yurchenko. Vitaly slouched in the parlor. He had turned on the television and was watching Billy Joel, who had a full light show cranking onstage. I'd met an Englishman on the plane to Moscow, a young trucker who had developed a booming business bringing in stage equipment for European rock shows. "At age thirty, Boris may be cheerful," Vitaly grumped. "Let's see what another ten or fifteen years do to his disposition." I left Vitaly Karpovich nodding his head in time to the music.

◆

Across the dooryard from the guesthouse, another stucco building served as the farm's infirmary. It included a hydrotherapy room. Yurchenko had decided that I needed hydrotherapy, and he'd gravely issued the key to the place from his big jailer's ring. "Return it soon," he'd said, and muttered about "our healthful machine."

The shower chamber was tiled. It reeked of feet. Farm residents took weekly group showers there. The schedule was tacked to the wall. "Our healthful machine" was a contraption that I imagined came from a Victorian-era spa. It looked like a harpoon gun, and hurled fusillades of stinging water bolts across the room. The hot splats sailed at me through the misty air, exploding on contact. I forgot all ironies; it was a fine machine. I understood Yurchenko's fondness for it.

Afterward I fell back asleep, shedding my cold, and awakened again thinking (this time) about farm chairmen. A chairman was, of course, more a bureaucrat than a farmer. The chain of bureaucrats was exactingly accountable for a sequence of outcomes none had a prayer of controlling. They therefore shared another alliance: engineering cover-ups. The highest of them, way far up top somewhere, may have spent time meditating on how to marry creed and practice. The next down were probably the ones who paid attention to national crop requirements. A next tier broke superiors' edicts down to tons per region, and another envisioned the practical ways for districts to carry their noble burdens. When the command finally touched plowed ground, the poor, squeezed, lowest authority in this orderly procession of fantasists was Farm Chairman Yurchenko, standing above a score of assistant experts on specific aspects of agriculture, record-keeping, village administration, ideology, procurement and distribution, all small chiefs with assistants.

The farm chairman was the mediator, and he absorbed, cumulatively, all the demands from the top, creed-based and practical, and squared them with the sloppy realities at the bottom. Superiors' edicts burned into a farm chairman like successive doses of radiation, in time making him weird and powerful. His success at the impossible — everyone knew a farm couldn't really run by edicts from a thousand miles distance and on suppositions determined five years back — mostly depended on how he brought off his relationship with the bureaucrats he bore above him, as if he were a circus tumbler attempting an amazing feat of balance.

A successful farm chairman, new or old style, needed to be a performer, costumed in bangles and agile enough to compensate — by personal charm, good-ol'-boyhood, material gifts, ceremonies of wining and dining, and facilitating connections for others — for the inevitable failures of execution inherent in a five-year plan.

In *perestroika,* regional officials won one strong power, the authority to blend resources of farms as needed. They took over more and more field assignments and equipment allocations from Kiev. This increased the illicit powers of regional administrators. Local officials might at any moment command one farm to delay its own work, lend trucks to the farm down the road, and absorb the costs.

More than ever, effective chairmen lavished favors on the Raion (District) Communist Party Committee and the Raiispolkom, the People's Soviet Committee that was local quasi-civil government. These officials required reports of how much milk got milked each day, what chores got done, what work brigades accomplished. These documents held chairmen in perpetual blackmail.

The local Party chairman's office and local soviet executive committee chairman's office (often, as in Belgorod, ruled by the same person) kept forty or fifty people checking farm operations — financial officers checked ledgers, veterinary officials checked animal health, fire inspectors discovered code violations, health inspectors examined kitchens and infirmaries — at the *raion* level alone. On *oblast* level, checking got checked. Officials from republic and all-Union levels looked over shoulders, too. There were also a bureau of statistics and a census bureau in the plot. They all needed hams and wheels of cheese. The chairman's fish smokery, his kiln producing scarce roof tile, sewer pipe, or brick, fit the Soviet puzzle here.

◆

I'd skipped dinner, and when I went to breakfast next morning, I found I was cured. Breakfasts at Yurchenko's resembled lunches and suppers. Visiting officials and sub-courtiers sought the chairman's opinion or promise on farm and local administrative business between mouthfuls. The same dishes showed up at all meals, always swamped with butter: the buttered *pirogi* with sour cream again, and the hot buttered borscht with sour cream, the chicken roasted to the point of fragmentation and afloat in its own fat and butter too, the black bread with butter, and a few times a week, my favorite, the crock of buckwheat baked in butter. Once there was homemade headcheese, hold the butter.

In the chairman's private dining room of Farm Victory of Communism, there was no food shortage. A stout blond cook made everything Yurchenko asked her for, and a serving girl bore it in on platters. I thought this room might have had the same mood and function under the tsars. The pleased smiles of sated officials drawing their chairs back, folding their hands over full bellies, might even have looked the same.

The farmers from Kaluga rose and shook hands with Yurchenko, and out front, squeezed shoulder to shoulder into a tiny car and drove off northward. Their trucks would come to pick up seed; they'd negotiated successfully. When Yurchenko came back inside, he was perturbed and animated — the only time I saw him agitated.

"We had here the Kaluga man praising the lease brigade — nice words, but I am skeptical," he said. He was pronouncing on their visit. Yurchenko epitomized his opposition. "I don't believe in that man. Why? I don't see any permanent ties between him and the state farm, or him and the state. He just chose farming as a place to make big money quickly. You answer me this: We give a man a tractor, parts, gas, a shop, all for free. He gets a salary and he works for all of us. Why should he work more carelessly than he would if we sell him the tractor and he has to pay for fixing it himself? Why would that make a guy work better?"

I told him the litany of answers self-evident in America — pride of accomplishment, risk of loss, and prospect of profit motivate small owners the world over, not to mention having loan payments to meet. He brooded and said, "Yes, we need to find new forms, but the lease brigade is not the form." I agreed with him. "I rent a tractor to a peasant for three years, then he can just drop it, leave it parked? And during the three years he can ruin it? Is that the attitude you're looking for? Perhaps there should be associations where farmers own tractors together." This was an old Soviet idea that had been dropped. I told Yurchenko I'd relish the chance to walk around an Iowa farm town with him at harvest time. He just nodded.

Seeing his beloved Soviet system slipping into disarray while news from the outside world demonstrated to locals that the West was doing better, he persisted in his strong conviction that the machinery of state ownership should cure things. He blamed "radical politicians" for disorder. "Meanwhile," he said bitterly, "I need tires for all cars here and I have to go around searching, like a pauper. A strong collective farm such as mine is now paid for production at a lower rate than a backward farm that produces little. Of course we need to improve things."

I wanted to offer the West's obvious answers, he wanted to blame his government's changing policies. I felt smug, he felt indignant. It was hard to resist debate. Instead I asked what advice he might hang on a classroom wall for young farmers to follow. Yurchenko was at home with that sort of thinking. He took the question to mean how would he advise young farm chairmen, not young independent farmers, and came up with a list:

1. You shouldn't be lazy.

2. You should be very concrete and detailed in the orders you give people.

3. You should use land conservatively, so it remains productive for the next generation.

4. You should be father to those you direct. The good father is an adviser to his children, but is also sometimes a severe judge.

5. You should have the feelings of the owner of the land — within the limits of your assigned job.

I was amazed by the last item. He comes close to espousing the very thing he questions most, ownership. "I saw a combine driver yesterday — he already has covered three hundred fifty hectares, delivering good crops. He's one of the best, and his machine is considered complex. But his work was not up to his usual mark. He's got two children, but nevertheless I called him down from the machine and I saw that he was running drunk. I punished him severely. He lost all his bonuses. He had just won a competition. We canceled the award. I felt he had put everybody in terrible danger. He could have made his kids orphans, or run over somebody. He could have destroyed the combine. He was absolutely wild."

I asked Yurchenko if the combiner might have felt more responsible if in fact he'd owned the machine himself. He argued the merits of nonownership instead of addressing my question: "He can make up to eighty-five rubles a day, normally. He doesn't have to fix his own combine, pay for gas — he just gathers and winnows crops. An American farmer who visited here told me he works from seven in the morning to seven at night. This combiner here rarely has to do that. The combiner on the next field doesn't own his combine either, but he is honorable — why was this fellow irresponsible? I expect four hundred people to appear ready to work every morning. One has a sick child, another a sick father, the third is sick himself. I have somehow to absorb these conditions and drive them to work anyhow. It's not easy but I manage, and the peasants are moderately satisfied."

Does he bear all burdens of his peasants' lives himself? "No," he answered, "I have help from the on-farm secretary of the Communist Party. And he consolidates the efforts of a hundred on-farm Communists. He helps them influence the mood and morale of the people in the fields and villages, and takes care of the cultural part of our life. He's a great help to me."

◆

Not all farms had resident Party officials. Farm Victory of Communism did, and the next afternoon Yurchenko brought Grigory to our parlor. On lesser farms a worker long in the Party took on this job part time, reporting to an off-farm superior. One way or the other, the office was filled on every farm in the country, never by the chairman himself. The Party officer had two jobs: ministering to (and watching) the people and assisting (and watching) the chairman. In the Stalin and Brezhnev eras, the watching part had been deadly business.

This Party officer was a man in a gray flannel suit, thirtyish, with a round boyish face and nice European loafers. In the Soviet Union, shoes made the man. No one with a choice wore Soviet shoes. Generals walked the streets of Moscow wearing pointy Italian shoes with their uniforms. Everyone wanted foreign shoes, but most people didn't have access to them. Grigory stared out of piercing blue eyes, intelligently, challengingly, even when he smiled, and then the corners of his mouth somehow stayed down.

He was altogether local, born a village away. He'd studied science education at Poltava Pedagogical Institute. Then he'd taught school nearby. He'd been "an obedient son." He'd joined Komsomol, the national Communist youth group, and "I had the evenhanded and compliant temperament needed for the elders to make me a leader in it." At twenty-five he'd become a full Party member. "If you calculate," he said, "this is the right age to join the Party, because joining is a sign of political maturity. You must really think about the political slogans, the programs. When you're just twenty, you aren't mature enough to think clearly about those points and come to personal decisions. At twenty-five, you can. But age isn't everything. There was a scholar — Yevgeny Paton, a welding expert? He joined the Party at seventy-nine, the year he died.

"I didn't have such a single moment of insight. My commitment grew. When you join, you accept more responsibility voluntarily. You must show more discipline, be more active, accept more risk. That's the way I put it to myself." I told him that I saw that he was earnest, but that I didn't understand what risk he'd shouldered. Did it have to do with switching allegiances — replacing local friendships with loyalty to the national organization?

"You should realize the Party does not as a rule make decisions that deal directly with the economy. Mine was not an economic risk. But when it comes to selection and promotion of personnel, our main business here at the farm level, I take risks. Here is an example: The old manager of a warehouse recently died. I recommended a Communist — not a very educated one, but one who had done good work. That raised a certain risk for my reputation. I couldn't know how he'd perform. But still the Party followed my recommendation. He's worked for two years now, and does well. That kind of risk." It sounded like the usual risk of bureaucrats — the risk of getting blamed.

Thinking of Vitaly Karpovich's about-face on my wish to visit adjacent farms, I asked Grigory if he agreed with all Party edicts. "I joined the Party when Chernenko was first party secretary," he said. "Do I share the opinion that his was a period of stagnation? Yes, it was. As for current politics, *glasnost* complicates my work, makes it more challenging and interesting. It has touched all our people, but has touched Party members most specifically.

"The Party was the initiator and the object of *glasnost*. The contradictions of our lives during the stagnation of Brezhnev and Chernenko weren't acknowledged. They were pushed under the carpet. Suddenly they show everywhere, so we Communists have to demonstrate the way to solve problems that until recently we denied were problems! The shortage of consumer goods — of course we feel it on the farm. We have no soap powder in our store. Sugar is there but only for coupons — which is painful here, because the big sugar factory is right down the road.

"So I meet people on the farm. I meet Party officials — sometimes I have to reach above the local, to district level, to get authority to solve some problems. An example: An old man from Mlini walked into my office a few days ago. He had a complaint. A few kids were driving cars wildly down the narrow street leading to the riverbank. They terrified a cow, which fell into a ravine. So the man came to me with a request that the street be closed to through traffic. He hadn't come alone, either. He'd gotten signatures from everyone on the street. Yes, I found the request legitimate. For this one, I went only up to the head of the local soviet, just next door. Today I wrote a formal document asking for cooperation of the motor vehicles bureau. Soon they will come up with the appropriate sign — we call it a 'brick,' because it looks like one.

"Widows, veterans, old people — that's my routine. I recently conducted a village meeting, not just for Party members but for everyone, because the people were concerned about how to get coal. It's the village's winter heat. I decided to solve their problem. Together with the head of the local soviet, I visited every house and spoke to every head of household about his need. I put the list on record and passed an order. And because it's summer and they aren't overburdened, I was able to convince the proper authorities to deliver enough coal. I won't hear complaints this winter." I thought about what had made coal trucks come around, back home.

"A final example: We have problem teenagers — it's not just the USA that has them. Some kids pulled up newly planted trees and heaved them into the pond in front of this building. Kids are kids, so some bragged. We found out who did it, and spoke to the parents, and then to the kids, who promised that at the proper time they would replant the trees themselves."

I asked about the mood of the dozens of Party members on the farm — if he'd heard resentment of Gorbachev's "liberal" *perestroika* directives. "I joined the Party; I'm still in it," he answered.

"I publish a newspaper on the farm with community news in it . . ." Two days later, after some hemming and hawing, he came by and gave me the folded single sheet of newsprint. The news was humdrum: crop yields one couldn't trust and meetings where Yurchenko had made speeches. The most fascinating thing was a chronological list of malfeasants, their fines and punishments. Anton Petrenko, stole bag of feed. Aleksei Fedorenko, found drunk. At the bottom of the chain of command, the Party's local man wielded shame to keep Yurchenko's villagers in line.

7

IT WAS NIGHT. The on-farm Communist secretary was off in his cottage eating supper, probably under a small portrait of Lenin that must have hung where a simple cross might were he an Iowa parson. In the guesthouse parlor, Vitaly Karpovich fussed with the big television. It plugged into a suitcase-sized cabinet of vacuum tubes — a radio-era version of a voltage-spike damper. Vitaly was catching up on the news, an unsettling daily experience. *Glasnost* policies permitting increased candor were so recent that frankness itself was an unvoiced theme of news broadcasts. Whenever I watched with Soviet citizens in those days, the released force of historic change was apparent. Every startling *perestroika* development sounded merely transient. Land leases, cooperatives, the right to hire help, the right to hold dollars, the occasional unrigged election, the lifting of much censorship — each point of slackening state control seemed just as likely to snap back the following day as to slacken further. No new development, or the thrust of new developments, seemed certain. And the end of Communist rule was not considered. No one even supposed that might happen.

Years of idly discounting official word and scanning rumors for their hints of truth had transformed Soviet citizens into news hawks. They were already skilled interpreters of tiny signs of change — a name missing from lists of speakers, a new seating order in a May Day photo of bigwigs. They impressed me as generally more inclined than Americans to bother trying to divine the news behind the news. Vitaly Karpovich sat slouched in his easy chair, his face morose, his expert eye on the TV screen.

"*Separation of powers worries some members of the Supreme Soviet,*" said the square-jawed announcer of the national evening news, *Vremya* — Time — "*who feel the government will act too independently.*" Vitaly nodded slowly with an expression of judicious agreement. His self-declared Stalinism, I came to realize, was consistent and showed often. The flow of everyday public events on TV ran contrary to it, and he appeared in pain as he watched. He must have been an efficient dean, a scourge, a good stifler of the autonomous. His indignation measured the authenticity of change.

The TV announcer said, "*A council is pushing to decentralize the Ministry of Interior and to make police accountable to local authorities.*" Police authority tampered with? Regionalization of political authority backed? Vitaly scowled.

"*Forest fires on the border of Finland destroy rich timber stands.*" TV cameracraft quickly got slicker during *perestroika,* although the editing wasn't yet lean.

The All-Union Supreme Soviet was in session. "*Gorbachev reported on his foreign trips. The Supreme Soviet has appealed directly to the U.S. Congress to end nuclear testing.*" Imagine them acting independently! Vitaly grimaced.

President George Bush's face showed up, bearing that same grimace, and looked back at Vitaly. A hijacking was mid-standoff. President Bush denied that America planned to invade Lebanon, even if a second hostage was killed.

In Nicaragua the Sandinistas worked on another new peace treaty with the contras. Vitaly's eyelids flickered. In Cuba, a collision of two trains killed thirty-three. Vitaly shook himself awake.

"*In Afghanistan, nineteen surface-to-surface missiles were used, killing one person.*" The camera scanned workaday Kabul. A young girl hurried across the screen holding a white sun umbrella high up; a marketwoman took money, folded a few yards of cloth, and nimbly wrapped it. Vitaly rubbed his eyes.

"*American warships docked at Sevastopol. The Yanks were allowed ashore. Soviets walked about the ship.*" The camera shot balloons, flags, cameras, then panned over to a World War II memorial, developing the contradiction of this renewed alliance with a current adversary. Vitaly's brow knit hard. He'd hauled me to every World War II monument he could find. (Advice to tourists, even in post-Soviet times: bear up when shown monuments.) Vitaly's piety was his strength. He was the moral equivalent of a good Kiwanis Club member. His heart swelled or ached with his country's fortunes. I felt as distant from this disposition as I did from that of his cousins-in-personality in Iowa. Here, strangely, I embodied the immoral spirit of capitalism for him (and for myself, too!), and he was out to show me the moral superiority of his way, even as it lost ground. Back home, I'd often embodied the immoral spirit of one who questions the sacredness of business institutions. Our Kiwanians give me the same scowls as theirs.

"*In an international ballroom-dancing competition in Sverdlovsk, a Muscovite pair took first place. The competition was sponsored by seven industrial concerns from the Urals,*" which the announcer listed, adding, "*For the most part, these couples are married.*" Vitaly tapped his foot and bobbed his head to the waltz music. Winning spouses glided across the dance floor, sequins glistening.

At the Chelsea Flower Show in London, the camera crew had concentrated not on flowers but lawnmowers, still rare in the Soviet Union.

In a few seconds, the sports segment flashed a gymnast whirling through parallel bars, go-carts drifting around hairpin turns, sprinters pushing out of blocks then lifting their heads in mid-race agony, broad jumpers air-walking aloft, skiers twisting through gates with thighs pistoning against moguls.

By the time the national weather map appeared onscreen, Vitaly snored in his chair. I left the set running in case he reawakened. The light from a puppet drama played across his childlike smile.

◆

We were in the breadbasket of a land of scarcity. Amber waves of grain surrounded us. I had come to report on the food problem, but was being fattened like a goose, force fed rich lunches and banquets at every turn. Within days my belt clipped only on its outermost notch, and soon I had to punch a new notch. Again and again I was faced with those white fatback squares with garlic, that sausage loaf, stewed chicken, stewed beef, thick borscht with kidney or liver, the wonderful buttered kasha, the sharp brown bread. The plate of boiled eggs. The plate of soft butter. The plate of pickles. The plate of fresh tomatoes, scallions, and dill. Again and again I waddled off like one of Gogol's officials and inspected fields or the local store. The feasts were relentless. Another awaited, banquet tables set in some unlikely back room, serving women peeking out from the kitchen at the arriving American delegation. We visited Gogol's Mirgorod, where the mud-mired intersection he'd described one hundred fifty years earlier was a tourist site.

The fields were, even on the show farms Vitaly Karpovich had allowed us to see, always so-so, never groomed cleanly. Even the best collective farms farmed carelessly. Between lush patches, workers left poor spots, stunted, pale stands, streaks of rough ground the harrows had missed, stands of weeds, stands plowed too shallowly, stands where the seeder had clogged and no one had cared. Sugar beets and lesser grains grew where corn made sense. Soy production was a novelty. Broken-down combine hulks and rusted-out manure spreaders strewed this most fertile Soviet land. Leaking oil smeared the working tractors' engines. A plenitude of workers in little crews poked away at jobs that machines or chemicals, and tenfold fewer workers, accomplished in the West.

Building materials were so scarce all over that collective-farm chairmen who managed to accumulate them gathered great bartering power. A few charismatic chairmen in the region had wrested exemptions allowing them to run sawmills and brick kilns. In 1989 such secondary on-farm enterprises had only recently become legal. We visited a small electrical motor repair shop in which a father and a few sons fixed dozens of motors a day from every farm around. The family took in thousands of rubles from their work, and shared them with the farm treasury. I saw the father rewinding a copper armature by hand, for want of simple shop tools and parts. Ministries guarded monopoly prerogatives of manufacture and distribution; they impeded farms' struggles to fulfill their Five Year Plans. Farms with their own barter goods played in the shadow economy, ran better, each subverting a bit of ministry power.

I sensed the intricacy and local politics of intra-enterprise wheeling and dealing in the guardedness that greeted my questions in that area. Yurchenko and other farm chairmen spoke generally about bartering for coal, cement, and iron girders in multistage deals. A chairman, I gathered, might arrange with a farm equipment bureaucrat to bump a farm higher on the order list in return for bricks, boards, labor, meat, vegetable oil, farm cheese. The factory would find clients for these things in other trades. Officials with access to trucks were in ambiguous roles, just a temptation away from being middlemen, an evil in the Communist worldview.

Perestroika policies did increase enterprise chiefs' autonomy from planners, but that exposed a limitation — few enterprise bosses had business experience. Party officials seemed to be taking the lead themselves; they were the ones with the money, power, and experience. Webs of once-forbidden direct dealings between enterprises were expanding, I was told, and included the Party. The heart of one strike in the news was miners' demand for fifteen percent of the coal they dug, so their organization could barter for itself. Like meat, coal was as good as hard currency. Rural cronies were patching together gnarled, restrictive little zones of mutual protection, inside which their overlapping interests played out — capitalism at its worst. These were enduring missteps on the path toward a market economy, substituting private advantage and loyalties for the public logic of supply and demand. Long after the fall of the Party, such alliances would help sustain rural power nearly as before.

Some local bosses made odd things happen, willing into being their utopian dreams. Yurchenko had those racehorses and Olympic riders. Another chairman gathered a substantial hardware store together, stocked with rarities — nails and screws and hammers and sickles — to ease his peasants' lives. The store looked everyday to me, but a Soviet citizen seeing such hard-to-find wonders as hand-cranked grinding wheels, rubber mallets, and crosscut saws knew at once that the boss was important. Vitaly Karpovich had scoffed at a chairman troubling to ease peasants' "backward lives with individual backward solutions." Vitaly Karpovich was browsing across the store, and finally presented us with Gorbachev's speeches — in Russian. In another few years, Vitaly Karpovich would be a modern patriot still, but pushing his gospel of progress in a separate Ukraine, with its own language and the world's third-largest nuclear arsenal.

◆

With him in tow, we drove down the road to visit "Nadia," one of the well-paid milkmaids. She received us in her best dress, face scrubbed, a farm wife on Sunday. Her large cottage was built of glazed tile, green and white and yellow, with a tiled roof and a prim garden. Her husband was a tractor driver. He pedaled home on a black bicycle for our midday visit, disheveled in his work clothes, smiled and leaned cockily against his bike. I gave him a pack of Marlboros. That at once felt like a mistake. He became awkward and tried hard to give it back. Waving Marlboros around got Westerners taxis at rush hour in downtown Moscow. The husband was my host, and may have felt paid. Still, with a conspiratorial grin, perhaps because of the ambiguity of a gift that was also the coin of bribes, he finally took it. I felt as though I'd tipped a friend, so I apologized, worsening the awkwardness. We laughed.

I was delighted. This interaction was intelligible to both of us, although we'd mimed it. How different our lives must have been. Yet I could imagine being him; so much was familiar. There was his wife, who laughed warmly at his miming. They took turns holding the kids. It was easy to imagine them loving and scrapping, working at life. I could imagine him sensing which bosses were straight with him. He must have had favorite foods, worried about middle age, wished for what more money could bring his family, thought about something a foreman had said that had disturbed his pride, and what a friend had said that had pleased his heart. I suppose I could look at a Rockefeller in a penthouse bank office or a Borneo tribesman in a rain-forest

village and think of such things, too. But I was not just considering the common condition of mankind. In this case, we had
connected. I'm sure we both knew it. I'd felt that way during the
open-hearted wanderings of my twenties, but seldom during my
curmudgeonly forties.

They led us into the house. I could have lived there happily.
Compared to flats back in Moscow, it felt spacious — a mudroom, a tiny kitchen into which a gas stove (scorched pots tumbled off it) and a table had been stuffed, a wide central corridor,
and three bedrooms. The cottage had indoor plumbing. They'd
neatly lined up a few pipe beds and chairs, but no table, in nearly
empty rooms. Rugs, in keeping with local usage, hung on the
walls as ornament and insulation. The bare tiled floors were
immaculate, save for a few toys scattered about. It was a warm,
tight house, and outside was a bountiful private plot.

◆

Beckoning his jeep and driver, who awaited him outside of wherever he was, Chairman Yurchenko took us jouncing through
more fields. One was impressive, heavy with a seed-bearing
grass he called *espertsa* (esparset and esparto grass are in English
dictionaries, variously as varieties of hemp or millet) and with a
tangle of vetch — which, if they managed to harvest it without
jamming their mower and to dry it without leaving it outdoors
through a rain or two, must have made an excellent legume feed.

He stopped the jeep at a crossroads. Improbably, there stood
a small café, identified as "Three Wells" by a little sign above
the door. It was the only such amenity I ever saw on a farm. It
was a small white building, sitting pleasantly by a fenced-in
spring that flowed into a fountain-sized box made of notched
timbers. A counterbalanced lever as big as a railroad-crossing
gate reached into it with a bucket mounted on the end. The
lever had been playfully constructed as the silhouette of a dick-
eybird. Yurchenko dipped me a ladleful.

He gazed over this scene proudly and delivered himself of a
toastmaster's oration: "I have changed the wood and pumps
three times in my life on this well whose water we just quaffed
— first when I came here, then when the farm was quite suc-

cessful, and recently, when I am strong and old and tough. I will
live to change them once more. What sort of a man would you
think me if I'd allowed such a source of pure water to get dilapidated? I've always kept it neat. In the next village, the Orthodox church will reopen," he said, "following a petition by
townsfolk. The holy water will be dipped from this well." It was
a ceremonious, boastful declaration of self by a *perestroika* sur-
vivor.

A man drinking coffee in the café limped up to Yurchenko and
said, "I'm old — I have one eye, one hand. I'm against the miners' strike." Yurchenko nodded. He was, too. Coffee was on sale
by the bag, at 4 rubles a kilo, probably a hundredfold under
world market price. What was the route of this subsidized coffee? Why was this substance, rare everywhere in the Soviet Union, here in this little farm shop? It also offered crockery mugs,
sunflower oil, bags of buckwheat, and sausage at 2.8 rubles
a kilo, the official state price. Behind the café grew a 250-acre
field of sugar beets. The yellow and pale green blotches on the
leaves were caused by misapplied fertilizer, Yurchenko said.
Two old babushkas gossiped in the driveway. A girl of three or
four danced in great leaps and wriggles before them. Her father
leaned on a car and watched her, and us, in the quiet sunshine.
This was a nice place on a nice day.

Yurchenko climbed back in the jeep and continued his patrol.
He'd just gone to a meeting of the local soviet — a show of democracy in his offices. There were fifty-five members. He was
"one of nine" on the executive committee, he said, "charged
with controlling the schools, the co-op shops, the cultural institutions, controlling local welfare, keeping the villages in order.
The farm is profitable — three million rubles last year, and
meanwhile the soviet has no money for roads. So our farm built
sixty kilometers of roads; if we didn't, no one would. We built
heated auto repair shops. We fix cars at minus thirty. At the
meeting yesterday we specified the size of cottage fences and
the paint color permissible. We demanded that the local co-op
store carry several varieties of bread, because bread is a product
of state bakeries. We checked the stores to make sure of some
things — for example, our people can tomatoes and we need a

supply of empty jars for fall. We assured ourselves the store has secured a lot of agreements with farms in Moldova — for watermelons, too. We assured ourselves that on September first, when classes start, the correct schoolbooks and uniforms will be available."

What would happen without his checking? Our keeper, Vitaly Karpovich, moaned, "Human nature means people must be policed to make them do things properly." From the front seat of the jeep, Yurchenko added, "We have had to put someone in the village street to fine people who don't throw cigarette butts in the containers. I don't want you to feel that the local soviet is a policeman, but we do need to keep up areas crucial to the community. There ought to be local-level management. In Stalin's time it was stricter. You could go to jail for not rotating crops as specified from above." We bumped over the farm's endless field roads, and he summed things up: "I create conditions under which hard work brings good results."

Were Yurchenko religious, one might suspect that the mortal sin that he harbored amid his many virtues was pride. The chairman was a puzzle. He was very conservative. Neither self-interest nor the joy of power seemed the object of his rule. He had been practical enough to abide Gorbachev's reform-Communist tinkerings. At an ambiguous historical moment, Yurchenko marched along. He'd sharpened his horse sense, and, in a job that for most of the century had required allegiance above efficiency, he'd warily and effectively devoted himself to his farm's advantage.

In the early evening, we arrived back at the main square of the farm. The village store he'd spoken about was still open. It had decent winter coats for thirty rubles, needles and thread and bolts of cloth, berets, combs, razors. In the food store newly baked breads tasted good enough for a Cambridge boutique bakery. Outside, a work crew hauled wheelbarrows of tar from a truck, filling potholes. "Finding the money for repairs here wasn't hard," said Yurchenko. "Finding asphalt was." The patron was proud. The village residents straggled back from work. Some hoed their gardens, others sat on benches in front of fenced yards, smoking, talking, staring at the strangers hosted by their fierce chairman. A scowling woman in a pale purple dress stalked toward us, staff in hand, leading a large, inattentive flock of geese, an emulation of the chairman.

♦

The next morning we moved on. Yurchenko shook hands, bade us goodbye, and locked the guesthouse behind us with his big ring of keys. With Vitaly, we drove several hours to Collective Farm Named After Kirov, and shook hands with the chairman, Savely Golovko. We'd again been passed hand to hand, as per the plan in our keeper's pocket. The introductions were friendly — call him Savely. He'd been chairman for twenty years — he was another of those who'd gotten himself firmly enough into position to farm somewhat autonomously.

Like Yurchenko, Savely, too, was full of numbers. He'd fattened 4,000 beef cows, and his 1,000 dairy cows yielded 8,000 pounds — fully half the U.S. average and very good for the USSR. He fattened 2,500 pigs a year, tended 1,400 chickens, and ran a specialized breeding farm stocked with Czech and East German goats. "We have thousands of applications from people wishing to buy our goats for breeding. Raising goats is mainly a task for individuals. Our old folks fatten goats and sell them." Savely's farm had 832 "members who work productively," not counting family.

We drove around his rolling farms, looking at good fields and good houses, at shops, a pharmacy, a fifty-patient hospital, and at an old-age home — a converted schoolhouse, dark inside, but spotless. Most residents of the home had gone for the summer to live with family members. Two tiny old ladies lay moaning in beds in separate corners of the big, wax-smelling building. "We have four doctors," said Savely. "I offer doctors superior quarters."

The average farm worker was only thirty-three years old, far younger than the national average, indicating resourceful management by Savely. He'd taken advantage of the lack of urban housing to strengthen his farm. He'd constructed nice houses and lured "the younger generation" from cities to occupy them. "We have 185 houses now. A peculiar attraction of our farm is we say, 'Here is an apartment key. You needn't wait.' It's for recruiting. I still need people.

"We have a forty-four-person brigade that just builds. This is my priority. Until two years ago, it violated state rules for me to pay cash rubles for building materials. Before that, I had to have permission to obtain them through the proper bureaucratic procedures." Savely's skill and long tenure and political heft had brought him access to lumber and bricks. He must have pussy-footed along the margin of the law.

Savely had an extravagant belly laugh that no doubt canceled debts for him. He was flamboyant. An audacious version of the mandatory Lenin picture hung behind his desk. It was not the glowering state-approved portrait, but expressed the new "socialism with a human face." Over a bright vermilion brush-textured base, an artist had painted a Rouault-like study of Lenin, bold and quizzical, outlined in rough black, three times life size. Savely worked while dwarfed by his nation's father. The painting was modern and trendy but still imposing — still rather reverential.

Savely was taking care, in the waning days of state subsidies, to stock up. Machinery that had been delivered, like it or not, to each farm now came only on request and if partly paid for by the farm. "I have three new Don 1500 combines because I jumped and got them for 14,000 rubles, with the state covering the difference — now the price is up to 50,000 rubles. For harvesting wet grain, the Don is better than earlier models, even though it's heavy and has big wheels that rip up the topsoil. I'd like to be able to choose among combines and to negotiate price — in paradise I could do that! But here, the Don is the only one made."

We washed up for supper and drove in a small fleet of farm jeeps to a freshly spruced up guesthouse by a pond. It smelled of paint and sawed wood. The outhouse was brand-new. "We would like, in the future," said Savely, "to entertain parties of hunters and other Europeans who wish to stay here. That's why we built this facility." This translated into a common transition-time Soviet sentiment: "We need hard currency."

Savely was a salesman, and he would likely succeed in any

regime. For the evening, he was joined by the district Party chief of agriculture, a dapper, dark, tall gentleman who said only the right thing, although he'd somehow persisted in appearing like a sophisticate among rubes. Savely was earthy — no sense that he came from the stuck-up side of the tracks. He admitted real problems right and left. I liked him. The Party agriculture secretary said with a straight face, "There are three pillars to this farm: discipline, confidence, and mutual understanding." The conversation flowed around him. He was a rock in a stream that was heading somewhere else.

Where it was heading was toward drunken confusion. I had successfully resisted the glum toasts of Vitaly Karpovich and those of a dozen hosts in Moscow. But in a moment Savely made me feel compelled and ambitious about partying.

He toasted my mother. I have a fine mother who is a warm wit and great natural storyteller. I took a small sip. Savely was short and roly-poly, and touched my shoulder imploringly. Looking with dog eyes, he said, "Ah, you insult your mother? Okay, then let us drink to my mother's memory, and I will be insulted if you do not drink bottoms up!"

He was so innocent and sincere, I tipped my glass straight upside down. And then I did the same on behalf of his nation, then my nation, then went back and made up for the slight to my mother. We saluted his farm, my book, his wife, my family. Soon, I loved him, and he loved me, and I slurred out a lucid observation: "I see why you are the manager of a large and successful farm."

Savely wanted to trade jokes. My translator on this outing was as cockeyed as I was, but tried anyhow: "There is an international drinking competition, American, Frenchman, and Russian. There is a small glass, a regular glass, a bottle, and a bucket of vodka. The American starts. He gulps the small glass and a bit of the regular glass, and can't go on. The Frenchman has the small glass, the regular glass, and almost reaches for the bottle, but he's all disconnected and out of touch. Then the Russian starts, with the bucket. He downs the bottle, the glass, and even manages the little glass. You know how they figure out who is the winner? There's an old Ukrainian expression: Only your soul knows your full capacity."

They all roared. I thought I'd understood every word, but I didn't get it. "Okay, here's another joke. The emperor wanted to kill an eagle. He believed that a duck was an eagle, see . . ." The evening trundled on.

I found myself outside. Peepers shouted from the grassy pond. I navigated around the pond with the district Party chief of agriculture, who somehow must have communicated his desire to stroll with me, and we pledged eternal goodwill, I think, with me yelling English and him nodding agreeably and yelling in Ukrainian, each of us understanding a few words and both of us making many curlicued gestures that looped off into the air, starting right from the heart. I can remember the stark white evening sunlight, and the heavy smell of new hay in the field behind the pond, and the fresh paint of the guesthouse. He kept uttering the same phrase as we walked back inside. We had it translated: "I don't change my message from year to year," he'd told me. "Shake."

I spent the next morning wandering around Savely's farm very gently, for fear of jostling my headache. I viewed crops and animals and combines in good repair and combines under repair. There was a modest lunch, and when I refused to consume more than the tiniest sip of the vodka they poured, Savely merely laughed and didn't press.

After lunch, we went to see the school. There was whispering between Savely and two or three somber gentlemen of the farm, who kept approaching to check on something or another. We walked into a big room at the end of a school corridor.

The room burst with song, brash, rich chords. Eight Ukrainians stood in brocaded and embroidered national dress, and their singing was thrilling. The ingratiating Savely had cultivated a traditional singing group to entertain at state occasions. There was a lead alto — a muscular blond milkmaid with a throaty voice who belted out modal melodies from the breadth of her throat while standing on the balls of her feet. She came to me and pulled me out on the dance floor; we danced a polka while the officials of the nether Ukraine observed. I was suddenly blessed with sure feet. We whirled around and around and threw in a few fancy kicks and stomps, and everyone applauded, including separate demonstrations of fingertip clapping by the district Party chief of agriculture and the local mayor, a sturdy woman in her forties who clapped soundlessly, hands not quite meeting. Eventually, we stopped.

A redheaded English teacher — who had by this point confided in me sorrowfully, in very broken English, that he couldn't speak English well enough to be teaching it — attempted to translate the whirling songs.

> Something is in the stalls.
> Rye was in the stalls.
> Everything has disappeared.
> It was barley. Where is it?
> There was fat. Where is the fat?
> You gave it to your relatives . . .
> You! No, you! You! No, you!

And:

> I was at the market.
> I saw a boy.
> He was not near the fish soup.
> He did not kiss me.
> He paid no attention . . .

My dear partner, the blessed alto, ran toward me as the crowd broke up. "Who are you?" she asked. "Why are we taken from work and told to sing for you? You must be very important for this!"

I told her I was not important, and could not understand it myself. Savely soon explained it. "You will tell of this group in America. Someone will want to hear them over there." The quest for hard currency was just getting started.

The blessed alto walked off with us, looking furtively behind her. "I have never had this chance before," she whispered. "I have relatives. In Saskatchewan. Can you tell them I want to know them, to come to them?" We asked where they were, but she could not really say.

8

EARLY NEXT MORNING I'd just half awakened when the Party agriculture secretary, Vasily Fyodorovich Zabolotny, showed up wearing the same good suit he'd worn the other night. I recalled groggily that shortly after our circumambulation of the pond, he'd pledged to pay an official state visit.

I wanted to engage him in sober reflection early on this dull gray morning. He embodied the demonized abstraction "local Party bureaucrat," the figure mediating a farm's practical needs and the unwieldy impositions of a state plan. If the power of the center was withering and that of the regions rising, he was a harbinger of the coming regime. He was brisk and all business.

Of the men I'd spoken with in city or country, Zabolotny, with his Italian-cut blue suit, his casual bearing, his ankle-high black boots, and his gleaming smile, most resembled an American executive. Appearances deceived: he sure didn't sound like one. He was a baby step past stodgy *apparatchik*, a new-style, progress-oriented *chinovnik*, a career bureaucrat getting ahead, not a pioneer of Communism. That he strolled with me at Savely's supper, came to call, and agreed to discuss his business set him apart from the usual run of regional Party figures, who stayed in the shadows and claimed civil authorities were in charge.

What was the main thing he did? "Organize." He organized: discussions, programs, budgets, plans, priorities for organizing.

"I correct mistakes." A joint-oiler, part of solutions. He did not see his considerable authority as part of any problem.

"Just last week, we brought together a council including all Party authorities in the district and the local soviet and discussed how to reorganize area agriculture so we'll be fed under current conditions and also fulfill our quotas."

In Europe and America, people thought his nation to be in mid-gale. But in the provincial Ukraine, the winds of change had barely ruffled Zabolotny's 1950s pompadour: "We decided what strategy to recommend and presented these findings to the Council of Chairmen of Collective Farms and Directors of State Farms. And so we formulated the district food program for the next five years." I thought about my still-warm bed, a room away.

He explained step by step the beauty of sound administration: "First, we planned a program to up soil fertility. We discussed how to produce organic fertilizer, and the fact that we should deliver fifteen metric tons per hectare in the whole district." I did not see the beauty in it. It was a nice high tonnage of manure, but the costs and mechanical problems of gathering and storing manure, composting it, delivering and spreading it at optimal dosage over a county have prevented even developed nations with enough trucks and spreaders and banks from doing it.

Soviet farms *over*fertilized at the time, with chemical fertilizer, wasting a lot in storage and delivery. They were also known not to use available manure, for want of machinery to handle it. So the plan seemed too hopeful, even at dawn. I didn't argue.

"Second, we discussed how to transform sugar-beet byproducts into fertilizer — our factories make two million metric tons of waste a year." Discovering "hidden" fertilizer sources had been a theme of earnest Soviet authorities for decades. But beet-processing waste usually found higher use as cattle feed than as compost. I wanted breakfast.

"Third, we decided to increase cattle feed production, and also grow more corn and soy not ordered by the central government, but for district use. We have low corn and soybean quotas now because we produce little. The authorities ask me to raise meat production, so they have freed me to grow what I feel necessary." The Ukraine was not only the USSR's breadbasket, it had

been Europe's too, before the Revolution. But the project of raising corn and soy production required what simply was not
around: the right seed for a climate at the dry and northerly
extreme for those crops, the right planting drills, the right combine harvesting heads, the right drying, storing, grinding, and
mixing technology. Voting for soy in a council fell short of delivering milled soy meal to full pig barns. I thought about corn
bread. I wondered what I'd do that day.

I asked what he did all day. "Mostly routine handling of complaints — from Communists, from non-Communists. I have
open office hours one morning a week. In Lokhvitsa, the district
seat, there's a campaign on to smooth a bumpy road and extend
it to reach all houses. I've helped the plan go ahead.

"A gravel pit constantly made one village's houses dusty. I
viewed the houses, then ordered the management to build a
bypass road. It's done and tarred now. As we say, The wolves are
not hungry anymore, and the sheep are still alive." I chuckled.

I'd heard that Lokhvitsa residents wanted to build a church.
Would the regional Party office be involved in such a decision?
"That's ideology. I don't get involved in ideology," he said. In
fact, he told me later, he'd previously been the secretary for
ideology.

A combine driver had told me he was pushing for a bonus he
felt had been unfairly denied by the farm chairman. "That could
be resolved on a lower level than I occupy. If they can't agree, I'll
get involved later. I must react, orally or in writing, to every
complaint. A water main burst or sewage plant leak or no electricity makes the people raise hell and ask me for help, but that
isn't my main concern. I discuss things vaguely because just
now the situation is smooth," he said.

Was the world wrong to think the USSR was in crisis? "The
extreme conditions under which sharp conflict takes place do
not exist now. My authority comes in if someone heads an organization and unhappy employees want to fire him. They complain to the district Party committee. Then a commission interviews workers, and we call meetings. We can recommend
removal of a manager, boss, or Party leader. We then look for a
substitute." He stuck with what he knew. I did too.

Did he control local hirings and firings of agriculture bosses?

Yes, that was "the most substantial control" at his disposal, although he soft-pedaled it: "It's not as bad as you make it sound. I just dealt with a brigade leader — he bossed twenty-seven people running a dairy of one hundred cows on 3,750 acres." That seemed large enough for a thousand cows to me. "I looked at their wheat, and it was crawling with bugs. The boss had pesticide applied at the wrong time, damaging wheat, not bugs. He was inattentive to people, and incompetent. The workers had lost a brigade bonus. So we got rid of him. Not because we felt like it — for good reason." I didn't ask about the inefficiency of feeding wheat — uncooked wheat — to dairy cows, which was a practice seen nowhere else in farming, nor about the level of productivity implied by a twenty-seven-worker brigade caring for one hundred cows and some cropland, a job four people might do in the West, with no administrators above them. And I did not ask if new local elections would alter his power to pick bosses. Such matters were deep rumblings, beyond the control of even a district Party chief of agriculture.

I asked how he felt about the fledgling movement toward privately managed farms. "Positive. All forms should compete." I'd heard that often. But had he taken action to promote private farms? "We had meetings in the winter on new management forms, one for ninety-six managers, the other for lower-level people in charge of brigades. I can tell you no one in our district obstructs this."

What about his own rise through the ranks? "I started in '68 as a laborer on a sugar-beet farm. I studied agronomy at Poltava Agricultural Institute, and joined the Party in '76. I managed a brigade, then was farm section agronomist, then agronomist for the whole collective farm, then director of a beef *combinat* — in 1980 I was elected by eighteen groups. Then I became chief agronomist for RAPO [the regional agri-administration], elected by the twenty managers of all-district agri-enterprises."

Having worked hard and risen through the ranks, how did he react to economist Nikolai Shmelev's well-publicized heretical complaint that none of the nation's 3.5 million agri-bureaucrats were needed? I told him friends in Moscow had described an ascent through rigid bureaucracy, each rise championed by a friend one level above. Didn't this way of selecting people ensure they'd be boss-pleasers? And weren't those headed for the top of the *oblast*-level Party offices sent out for a year or two of adult education, then handed advanced degrees in various fields so they could be placed as leaders in research institutes, although they weren't scientists at all but administrators loyal to their own Party supervisors?

He kept smiling and responded sharply, which wasn't surprising, considering my frank question: "How many managers are employed in American agriculture? Let us take care of our system ourselves! Your bureaucracy is no smaller, if you count noses. We may do wrong by cutting ours! The process of finding a better way is going on right now. I'm an adherent of *perestroika*, the sooner the better. But the right changes will be learned from the people at grassroots level."

We promised to meet for another circumambulation of Savely's pond in a year or two, to take inventory of what had changed. I went off to breakfast. No curlicues from the heart had emerged this walk around.

◆

Across the Ukraine, the outlandish red-haired high school English teacher whom I'd met at Savely's musical surprise kept popping up, probably locally assigned both to eavesdrop and to be helpful. He was from the village of Lokhvitsa, he said, and his name was Yuri Aleksandrovich Plakhtienko. After a long day of field inspections, I'd staggered back to "Motel Poltava" — not a motel at all but a big, clumsy hotel. He stood out front on the piazza, grinning, offering services with wonderfully British manners, bowing and muttering, "Well, I say good man," and "Well, of course, now I have just forgotten the word, of course." But he'd never before been able to get near a native English speaker. I bowed back and smiled, and went on in, feeling beat but rare.

The fattest mosquitoes in the universe had just grown up in Poltava, and the Soviets hadn't yet invented screens. It was far too hot to close the windows. I turned to the BBC World Service again for solace. It was broadcasting interviews with unhappy Miskito Indians in Nicaragua.

A year earlier, on my previous trip with Yuri Chernichenko,

the Marlboro debacle had taken place in the restaurant at Motel Poltava. Marlboros were the *baksheesh* of *perestroika*-era small favors. A pack had gotten laundry done in Kiev, and another had bought an hour's taxi ride across Moscow. Parched after a long day, my interpreter, the beefy ex–soccer star named Pavel Pavlovich Sorokin, was determined to get us beer. "No beer" — the waiter had cut him off abruptly. Sorokin had pointed to beer aplenty an arm's length away on the next table, then handed back the menu with a pack of Marlboros ostentatiously tucked inside. "Beer," he'd said. The waiter had smiled and bowed, softened his gestures, lingered solicitously discussing our order. He had come back — half an hour later — and said, "No beer." He hadn't returned the Marlboros. Sorokin was new to capitalism then, and had just learned not to pay in advance.

I now noticed the same waiter as I again walked into the restaurant. As if preserving the barmy nature of the place, an angry-faced old man in a heavy brown suit with a tangle of medals on the lapel rushed at me shouting, "What have you done with the colonel?" The old guy's buddies stepped between us. He squinted and melted away, bewildered.

The waiter smiled without recognition and kindly placed the foreign guests at a choice table right in front of the loud, bad band. Poltava's hip, glamorously togged teens danced — quaintly to my eyes, but with glee — to newly permitted Western rock and to Ukrainian stomps. An indignant woman rushed off the dance floor and thumbed me out of her seat. We shared their table. Her escort was an East German engineer, heading home from a thrifty Azov Sea holiday with his mistress. She was a nurse. "If the Berlin Wall would be removed, I'm not sure many people would stay in East Germany," he said. "I certainly wouldn't." This was five months before Germans demolished the wall. I dabbed thin beef gruel with bread — bread made with imported American wheat. We drank beer, for which no Marlboros were needed, and toasted international friendship.

◆

In the morning, the red-haired English teacher had drifted back to the hotel piazza. The Soviet delegation, he was honored and pleased to let me know, was present to fulfill the scheduled mission of showing the American delegation the significant regional museum in the provincial town of Lokhvitsa.

It was clunky, local, small, and revealing, a shrine of sorts to place and state. The first room had dioramas full of hairy trees and varnished rocks, and multicolored charts and nature-lore placards by glassed-in stuffed muskrats and porcupines, and a hare as big as a knapsack. Rows of rock cores. Explanations that started out, "Millions of years ago, there was an ocean here . . ." Rows of mammoth teeth. A tableau of bird eggs ordered by size. "There are 8,000 kinds of birds known on our planet. There are 350 kinds in our Ukraine. There are 150 in the Lokhvitsa District. The biggest, the domestic goose, the smallest, *reones*. Our district is rich in gas and oil . . ."

The next room added human beings to the natural inventory, exhibiting relics of civilization from fourteen thousand years ago. The town had been around since the year 1000. "There were many enemies then. Most awesome was the Tartar, who destroyed all places." There were mallet heads with handle holes, and daggers. "Here are the weapons of our enemies." "Here are the weapons of our defenders, the Russians." The exhibit had a political tilt. Cossacks "came to help fight," and stayed. "Here is a specimen of the peasant from the seventeenth to the nineteenth centuries." "Here is an early-twentieth-century peasant."

And the next room showed off artifacts of the revolution of 1905. "In Lokhvitsa, on the 14th of December, peaceful demonstrators were shot, including the local poet Teslenko. Here is the highest decoration . . . and a proverb: If you move slowly, you'll travel farther."

The biggest room portrayed the victory of Communism. The red-haired English teacher presented the room, bowing shyly with arm outstretched. Banners, arms, smiling photographs of bedraggled revolutionary heroes jammed glass cases. I'd said not a word about ethnicity, but the curator said to me, "We have the documents of Esther Pipshitz, Jewish Communist Party official. We had a lot of Jews — most later exterminated by the Germans. The country was in horrible shape. The Party taught people to write." Party artifacts went up to the beginning of the Second World War.

I asked about the collectivization of farming: wasn't that prewar era when there were forced marches here, and confiscation of thousands of families' winter food, and arbitrary executions? In conversation over the past few years, many peasants had told me awful stories about missing grandparents — stories their parents had whispered and cut off half told. Now that articles had surfaced saying that perhaps fifteen or twenty million citizens had been killed during the collectivization drive, not by Nazis but by Communists, was this part of history accessible to museum goers?

The curator and some anonymous gray-suited gentlemen and the red-haired English teacher conferred. "We have a few items," the curator said. "With the new openness, we will talk about some things more, but we do not yet. We have in this case the *Atheist*, a Kiev newspaper from 1930. This article just says that in the village of Bichovska, people decided to organize a collective farm. Here's another interesting clipping — it unfortunately represents the mood then: local nuns who wanted to sabotage collectivization started rumors that if you join a collective farm you'll sit on a hot frying pan in hell, so peasants refused to join. Here's another article: opportunists help *kulaks* and church activists 'assisting the forces who want to wreck collectivization of the people's agriculture.' That's all we have." I asked if schoolkids could catch the meaning of those clippings. "No one ever mentioned them," the curator said.

The next room memorialized another twenty million victims, those killed in World War II. That carnage was not secret. Flags and guns and helmets, battle maps with pins, bashed-up ammo crates and photos of the Soviet Mothers of Poltava filled every nook.

Their sentiment stirred by this last room, the Soviet delegation swept us into vans while the English teacher shouted, "Come up, come up!" Where to? "To famous memorial on Germans' Poltava battle *platz*." I recalled the memorial depicted on the train curtains.

We solemnly crossed a wide lawn. The place teemed with ten-year-olds, who were shouted into groups by their teachers. The groups stood before a colossal statue and stared at an eternal flame flickering next to a gigantic polished-stone platform suitable for blood sacrifices. A loudspeaker blasted marches. The monument's director, a chubby woman with clipped, severe gestures, ran out with chugging gait and pumped my hand. She had a soothing voice. Above the sound of her greetings another voice boomed a recorded spiel, an encompassing amplification, the Mother of the Motherland herself weaving a tale of passion, patriotism, and sacrifice. "General Mikhail Petrovich Kirponis," said the recorded voice, "recreated in this statue eight meters high and weighing thirty tons, was surrounded by German troops right here. His brilliance allowed us to hold out for three days and three nights. The general showed enormous courage, then died of a gunshot" — perhaps, Mark whispered to me, by his own hand when capture was imminent. "His troops, pinned by enemy fire, couldn't remove the body, so they buried it." For a moment I imagined these secret gravediggers who knew they too might soon die, and then I caught myself. I was feeling something close to reverence — what the site was designed to induce.

"See?" Mark said. "On the statue, the general's name ends the Ukrainian way, spelled -*is*, not the Russian way, -*os*."

Although several hundred thousand soldiers died, a handful of the general's gravediggers survived, told the tale, and, in 1947, the Soviet Army located the body, "miraculously preserved." They carried it to Kiev. Experts studied it. A decade later they reburied it in this park. In appreciation of the sacrifice of the heroes, the booming Mother-voice said, Soviet citizens insisted on contributing half a million rubles for the statue.

Memorials were the only well-tended sites in the nation. The grass got clipped here and nowhere else. The loudspeakers that intoned this durable tale of devotion and duty were of full timbre, distortion-free in spite of the volume, and the message. The Soviets memorialized well — and, in this case, cannily. General Kirpon*os* was a genuine Soviet hero, qualified for official memorialization; he'd been a Party member since 1918 and had risen to the command of southwestern-front troops after Stalin's prewar purges had killed off many of the Red Army's skilled leaders. The canny aspect was that in his embodiment as Kirpon*is*, he also qualified as a Ukrainian proxy-patriot — at least he'd died defending his native land against the Hun, and near where the original battle of Poltava had been fought in 1709, when a Russian army under Peter the Great defeated Swedes and a small group of Ukrainians who'd joined forces. The victory had set up Russian domination for nearly three more centuries. Ukrainian separatist longings had never ceased itching around Soviet patriotic sites. A few weeks before, Vitaly Karpovich said, the ceremony commemorating the 280th anniversary of the Battle of Poltava was abruptly canceled to avert a demonstration by nationalists.

Facing the general, a wedding party lined up in close formation. They stood behind a big, shiny-faced, smiling bride and a tiny groom in a huge blue suit. Their parents beamed at them. They looked happy and confused. They awaited something. In the atheistic USSR, wedding parties linked up with the power and glory of patriotic sacrifice at formerly sacramental moments. And because General Kirponis had died protecting the Ukraine, the wedding party's devotion felt authentic. They'd brought pride intact to the ceremony before the big, granite, dual-purpose general.

The redheaded high school teacher pulled me urgently aside. He wanted to conspire with me. His script called for whispering here. I could barely understand his brand of English even when he spoke up. Would I do him a special favor, he hissed, "Weell you bless me beeg thing speciaol if pleece, kind sirrr?" These were close friends of his. Yesterday, he'd told them he would produce the American — could I possibly? I'd been on the road for a month in my rumpled blue jeans. He relayed my consent to the wedding party with great, bouncing nods and jubilant waves of his arm, as if he were signaling in an aircraft to land.

The bride's mother ran up and shoved a wreath and a bouquet into my arms — plaited red gladioli — and the high school teacher gestured that I was to lay the wreath on the polished altar, at the feet of the gigantic general, on behalf of the bride and groom, and speak to them. "My speciaol friends," he said, nodding knowingly, shrugging apologetically, pointing across to the bride and groom, who stood as still as cake decorations.

The eternal flame flickered. Martial music blared. The sun glared down. I paced slowly forward, in step with the music, composing my face into a solemn blankness, the wreath in my outstretched hands. I stood a respectful moment, thinking about the great terror of battle and lesser terror of marriage, and noticing that even that was not reflected in the groom's eager grin.

I confabulated a very short speech. I commenced by issuing international blessings for world peace, and followed on with observations to the effect that each marriage is a thread with which to weave a strong nation. It was received in silence. Then the high school teacher shouted at the crowd for five minutes, translating far more than I'd pronounced. Everyone clapped and smiled at me then, nodding agreement repeatedly. Finally he pushed me toward the bride, who stood rigidly. I bent and kissed her cheek, noticing her sweet scent, and handed her the wilting bouquet. She didn't even blink.

The bride and groom glanced up, smiling at each other, just plain happy. Ceremonial speeches flowed in full torrent as we drove off into the slow summer sunset. Normal lives played out here, too.

The driver made my own life flash in review several times. Soviet drivers reflected national history; they simply didn't stop for pedestrians. Anyone behind the wheel was an aristocrat among peasants. The lot of common folk was, as ever, to leap aside.

A year before, I'd been in a black Volga taking a carful of reform-minded academics home from a picnic. The chauffeur must have been doing forty miles an hour on a dirt side street among the *dachas* of the Moscow gentry. We'd struck a boy on a bike. He'd been pedaling carefully along the verge of the narrow road. The car had snagged his handlebar and flung up the rear tire, then grazed him as he fell. He'd flown sideways past the window and landed belly-down in a ditch. The driver had touched the brakes, slowing, turning his head and watching as the boy eased up onto his elbows, then onto one knee. The father was running across the road behind us. The driver had stepped on the gas and left.

My fellow passengers, reputedly the most liberal and compassionate reform thinkers in public life in 1988, had laughed at my dismay. As the car sped many miles from the scene, they'd chided me: "The boy will be all right. You know he got up. His father is with him. Our driver would have such trouble if he had stopped. It simply wasn't our driver's fault. You saw how the boy steered the bicycle into the road suddenly."

Wouldn't the authorities track down the driver and question him? "No. Chances are that seeing the sort of car this is, they will hesitate to report it, because it would mean confronting someone unknown who probably has considerable power. Better to let it go."

On the Poltava road, our van hung up behind two manure spreaders, and we drove tamely at walking speed for minute after minute. The road twisted. Traffic streamed toward us. There was virtually no national highway system. The USSR, for all its size, had one fifth the road mileage of America. Intercity roads were usually two or three lanes, and bumper to bumper. This was part of the bad infrastructure.

The road bisected fields of sunflowers as big as skillets, all arched at the same angle. Two boys and a tethered cow lay flat on a grassy strip by the road. One boy read. The other stared through the fine mountain ash trees quavering over him, up into the sky. And the cow chewed grass.

Near town we slowed again, behind another farm wagon. Slow drivers had no habit of letting anyone by — it was not done. Our driver chain-smoked black tobacco. The Party agriculture secretary of Poltava, the secretary's assistant, and Vitaly also lit up. The van grew foggy and hot. Soviet health theories included the wisdom that one should never sit in a breeze, no matter what. I opened the sliding rear window. Vitaly reached back and slammed it shut. The driver saw peasants selling tomatoes from their tiny private plots by the roadside. He wanted some for his wife. He slowed. Vitaly yelled for him to drive on.

Motel Poltava, when we reached it, felt like home. The dining room blasted its horrid music, and hadn't run out of beer. I went upstairs early. The BBC held forth on the porcelain collection on view in the Victoria and Albert Museum, where it could give great pleasure to all.

9

EARLY IN THE MORNING we jostled away from Poltava, heading two hundred kilometers south in an orange Gosagroprom van. Vitaly Karpovich Chuiko's personal aide drove, chatting with his boss, laughing and smoking his way through a first pack and deep into a second pack on the slow roads. We were heading for Farm Beacon of Communism. The wholesome names given collective farms continued to amaze me. I'd been listing a few: Farm Precepts of Lenin. Farm Dawn of Communism. Farm Friendship. *Red* anything — Red Dawn, Red Victory, Red Army, Red Banner, and Red October farms. October Revolution. Twentieth Party Congress, Twenty-first Party Congress, and Twenty-third Party Congress farms. Farm Stalin. Farm Molotov. Farm Comintern. Farm Forward. Farm Tolstoy. Farm Chekhov. Farm Progress. The shaggy fields we drove past looked the more inglorious behind those fearsome designations. Issued during that short period of forced collectivization in the late twenties and early thirties, the farm names sang a sad song — a jaunty forced march that still echoes in every rural life. Under red banners on which village women had been compelled to stitch the cheery names, peasants and smallholders were joined together in abject compliance, terrified into signing away hay fields, barns, homesteads, horses, and chickens. The names the women sewed proclaimed bold new alliances of once-enslaved souls losing their chains, throwing their goods and lives and lots together in the spirit of Marxism-Leninism, for their collective benefit.

What many peasants must have shared first was their mourning. It would have been stifled, secret mourning. They'd have sensed spies and snitches all around. Friends and relatives and gardens and usual lives would have been freshly torn from them in a tumult of executions, exiles to cold places, and enforced starvation. Stalin's soldiers would have been patrolling the countryside, shutting the last monasteries, leaving bewildered believers to pray in silence. Cadres of zealous Young Communists were about in each village, issuing harsh, enthusiastic edicts, and promises.

There'd have been stubborn holdouts in the earliest days of collectivization, and they would have been suffering. There'd have also been toadies, and they'd have been riding high. Some historians say the poorest peasants at first did welcome collectivization. They'd have gained from sharing others' farm stock and tools. So would opportunistic officials, tempted by the prospect of safety, rank, and the power to scare. Such cadres declared peasants with any wealth *kulaks*, paraded them as class enemies, killed some, drove others out of town with no papers and nowhere to wander, shot wanderers for want of papers. A cow or a plow horse could have damned a family. A tin roof was fatal evidence of class betrayal. Anyone discovered concealing grain for his family in the hard winter that followed would have been arrested; the will to survive itself had constituted evidence of *kulak*hood. Families that couldn't meet mandatory grain contributions were also traitorous. Villagers had been gathered for obligatory sessions of vitriol, to hate class enemies together. The destitute, it has been said, were set to robbing the poor. Millions of *kulaks* died, their goods and land secured for The People.

In this manner and under those elated farm names, virtually all agricultural land was soon collectivized. The despised *kulaks* had included most village leaders, the ambitious, those with know-how and force of character. In the aftermath, survivors would have harbored secret memories of the lost ones, forbidden and therefore whispered. Terrible hunger followed collectivization, especially in 1932 and 1933. Many peasants had eaten or spitefully destroyed their livestock before joining. In the hard times, they'd scavenged and eaten seed grain; there was nothing to plant. The spirits of families, of whole villages, broke in those winters, and stayed broken for the remaining sixty years of Soviet power. The happy farm names grimaced from monumental gateposts, still left from a past only now opening to candid reexamination.

A friend from Kiev, the Ukrainian writer Kostya Vronsky, jokes about zealous street names: "First Lenin Dead End, Second Lenin Dead End! Collectivization installed not just funny names but perpetual food crises, and so it sealed its own demise. The terrible 1930s were a theme in our family," Kostya said, "because my great-grandfather had been declared a *kulak*. He'd had a big, scattered farm in a small town near Minsk, lost to collectivization. He had excellent health, but ten years in prison broke him. One of his sons became chairman of a large collective farm. Another — the one who was later my grandfather — worked as a printer at a local newspaper. One morning the editor told him an article would run that very afternoon about the chairman's brother — my great-uncle — declaring him *vrag naroda*, an enemy of the people, because he had recently not let his peasants use the farm horses. In fact the horses had gotten a morbid disease, and work would have killed them. After the editor warned my grandfather, my great-uncle cleared out of the city in an hour. That evening, security forces came to my great-uncle's apartment, but he was gone."

Famine always has political beneficiaries; left to work their fields and trade in the markets, people figure out ways to eat, even in hard times. Stalin consolidated his grip on the rural Ukraine by forced starvation. He applied the same policy there after the Second World War, some think, to deflate pro-German sentiment. That hunger is recalled as sharply as the previous one. Viktor Lishchenko, the agricultural economist, described his boyhood near Odessa:

"My parents spoke about the collectivization — it happened a year before I was born. I knew we'd lost millions in the Ukraine to execution by hunger in the early thirties. It happened again in the winter of 1946 — that one I recall. Memories such as mine are widespread and helped shape the country's political life. Right after the war, Stalin saw that many Ukrainians had betrayed the Soviet Union and Communism and worked with the Germans. It was true. Many had been glad when Germans ended Russian domination. In the western Ukraine, a lot of people felt Germans would be better masters. Germany's army had a number of voluntary battalions of Ukrainian soldiers. But Stalin won. And after the war he sent in soldiers again, and they grabbed away food. They forced farms to turn over all their crops. It had been a dry year, too. In 1946, while we starved, Stalin exported five million tons of grain.

"I thought about food all the time. My only idea was how to find food. My thoughts belonged to my stomach. Violence increased drastically. A starving society goes out of control. Every morning we asked the neighbors, 'Any thieves?' And always, somebody had been killed and more thefts had happened. Some houses had dogs and shotguns to protect them. My mom lived with an ax under her bed. I saw so many bodies. I saw killing.

"My school was near the station. That winter, people were moving around by any means of transportation, and they froze to death by the hundreds. Every time a freight train pulled in, I saw a special group of workers with metal hooks walking alongside the train and everywhere around, while people ran off. The crews groped under the cars with the hooks, pulled off stiffened bodies, and threw them in a trench. Only many years later did relatives dare to look for the dead; families were too scared to search then. I was terrified. People in power were willing to sacrifice other people. Knowing this made me adult very fast. I became a young old man.

"Sugar beets were piled near the railroad station. Nobody could touch them. All day, a guard with a rifle stood over them. A little boy ran up and took one sugar beet. The guard just fired — I saw it — seven years old the boy was, running with one sugar beet in his hand, and he fell, wounded. I see hungry children from Africa on TV now, and I remember it. This experience made me politically cautious. I also decided to work for agriculture then. I can't tolerate seeing a child with hungry eyes.

"The only food in 1946 was rationed bread. No one even spoke about meat and flour, which didn't return to stores until

'51, '52. I spent all my childhood in bread lines, waiting for a horse cart bearing loaves. I can smell it still; the driver was the most important person, and the baker wasn't dying either. We had so-called school lunches — but they were just small pieces of nougat. Our teacher stood, touching all pieces, counting students, cutting, licking her fingers, and I was jealous that she was closer to this food. I was pleased if one child was missing, so we'd have bigger pieces."

Viktor had looked up — it was fifty years later, and Gorbachev's mild attempt to modify the absolute control of central planners was just slipping out of hand. "That's what we're going to have this winter — we're heading toward hunger!" Viktor had said, shaking his finger. He felt safest with plodding reform, and his way was prevailing, although his dire prediction of famine in Russia did not come true because of private gardens and because boatloads of grain still arrived from abroad.

◆

The Gosagroprom van stopped in a dirt farmyard, and the American delegation gravely met, with bows on both sides, another regional agri-boss, Kosiak. He headed RAPO, a *perestroikan* tweak of the old system of top-down decision-making. He was the new-style *middle*-down decision-maker, and his new middle-level governmental organization reflected Gorbachev's plan to shift some authority, but not much, to a local, not a Kievan or Muscovite, boss. RAPO decided *how* to carry out the same old centralized Five Year Plan with mandatory crop deliveries. RAPO determined local farm, field, and work schedules locally. Kosiak was a human face. But the Party agriculture secretary hadn't disappeared.

Kosiak was joyful, a vital man. Vitaly Karpovich performed the introductions. With an ecstatic, hard-lipped smile Kosiak opened his mouth wide in silent greeting. His small eyes gleamed. He was built like a huge terrapin, broad-jawed, short and wide. He'd fattened laterally rather than ventrally, belly broadened at the ribs, but unpaunched. His shoulders and back bulged. He enclosed my shoulder in one beefy hand, nearly cracked me forehead to forehead, told me he'd been a professional wrestler, and crushed my fingers in a paralyzing hand-shake that ignored the fact that I had not been a professional wrestler too. "Do not put off eating until tomorrow and fuck-ing for old age," he growled, then he nodded, emphatically and stiffly, twice.

He'd been a collective-farm chairman. I saw the spirit that had propelled his clamber up the agri-bureaucracy. "My new role is more of the same," he yelled. "I'm a reformer!" He yelled every sentence as my translator whispered the previous one. He had just one gear, slow and fully powered, like a piece of heavy equipment doing a hard job. He was hearty and he was so glad. He wanted to explain things, show things, convince me of things. All the while we talked, his eyes searched me with the scrutiny of a policeman gripping a perpetrator. He was a force, a steady, impelling, kindly force, and a dedicated host.

We climbed back into the van and rumbled on into drier ter-rain. Kosiak supervised the entire panorama. His gestures com-prised a proprietary dance. Arms up, inscribing a circle, he gazed across a breadth of endless fields and announced, "The steppe continues to the Black Sea," which was far out of sight. His hand swept the land and cut the air where seashore marked the boundary in his mind.

"I ran for office, won my job in a *contested* election in 1989," he said. RAPO was soviet — civil, not Party — the acronym translated as District Agro-Industrial Association. It was a mod-ification that tinkered with an existing office that already had offices, motor pool, staff, agronomists, engineers, and account-ants. It directly controlled farms and interfarm entities such as a feed plant, a power plant, a brick factory, and — soviet enti-ties always included "social" divisions — a music school and a resort. The fact of the brick factory impressed me. Bricks were barter power, as negotiable as hard currency. As with Yur-chenko, the right to make them symbolized political heft.

Was RAPO a reform, as officials themselves claimed, that put civil "soviet" power ahead of regional Party power? Kosiak looked amazed at this question. "No! Of course not!" One couldn't manage anything in this area unless the first secretary of the Party and also the chairman of the Party Agricultural Commission opted for it. And yes, since I'd asked, Kosiak himself was indeed deputy chairman of this Party Agricultural Commission, in addition to bearing his other heavy civil burdens — and mind me, his was not the number-one office on the commission, please understand, *chairman* was, and he was just one of several deputies. And yes, since I'd asked, those titles of his did place him in two chains of command, soviet and Party — a strategic position that remained, as ever, the locus of practical political power long inherent in the system. The *perestroika* shift to civil authority diminished in my estimation.

Had the people on the farms he administered elected him in that contested election? "No, other farm chairmen did," he said, and, "Yes, that is democratic reform! I impose the *zakaz* quotas on the very chairmen who elected me. The *zakaz* was enforced field by field from Moscow, but now Moscow gives me only a regional quota. Then I rob Peter to pay Paul. I relieve one farm of some burden and spread it elsewhere. I push development of regional food processing. I ward off capricious interference by other bureaucrats. Farm chairmen aren't my great friends now, but we respect each other. Our alliance is built from helping one another figure out how to share limited resources." Kosiak pointed to a farm chairman in our group. "He sold me bean seed I needed back when I was a chairman too. We logged together twenty years ago. I sent him beet pickers."

The chairman he'd pointed to, N. V. Panasenko, took over the tour when the orange Gosagroprom van stopped at his own farm. "In this test field," he said when we'd driven to a grid of garden-sized test patches of ripening soybeans, "I am proud to say I grow American soy. It grows easily here. We have land like Indiana, Illinois, Iowa, Minnesota, but it's warmer there and there's a longer season and more rain. We get nearly half a meter a year. Soy can survive. If we can get half the yield they get in America, that's okay. Soy helps animals utilize the protein in other types of feed. It saves a lot of grain. There's no substitute. I learned this visiting America.

"That visit was important. I test-drove an International Harvester combine. Superficially it looks like our Don 1500. The farmer I was with had the stripped-down version — open cab, little automatic equipment. But in eight years he'd not had one major breakdown. He said, 'This will last to the end of my life.'

Not our Don. Our Don is complicated! The International is tender to the grain as it harvests. The rotor is good, so you get clean, uncracked corn. At the output end of our Don you find damaged corn. After a harvest with the Don you have to run the grain through a separate cleaning machine — one more handling. And the International is lighter. It floats over the field!

When I eventually read Viktor Lishchenko this interview back in Moscow, he said, "On a farm, all things are related. If you have soy to feed with your corn, it balances the protein in other grain, and the pigs absorb far more nutrition. I'd like to assemble a small American pig farm with the right technology, to show people." Viktor had arranged the soy project on Panasenko's farm, and had pointed me toward it. It was top-down reform, *perestroika*'s typical direction. "This is grassroots change!" Kosiak had shouted. "*Perestroika* has started to fly here — but we don't yet see economic results."

Panasenko, who had been in the United States, and Kosiak sat me down and grilled me on how the Chicago Grain Exchange works, how cattle are marketed in Iowa ("Who decides to sell a cow?"), how farmers arrange crop insurance, why milk is not usually processed on American farms. They got into it. They were interested. Vitaly, our keeper, made his cross face, and after a while it turned red and he angrily proffered misinformation: "Your farms do process butter and cheese and milk: And our government does the same thing as a Chicago exchange!"

"Should we imitate your mandatory crop-quota system?" I asked.

"Then your farmers wouldn't be so insecure!" Vitaly answered, nodding smugly. That capped the discussion. By the end of lunch, we were laughing. But Vitaly Karpovich had again done his job. Kosiak and Panasenko asked no more about America.

♦

I wandered from the farm dining hall across the village square into the store. It had the basics — thread and needles, rugs, blankets, boots, coats, work pants, and pans. The citizens had shelter, clothing, and food. They lacked variety and the twentieth-century digital technology that fills malls — an absence with some redeeming virtue. On this rich farm they were secure, and that was a leap ahead of the recent fearsome past. The older generation remembered, and would be a long time turning on those they saw as responsible for their safety.

A proverbial little old lady, well under five feet tall, her face overpowered by black, thick-framed glasses, stooped by the shirts, counting stock and entering numbers on a clipboard. She spied me, beamed, marched over, asked, "Are you the American writer?" Her mop of white hair bounced when she spoke. "I want to talk to you."

Vitaly Karpovich stepped in — we have a schedule, our American writer is relaxing, may I help you? Her determination and the publicness of the place made frustration flicker on his face. She saw his well-exercised glare. Kneeling by shelves of shoes, I took my laptop out of its knapsack and set to work transcribing the monologue of Uliana Kharitonovna Ketman:

"I am a retired teacher at the school here, a widow. My children have moved to the city. I am too old to care if they do not want me to talk to you!" She expressed herself in emphatic, short bursts. "Probably no one has spoken about collectivization. I am old and remember the forced starvation well. I want to tell you about that." She was organized, and knew just what she wanted to say. Vitaly Karpovich repeated his objections. I reminded him of his pledge to let others speak freely, and added insult by asking him to back out of the conversation. The glare turned piercing, but he retreated a few aisles.

"I was born in 1917," the woman said. Her voice was strong. "I lost my father in 1938, a few years after the collectivization. He was an accountant. He had a big library, but he was safe at first because he was active during the collectivization. He became the first chairman of a collective farm — an interesting one, where most of the farmers were middle class — they were *kulaks!* My father organized that farm from 1930 to 1933. Soon, though, Stalin and his henchmen forced this farm to disband. 'Now they will work on us,' my father said when that happened, and soon they did.

"All at once, carts and trucks took all the wheat from all our peasants. The worst famine around here hit us the winter of

1932 to '33. At that time, my father was lucky enough to become bookkeeper on a state farm, so we still had a salary and access to food. We were saved — at least those nearest in the family were. But there were many relatives we couldn't help, and they died.

"You can't forget starving. It's a wound that can't be healed. My grandmother and my grandfather died in the famine. We walked down the street and corpses lay all around. I went off and studied in town, at a teachers' college. There, the only people who stayed alive worked in the communal dining room or were students or officials. We found no one else living. I like to think that some just ran away — but to where? There were only corpses. The famine has lasting effects on the mentality of all people around here. I tried to help however I could, but I made no money. Amazingly, under these conditions, the government kept the school open and I kept studying. What else was there to do? I had to eat. I grew weak from malnutrition.

"I visited my mother and she saw this. She had golden earrings. She handed them to me, and I went to a special store — a place of trade for foreigners — and I surrendered the gold. They didn't give me money. I walked out with flour and butter, and in this way I survived until the end of the famine."

Vitaly had edged back closer, shelf by shelf, during our conversation, finally standing back with us. "Couldn't you remember anything nice from your seventy years?" he asked, cutting her off.

She handled him easily. "You want to know something nice? I love my country — and I love the Ukraine. I believe in Gorbachev, and in *perestroika*. I support it with all my heart, because it is really necessary. The two big powers will accomplish everything. They'll guarantee peace, happiness. It is a good change." She'd retreated, scattering those pro-regime niceties with her, perhaps mockingly, perhaps not. A keeper's work is never done.

A few minutes later, she ran into us again, outside the dining hall, and she hugged me. "I am kissing you as a son," she said. "Mine died in a forest accident, in unclear circumstances, looking for gas and oil, something classified, involving putting more detail on a map out in our far east. Are you religious? I always have been."

Religion did it for Vitaly Karpovich. "We are late. Others have made plans. Come now, please," he beckoned sharply. She hugged me again.

◆

A traveler lives in a zone of self-importance. Experiences stain the mind as bright light stains the eye, afterimage decaying while happenstance wobbles forward. In sparkling sunlight, the orange van drove into the large delivery yard of a grain mill. At the far end, grain elevators loomed, enormous cement storage silos. In the glare, the scene reminded me of a visit the year before, with Yuri Chernichenko, to a huge Bunge Corporation grain elevator on the banks of the Missouri River. In a waiting room there, Yuri had leafed through a catalog from the Aldon Company, of Waukeegan, Illinois. It pictured tracks and signals and bumpers and other railroad-siding supplies to make grain elevators run efficiently. *Fax your order,* the catalog had boasted. *Request 24-hour delivery!* "One day telephone, next day come?" Yuri had asked, and when I'd told him they probably meant it, he'd sadly said, "Getting access to these materials at home would take many years. Then they would be bad materials. I see now it will take us a long time, a difficult time, to catch up."

These Ukrainian elevators were frescoed with abstracted wheat sheaves. It was a hot afternoon. There was little shade by the high barbed-wire fence ringing the mill. Dogs and a guard patrolled the fence. Uliana Kharitonovna Ketman's tale of hunger played in my mind.

"Why do you need this?" I asked Kosiak, pointing at the fence.

He shrugged. "People!" he said, echoing the explanation for guard dogs back in the Michurin apple orchards in Lithuania.

The air hovered, hot and foggy with grain dust. Below the towers sprawled a noisy factory turning out animal feed. We wandered, shouting over the clanking of machines, clambering along catwalks and by giant scales, ducking fat-stovepipe grain chutes, bellying past vibrating tank-sized grinders. It was a Saturday. The work force wasn't full strength, but a lot of people busily processed grain from thirty local collective farms. The mill tithed grain as payment.

We talked reform bureaucracy. The government in Kiev paid Kosiak's organization, RAPO, to administer this plant, the only one around. The organizational chain of command ran uphill, Kosiak shouted: the lowest link was a collective farm, and RAPO was next, running the farms and entities such as this mill. Above RAPO were a Poltava Oblast Agro-Industrial Association, Oblostnoy Agroprom, then a Ukraine Agro-Industrial Association in Kiev. RAPO was essentially local-level Gosagroprom, and did I know Gosagroprom had now formally ceased to exist at the all-Union level in Moscow? This shift increased power to Kosiak and to his boss, the regional Gosagroprom chief.

"Power comes to the person who occupies several jobs, uniting Party and soviet chains of command," Kosiak said. Did I know that this man, Vitaly Karpovich Chuiko, my keeper, standing right there smiling now, not glowering, was not just a dean but also deputy chairman for research of the regional Gosagroprom? Did I know his immediate boss was the chairman of Gosagroprom for the entire Ukraine? "So Vitaly has the highest-ranked boss here," Kosiak said. "Vitaly Karpovich is so able he has many jobs." No, I had not known my keeper's rank, although I had suspected it.

The regional Gosagroprom research he supervised included a soy-milling experiment, right here, and would I like to see it? I would, and would they also clear up a question about these double lines of authority for me? Gosagroprom, the *soviet* or civil line, supposedly now went only as high as Kiev. But didn't the *Party* chain of agricultural authority — which could overrule the soviet chain — continue from local Party committee through to the regional Party committee secretary for agriculture, then to the Ukrainian Party secretary of agriculture, and then to Yegor Ligachev, Gorbachev's archrival, head of the Communist Party Central Committee's Agriculture Department in Moscow? Well, yes. So didn't that mean that on important reform questions, Moscow Party authority no longer faced a similarly ranked civil Gosagroprom authority? "Yes ... but ..." Perhaps it wasn't a relevant point to them, because in their experience civil and Party authorities were never adversarial. The maze the bureaucrats had built confused and contained reform.

The sluggishness of reform showed in the mill's meager soy experiment. In a corner of the yard stood a small wooden garage. We climbed in over a high doorsill. A hodgepodge of grain grinders and chutes and pipes and bins filled the room. This room contained one of the great hopes of Soviet farming. Here was the empire's attempt to learn at last how to mill soybeans — an easy technical mission that could have the serious national purpose of saving billions spent importing grain. Only with *perestroika* had Soviet officials even acknowledged their lack of high-protein feed to fatten animals efficiently. It was a homely but tremendous problem — pigs and steers that took twice as long to fatten as Western animals did also needed barn space, labor, feed, and investment in all these things for twice as long. They needed twice the facilities for the same result.

By edict, the authorities had initially tried to solve the problem by pouring hundreds of millions of dollars into experiments with an industrial, nonagricultural solution — manufacturing yeast-based protein. That was a science-fiction solution, manna for workers' paradise. High production costs brought it down.

Gorbachev, who had been first Party secretary in the agricultural district of Stavropol, finally had accepted soy cultivation as a useful alternative. But the system was as innovation-resistant as it was starved for innovation. Soy production had stayed infinitesimal, partly because soy needs special milling. Chemicals in fresh beans prevent animals from digesting soy protein well. A milling process eliminated the problem. An "extruder nozzle" that heated soy meal above 160 degrees Celsius during grinding "disinhibited" these inhibitors. This simple, crucial nozzle, standard hardware in the West for fifty years, wasn't made in the Soviet Union. Hard currency had not appeared to purchase even a few foreign nozzles. Soy production might have been the path to self-sufficiency, but here *perestroika* had bogged down along the way for want of nozzles. Mill workers had cobbled together extruders, and they sometimes worked.

"They're ten degrees cooler than the model we are imitating, and they break," said the plant manager. He had milled small quantities of soy, and was doing feeding experiments to prove that soy was good for Soviet animals, too.

The manager, a retired navy pilot who'd taken up yoga, was a rare case: a thin Soviet male over forty. Careers, he made clear, were at stake, and loyalties on the line in this soy experiment. It was politicized. In this grain-poor nation, freeing land the *zakaz* had already assigned to wheat was close to anti-patriotic — especially for a "Western" farming experiment. Wheat was traditional. Planners didn't want to grow less wheat. They were scared to make mistakes; the old way had already been approved. Soy implied restructuring agriculture. That wasn't simple. These soy experimenters felt vulnerable. In this hut full of soy adventurists, excited and dismayed by their tiny project and homemade equipment in the middle of the vast, fertile, unbudging Ukraine, I understood why only Gorbachev's top-down reform had even begun to cut through the sturdy old system.

"I learned from my many years of struggling over soy policy," Viktor Lishchenko had later said in Moscow, "that you can't change a system from the top. I have made many tries. Resistance I couldn't conquer came from the collective-farm bosses and from bureaucrats. I lost my hope. That small experiment in Poltava was remarkable. In two years we brought experimental plots to U.S. levels of soy growth. The farms even made a little money selling beans as seed, not milling them — two thousand rubles a ton. But they needed real extruders. They needed banking too, and credit, and they needed know-how from the state, and they needed new, very expensive facilities for crushing soybeans and refining soy oil. Soy, in America, is an agri-industrial package. We have sunflower-oil processing plants, but they're not fit for soy. Farm bosses stay with what they know. Soy would take new herbicides, adjustments to planters and combines. For what? It's just more headache to them. Only a market economy could change the situation from the bottom up. We failed since the 1930s." It was a surprising speech, uttered very late in *perestroika,* by the usually cautious but surely exasperated economist, who continued to support collective farming even after the Party's fall.

◆

Back at Farm Beacon of Communism, I found another lease-brigade farmer — one of those early pioneers who had braved the social gale stirred when farm members left the collective and struck off on their own: "The contract we made with the lease brigade has many points," said the chairman. "We calculated the cost of production. If they use more money to get there, they lose. Less, they make money. It's the second year." That sounded sensible. The bewildered farmer walked into a meeting room. He was wiry, blond, about thirty, smart in the eyes and tough in manner. He sat tensely, as if ready to leap up and brawl. His voice was quiet, and as we spoke he eyed his chairman uncertainly, perhaps uncomfortable about speaking on unapproved subjects, at least at first, and looking for cues. For an hour, Viktor Vasilievich Vasiuta told his story:

"I am a trained driver, I have operated a truck, car, or combine since I was fifteen. After the army, I came back to the farm. This lease brigade wasn't my idea; the RAPO chairman chose Collective Farm Beacon of Communism because our chairman likes new ideas. The chairman chose me. I was amazed. I'd had the same idea for five years, but how could I come out with something unheard of? It came from the top — yet I'd been thinking it, so it's sort of the fulfillment of my dream.

"If you compare me to an American farmer, I have heard that there's a long way still to go toward independence. It is difficult to change generations of practices. For example, I have to get tractor oil at a warehouse twenty kilometers from here, which takes all morning, and I wasn't sure they'd give it to me. I can't get any from the collective farm's supply."

This shy man spoke with the other Mark, who was interpreting, as though both were Soviet citizens and Mark would translate the man's puzzlement with this conversation tactfully: "Well . . . I can't tell you the bad things, just the good ones. You see, I was interviewed a lot the last two years, and then I was in trouble, called disloyal . . . Well, I can say this about the new situation — before we were 'building socialism,' but now I work more for myself. How much more should I say? We have an expression: If you throw dirty laundry out from your hut, everybody will talk about it.

"In brief, I got in trouble already for telling this story: My contract gives me the right to have equipment fixed in the farm's big shop. But whenever I brought something in, the guys were envious. They said, 'You have the land and the contract — take care of yourself.' A journalist in Kiev wrote an article in *Ukrainian Youth* that said this collective farm hampers the lease brigade. The headline was 'Commune Clips Crane's Wings to Keep It from Flying.'"

Vitaly Karpovich, who did not think much of lease brigades, broke in with a gratuitous accusation: "Poor organization of labor is the big problem — laziness, incompetence."

The farmer smiled uneasily, and reverted to the official reform line. "If you are hunting for the big problem," he said, "I'll say it's that we've lost the feeling of ownership. We tried for fifty years to create the feeling of nonownership, of common property. We can't reverse that in a year; it will take decades. When I can pass land on to my son, that's when I'll feel ownership. My actual problem at this moment is more realistic. I have to install a bearing in my grass chopper and test it. I had so much trouble getting spare parts. I was doing that when the chairman summoned me here.

"Anyone who sees how hard we work ought not to envy me. My grandmother is in a regular work brigade. She is a distinguished member of the farm — she has war decorations. She disapproves. My brothers went to the city, but I make more than they do. One may join me, and he's a good driver. My dad built him a house and it's waiting for him. In theory, we'll be able to buy our own equipment soon — but we can't yet. We lease from the farm. And we have to sell every bit of our production to the farm. We ourselves decide how to farm — with advice from the collective farm's chief agronomist, of course."

We piled into a truck and drove through his fields. His corn was dark green and already shoulder high, and his mates were plowing a grain field after early harvest. He'd plant sugar beets on it. The farmer smiled with pride and asked a shy question: "Is it true that your farmers don't grow food for their homes — they buy it?" And another: "You have turnpikes? You pay to use them, and the roads pay for themselves?" And finally, "Is it true you have sixty TV channels?"

◆

At the end of my time in the Ukraine, I shook Vitaly Karpovich Chuiko's hand with gratitude. He'd chilled a few conversations, but in return he'd taught me his stolid, patriotic vision of social- ist reform. Vitaly was loyal, idealistic, and obviously righteous, and he'd lived in line with his convictions. He put the other Mark and me on the night train back to Moscow and waved us out of sight. At sunset we rode between endless golden wheat fields nearing harvest. We awakened to Moscow's drizzling gray dawn. Commuters gripped black umbrellas. A few peasants tended railside plots. Seeing me staring out the train window, an office clerk in the corridor said, "It will rain for three or four days, maybe forever. The rains are very long here. One of many Soviet paradoxes is that it rains wherever the soil is poor, and doesn't wherever it's good."

10

I'D PLANNED on R & R in Moscow — Vitaly Karpovich, with help from Nikolai Timofeyevich Yurchenko and Kosiak, had fit all he could into eighteen-hour days. Nights had ended with too many toasts to motherhood. But the same urge would beset hosts in Moscow.

Showing one's world to an outsider authenticates it. The Star Market in Boston, where my wife and I buy groceries, becomes a Beacon of Capitalism after Russian guests touch down. I have dragged them in yawning, straight from long flights and nasty ordeals at customs. I have the spirit of my keepers: jet lag be damned, it's welcome to America. Their drooping lids go wide-eyed, and I've proven the splendor of my world.

Sergei Ionisian met our train and drove the other Mark and me directly to the extraordinary Moscow graveyard at Novodevichy Convent, at a speed that made me worry we were late for a funeral there. "This is off-limits to most people," Sergei said proudly, approaching the iron gates and the suspicious babushkas who guarded and polished the place, "but it is open to me." His grandfather, a famous car engineer, was buried in the wall. "The wall is pretty good — you will see — but it is not the dirt. In dirt is better," he said. We would locate Grandfather. Sergei flashed his identity card. A babushka gave a small nod. Even after death, rank counted.

The cemetery was upper crust, but a crowded neighborhood.

Rows of dingy white graves, many of them once-grand statuary, others tiny arches of leaf-stained granite, filled the courtyard of the old convent. Soviet monuments weren't just good. If there was one thing at which the Soviets were world's best, surely it was memorializing. Monuments in the USSR won me over, again and again. This was a graveyard full of stone melodramas — of heroic children dying in battle, muscular workers rising fiercely from their chains, fiery orators excoriating rapt audiences. My frank translators frequently layered extra information into the glorifying descriptions of official guides: "This was a legendary airplane designer who helped the air force. *This guy was shot by Stalin.*" And, "A formidable industrial organizer, awarded the Order of the Red Banner for his work on metal molding . . . *disappeared in prison in 1937.*"

Novodevichy cemetery was the top spot, the ultimate, enduring privilege for Soviet society's builders. Status accrued to their heirs. Marxism-Leninism's optimism survived in this netherworld long after it had dwindled in the workaday world. A yard-wide hydropower dam rose behind a bas-relief of its cheery architect. A triangular granite airplane wing jutted under the majestic stone face of Tupolev, who designed Aeroflot jetliners and Soviet Air Force bombers. The bas-relief crew of a downed dirigible congregated along a far wall. Slender fingers gathered definition as a skilled surgeon's hands thrust clear of a boulder, as if the doctor were just resurfacing from a life below.

The inner circle of power was always small; many of those in it knew one another. Here were the makings of a hearty hereafter party: marble piano keyboards and granite scores awaited late maestros and divas, stone toe shoes were there for ballerinas, even a soapstone seal sat, nose pointing heavenward, above her circus trainer.

With the slightest flick of her faggot broom, a babushka pointed us toward Khrushchev's calm granite orb. Although he'd spent his last decade under house arrest, and was parked far from the Kremlin wall, his grave was big enough to hint at lingering esteem of his office. Interlocked black and white slabs had been sculpted by Ernst Neizvestny, an artist he had banned but later befriended. The sad bust of Stalin's second wife, a suicide, peered from a plastic case in a quiet corner of the yard. Sergei found his grandfather's place in the wall. A porcelain plate marked it, and behind glass, Grandfather's tiny knit-browed portrait. Grandfather concentrated, his expression matched by his grandson, who stared back at him.

Sergei Ionisian was a man for Russia's future. He'd made me understand what it meant to have had the substantial landscape of his life — his opportunities, forbidden roads, proper behaviors, in short, what was sensible to consider in life's navigation — shifting like a blowing dune as he came of age. Sergei grew up mild, and Orthodox. His father died young. At thirty-three Sergei still lived with his mother. They spoke Armenian at home. Sergei had studied automotive engineering, found his way to the Institute for the Study of the USA and Canada, and earned a doctorate in agricultural economics under Viktor Lishchenko. He was good at business and working with foreigners, an insider to lead the right outsiders through the maze of official obstacles. I watched him hold his own disputing with a hotel manager who wanted me reported to the police for having slept at Viktor's apartment. Sergei had maintained geniality, kept advancing practical points, and won ground by inches until the manager capitulated, hands flying up.

He hadn't joined the Party. Non-Communists were mostly kept off the fast track, but he'd stayed away. Now, after the direction of *perestroika* has become clearer, he seems to have been prescient. Even in the thick of setting up early agricultural joint ventures, he had a strong overview of the problems facing his country: "We have national problems with animal feed," he'd said to me. "But to deal with it, first we must build houses for farm workers, infrastructure to develop and transport crops, new roads, warehouses, grain elevators, and devote ourselves to improving agricultural equipment. We need technicians, construction enterprises to modernize farm and food equipment factories — too many people build each machine — and we must raise equipment quality. Our machines don't compare to Western machines. Such plant rebuilding will take years. We need good roads, especially in central Russia. We can't deliver crops properly from farm to factory to consumer. It's part of the reason for that now-famous number — that we waste thirty to forty percent of our crops. Soil erosion is bad. Some ways of raising more food are bad for soil. Irrigation leaches chemicals into lakes and rivers.

"We also need new market relations so there are wholesalers, dealers, and choices for consumers. We have a distribution system — one factory makes something and it is sent places that theoretically need it. To fix all this, we need a new system of financing. We'll need a new central agricultural bank and agricultural science institutes. Maybe in a decade we'll see the first increment of improvement, results from changes. The bureaucracy has such power still! It's hard for them to turn power over to those working the land. The consciousness of people has an inertia to it.

"Here's a story: At Collective Farm Vesna, only fifteen kilometers southeast of Moscow, they grow corn and feed livestock. The land is hilly, but they used no erosion control, so their soil has gotten poor. They used more and more fertilizer, costing them more and more. I drive past, going to my *dacha,* and see them spreading it. The economic plan ties up the farm chairman. He is not a real boss in the Western sense. He must check with district leaders and many others.

"But individual technical fixes aren't the answer, because every part of the system must be improved. But even if the new Don combine were good, how much help can a new machine alone give? It's like trying to practice ballet dancing in the middle of a rose garden — a futile and painful place to dance.

"International help will be hard to get until the ruble is convertible, and that may take a decade. We produce five times as many tractors as you do, but they don't work — how do we improve their quality? The word *manager* is brand-new here — we have borrowed the English word. Our management is poor. They practically don't understand what the job means!

"My English has helped me see all this. I've learned a lot reading paperback mysteries, believe it or not. When I was a boy, my grandmother said, 'Learning English is a job. If you want to play soccer for an hour, learn English for an hour too.' I hated it. 'Every intelligent man should know English and French,' she said. Grandmother was progressive. She knew our dealings with foreigners would increase.

"Don't misunderstand — she was a revolutionary. At fifty-five she went and got her doctorate. Her husband had one already. Unlike some of our leaders, she thought there should be no boundaries of knowledge. Anyhow, that's the influence that prepared me to meet these new times. I am lucky, yes?" It was her husband who was buried in the convent wall. In that way, Sergei was lucky, too. He was among the few ready for the new Russia.

◆

I had a supper appointment with a difficult man. I'd met him a year before, in 1988. He was from the other side — an anti-reformer, an archconservative, pro-Party, pro-status-quo-ante-*perestroika*, a writer, a member of the conservative Russian Writers' Union, a Russophile. He was allied with and had served as a publicist for Yegor Ligachev — Gorbachev's once-renowned rival, pushed aside a few years after Gorbachev took power.

I'd heard about the writer from a banker in Iowa, John Chrystal. Chrystal had once arranged for a few dozen Soviet farmers to spend some weeks in Iowa. Ligachev, head of the Party's commission on agrarian policy (which essentially set policy for Gosagroprom), had contacted the American organizers days before the trip. Ligachev's friend wished to join the group. The friend was Anatoly Samoilovich Salutsky. Chrystal complained that the group had brought only one interpreter and that Salutsky had often commandeered him for his own uses.

Salutsky had come to Boston on business the previous winter, and called me. He'd heard that I'd visited with Yuri Chernichenko and that I was writing about him. I invited him to drop by, and he'd shown up in my kitchen that afternoon. He wore blue jeans and a flannel hunting shirt, and had a genial smile, rock-firm handshake, and warm laugh. I hypothesized (as one does with strangers one is sizing up) that he had the manner of a kindly schoolteacher.

Then he had turned to his topic, and I soon tried on another hypothesis: that he was a driven warrior, embroiled in intrigue and insult, himself alone with his few allies, taking what he may have considered a heroic stand at the bridge, battling to guard high ideals against self-interested pretenders. It seemed to me that his counterparts in the United States were the moralistic accusers on both our right and left wings. They all shared the air of noble, indignant certainty he brought to my kitchen in Boston. We'd settled down with coffee, and he spoke bitterly.

"In my essay," Salutsky had said, referring to a piece just published in a nationalistic Soviet journal, "I criticized how highly decorated collective-farm chairmen — you know, the ones with the gold stars for egotism — how their farms prosper while in general the availability of food diminishes. The food situation at home deteriorates, it doesn't improve." That much of what he said seemed accurate to me.

But the next part seemed calculated to insult, and distorted the views of Yuri Chernichenko, which I knew pretty well after over a month of travel together the previous year: "I published this essay and was severely mocked by your friend Chernichenko. Do you think he is a rebel bringing on an age of capitalism? . . . He was the pro-Party one . . . People like Chernichenko made careers under Brezhnev, and are actually not changing tunes. They continue to say current policy should support the strongest and dissolve the weaker — it's these people like Chernichenko who fascinate you." His words "support the strongest and dissolve the weaker" indeed described the stance of a nascent capitalist, but from a perch that made it sound merely nasty, and left out the constructive results of competition between "the strongest."

He had also asked some hard questions, which were cautions against my own temptation to think market solutions might translate easily to Soviet society: "What would happen to an American family farmer if you removed the highway, tractor dealerships, special types of seeds, the market for buying cattle feed? Then you'd duplicate our conditions. I say if you have no infrastructure, what's the difference if you have independent or collective farms? We must release *farms* from administrative orders and subordination — not *individuals* but collective farms themselves. My image of the Soviet agriculture of tomorrow is a troika — that cart with three horses. The strongest, in the middle, is collective farms, and the horses on either side are family farmers and citizens with private plots."

I too could imagine collective farms freed to finance and manage themselves, and doing so with fair entrepreneurial thrift, in

the manner of big Western corporate farms (that is, pretty thriftily, but in fact not quite as thriftily as largish family farms). But
at that point, why ban taking them private? Why ban private
land? Salutsky's vision seemed to posit autonomous farms but
not individual owners. His questions were strong, but those he
opposed vituperatively were also asking them.

He had closed his chat in my kitchen by invoking the nobility
of peasantry and peasants' family values. Brezhnev's policy of
depopulating "nonprospective" villages, he'd said, "cold-heart-
edly tore peasants from ancestral homes and created the poign-
ant sight of log huts sagging to the ground, roofs collapsing."
Who wouldn't be against that? A sad balalaika tune played in
my mind. When I went to such a village, several years later, I felt
the loss, too. But Salutsky's reproach painted those who differed
with him as destroying family, tradition, and morality itself. He
was the defender of existing authority against the specter of
moral chaos.

Salutsky had been so forthright in Boston, and so different
from my other sources, that I looked forward, in the evening
after the excursion to the Novodevichy Convent, to hearing his
latest views. Influential Muscovites somehow managed to make
their apartments cozy, although stores offered few choices of
furniture and fixtures. Doing so was a Soviet fascination. Salutsky and his wife had outdone everyone — they'd managed to
transform their tiny flat into a baronial German mansion.
They'd found animal heads and emblazoned coats of arms and
ancient rifles and hung them all on the walls. They'd loaded an
antique oak breakfront with bric-a-brac. On a rococo desk, Salutsky's old manual typewriter sat hip-deep in a familiar rubble
of discarded manuscript. I recall a rug or two — or were they
tapestries? — also on the walls.

Salutsky's wife served a royal supper — a rump roast and
baked potatoes, fresh beans, sweet cakes, and whiskey, a remarkable meal to have assembled that month of that year of
scarcity. She stayed silent through her husband's hours of conversation, then, five minutes before our departure, confidingly
said, "My husband raises his voice and shows his emotions, and
I've been watching you, and you don't know if he is serious.
He is."

Salutsky's argumentation still included slighting the probity of my acquaintances among the reformist intelligentsia. Once they said one thing and now they say another, he complained, seemingly forgetting that they had been suppressed and now could speak out. He smeared them with innuendo about lack of patriotism. It was a tense supper; he was indignant to his bones. His emotional counterparts in the West who also had instincts for *ad hominem* attack would have likewise appealed to religion, purity, motherhood, and the dignity of high office and motherland in the interest of preserving authority.

That's what I'd come to hear. I refrained from debate. He styled himself expert on the efficiencies of American agriculture, to support his argument that collective farms could be more efficient than anything America offered. "I assess highly the activities of American small farmers. But facts and statistics show they have become a way of life, not efficient businesses making money, selling products. Therefore the correct thing to do is compare part-time American farmers to our private plots." An absurd notion — part-time farmers in Iowa are often schoolteachers and mailmen who finish work at three P.M. and then tend a few hundred head of beef or a few hundred acres of crops. Soviet tillers of private plots were peasants who dubbed along, having to swipe feed for their cows and pigs, forbidden all but hand tools, but still feeding their families on an acre of garden apiece and bartering the leavings.

"I wrote this in a very important article," Salutsky said. "I was called to testify before the committee drafting our law on land ownership. I was invited because my view is special — opposite Yuri Chernichenko's, and he also spoke. Why look at reforming our law against private land? We should compare the production potential of collective versus private farms." I wonder if he knew that larger farms owned by families in America grew wheat or tomatoes or produced milk at lower per-unit cost than did farms that were subsidiaries of conglomerates.

"Some people want to create a stratum of landowning small farmers who would ally themselves with the urban stratum running cooperative businesses. Growing food is secondary to them. They want political gains. I reminded the committee that peasant reform always occurred in an atmosphere of intense struggle. Reforms always touched not just society's economic side but its morality and ideology. I scolded the group for being a secret committee, a narrow circle. We can't privatize land until we solve the more basic problem — what is our aspiration as a society? I am perplexed. Not one *perestroika* law works as intended." That part I agreed with.

"Remember Lenin's words, 'The small farm owner will always be in debt.' That committee absorbed my every word. The only guy screaming was your friend Chernichenko. Everyone else agreed — go slowly, there is a lot still to understand. But two weeks later, at the Supreme Soviet, ignoring Ligachev's agrarian policy commission, they decided to approve reform legislation. *This is an attempt to break the unity of the working class, to deprive it of its strength and power! Who was active in developing this scheme? You must not subdivide the Soviet working class! Attempts of theoreticians to split it fail. Chernichenko is anti-patriotic. I want you to publicize ME in the United States!*" So I am. On my laptop, I even put the lines he yelled at the end of supper in italics. The people who think as he did — including a sizable "peasant lobby" that had successfully warded off land reform — make similar arguments. At the same time, Yuri Chernichenko's continuing efforts — in the Russian parliament and in creating a rural party favoring private farmers — have gathered little support in the face of such sentiment.

◆

In the street, the other Mark and I flagged down a small white Lada — a private-car owner making money as an after-hours Moscow taxi driver. We climbed in and fled Salutsky and his antlers and eagles. We were borne away in the chariot of a long-haired young madman who loved dollars. Two dollars, he insisted. He was not a theoretician. He was a TV serviceman by day, but made much more on the side. He accelerated to 120 kilometers an hour and kept the hammer down. His Blaupunkt tape deck blared heavy metal. He'd replaced the gearshift knob with a coiled brass snake. "I want make money. *Ya Lubliu Ameeeereeeeeku!*" he whispered half in English, under the throb of his music, eyes gleaming. "Greeeeen. Make money there." Maybe his grandmother, too, had told him to practice his English as though it were a job.

I was beat, but the evening insisted it was young. I walked up the ten or eleven flights of stairs back at the Central Hotel (elevator under repair). I had brought in a few dozen pristine packs of Marlboros, for smoking and for trading. I went in search of matches. I wanted to eradicate the bitterness of supper with Salutsky. The ubiquitous corridor lady was not in the corridor. I wandered down a floor. A small, black-haired woman — Maltese, as it turned out, on vacation with her sister — stood in the hall probing the cork of a wine bottle with a jackknife. She gave me a light and I got a corkscrew. Her sister showed up with another bottle. I opened both. The corridor lady appeared. Corridor ladies of epochs past kept careful track of foreigners. One had once detained me at checkout time, and phoned down to a desk clerk who spoke basic English. "Where is the glass for water?" the voice on the phone had asked sharply. "Next to the window," I'd answered. I'd put that corridor lady back on the phone. She'd heard the news, fetched the stray glass, and only then given me the receipt for completed room inspection, which I had to sign to get back my passport.

This corridor lady was different. She was sweet to her three-year-old Olga, cuddling her. She brought us uninventoried water glasses, no signatures required. She joined the Maltese sisters and me. We drank rust-dry Maltese red wine at a table in her hotel corridor. Three skinny Finns came by — two affectionate men, perhaps both husbands of a gaunt woman. A lush Spanish lady (who had traveled with the Finns for the day) showed up. A prototypical tall, dark, handsome man, a Russian engineer, surveyed the party and pushed in next to the Maltese sisters. A beaming Azerbaijani carpenter materialized, and a dour old Georgian who said he was a salesman, which was surprising in an era and place where almost nothing was for sale.

Everybody put something on the table, which was soon covered with cigarettes (Aeroflot brand and my Marlboros), wine, chocolates, Georgian *shampanskoye*, French *biscuits*. The sisters brought out postcards, then key chains — souvenirs of Malta for everybody. I fetched plastic dinosaurs for little Olga, then more for the Azerbaijani's six kids. I played "shy dinosaur" with the carpenter while Olga watched. The shy dinosaur ran away and hid behind wine bottles when other dinosaurs appeared. She smiled and joined the game.

The Azerbaijani, with olive-skin and long arms and huge gray eyes, palavered with everybody in smatterings of several languages. He touched, imitated, shared glances, poured his soul into the act of communication with foreigners, which marked him as joyously un-Soviet, and the corridor lady joined right in with his clowning. They hummed a tune. The Spanish woman started singing songs in earnest after her third tumbler of wine, first a Finnish song, then "Kalinka, Kalinka." The Azerbaijani danced sinuously to the song, circling us. He was all elbows and knees, with large hands he used like fans. One of the Finnish woman's husbands was priggish, and said, "Watch out, don't encourage him," in a nearly perfect Oxbridge accent.

The Finnish wife was red-haired and leggy and wore a miniskirt. The Russian engineer could not look at anyone but the younger of the Maltese sisters. She had doe eyes and a leprechaun's smile. The older sister said, "In Malta the guys are handsome and the girls are all pretty, and you can have any one of them. Come to Malta!" She slid down and played on the floor with Olga. The sisters worked in a factory, stitching clothing. Their hobby was "language," she said, and they were here to practice. They had studied all winter for this visit.

Our lack of common language was our bond, and we drank for hours, laughing, singing. Every now and then I thought of the Salutskys, sleeping across town in heavy pajamas, side by wrinkled side, dreaming ponderous, righteous, fearful, all-Union dreams. Olga fell asleep on the floor, smiling, and the Azerbaijani carried her over to the couch beside us and lay her down gently.

PART IV

IN CENTRAL RUSSIA

1989 AND 1990

11

THE OTHER MARK and I comprised the American delegation, guests of the Writers' Union and of the Institute for the Study of the USA and Canada, with official backing and friends in high places. Nevertheless, our train booking northward to the cloth-manufacturing city of Ivanovo fell through. This was a telling nonevent. It showed that the rail office no longer jumped at a sort of back-channel command it had recently obeyed.

Our friends, who were merely moderately influential, had earlier routinely wangled last-minute reservations. Perks and amenities accorded Party bigwigs had been presumptively granted us as foreigners, too, because only official Western visitors had traveled non-Intourist routes. Intourist got all the sightseers, and also got their hard currency. A small payment, delicately offered by a third party, eventually fixed things. But it took three days, during which I roamed around Moscow.

On one of those evenings I strolled with Viktor Lishchenko, the economist. "I'm getting old," he said, although he wasn't yet sixty. He'd had a heart attack, been in an American hospital in Des Moines, and been to a Party sanatorium south of Moscow. His head and his heart ached. We looked at the squat milk-bottle columns, belfries, and scalloped eaves of a prerevolutionary merchant's house. He savored the pale old buildings and winding back streets.

On the Arbat, the newly renamed walking street, Viktor proclaimed "both pride and shame" for the city. Lounging young men ogled streetwalkers. An old woman shouted protest poetry, reading from a handful of tattered papers. Teenagers knotted around a bad guitarist, chanting along with mild protest songs by the popular late minstrel, Vysotsky. Passing soldiers listened; in or out of uniform, the audience was curious about the new openness of city life. Three college students had set an amiable sign on a table: ASK US: WE WILL ANSWER ANY QUESTIONS.

The impudence! For a long time, so many questions simply had not been asked. They cheerily repelled charges of anti-patriotism spewed their way by a pair of conservative workers. Amazingly, the debate was on. By a news kiosk, Viktor proclaimed, "In a thousand years the presses have never been as free as now!" Such openness had struck before. Several rushes of liberalization, equally sudden and convincing, had proved brief, Viktor said: the liberal reforms of the 1860s, the days of the October Manifesto in 1905, and the Khrushchev Thaw of the late fifties.

The novelty of change itself seemed to have depressed him. He was coming to terms at the same time with his treacherous heart and with the unreliability of the society to which he was accustomed. His strength had faded, and a telltale headache haunted him like his own ghost. Few in Moscow trusted that *perestroika* was for keeps either. Some even contrived conspiratorial explanations for it. Viktor thought Brezhnev-era strictures might soon muzzle the press again — and put food back in the shops for a while. The public candor of the press was not always matched in personal conversations, for fear that openness might soon be valved off, and outspokenness remembered.

Under the old regime, Viktor had labored long for the cause of improving Russian farming and food processing. He was valuable to men near the top, a loyal reformer with the seemingly oxymoronic goal of efficient Communism. He was "puzzled now." Reform was suddenly all around him, and in that new context his efforts seemed, even to him, not crusading but supporting a system he knew had retarded development and might switch on full strength again. In his loss of certainty he said simply, "The old values suddenly don't apply."

We walked and walked. We'd started out hungry. Whenever

we came to a restaurant, we tried to get in. If we weren't ignored, we were treated rudely. Doors shut as we approached. Waiters left us standing at entrances. We tried cafés and hotel dining rooms. The moon came up. Viktor's headache sharpened. At last we ate in a cooperative restaurant recently opened near his office. Our meal cost fifty rubles — a week's pay for a laborer. How had these private restaurateurs won space in the people's building? How did they get and keep their permits? And how could workers quit state jobs to work for the restaurant without officially being declared "parasites"? Viktor smiled at my questions. The cooperatively cooked borscht, fresh green salad, stewed beef, and fried potatoes improved on usual bought fare.

◆

Our railroad tickets north to Ivanovo came through. The Yaroslavl station was as crowded as the Kursk station, with its southward trains, had been. Wiry Uzbekis and Tartar women in black shawls clung to squalling toddlers. Their teenagers' fashions confirmed the rustiness of the Iron Curtain. Teens sported doubly garish Day-Glo orange copies of Western running jackets, purple and iridescent brown clodhopper knockoffs of Nikes, and baggy but embroidered jeans. Such variously dressed families dozed, leaning on each other, awaiting the rush for space on night trains. We settled into a two-person, soft-class cabin. The next cabin filled with drunken clerks who collaborated in a snoring chorus that went on throughout the night as we clattered toward Ivanovo.

The first soviet, or workers' council, had been organized in Ivanovo in 1905, a date celebrated as the advent of Soviet power. Yet the place had come to represent the darkness of central Russia. Russians also knew it as the "women's city." One quarter of Soviet cloth spit from Ivanovo's looms. Young women, many from far away, moved there to run the looms. They lived in dormitories across the squalid, sprawling, still vital city.

The day was clear. Steep streets sloped away from the station, glowing with yellow slashes of sunlight. *Izbas* settled into the mud, their tar-paper roofs patched with tin. They looked organized and dowdy in the wonderful light, blue filigreed window trim gleaming against blue sky. Down on a broad commercial boulevard workhorses harnessed with arched wooden yokes pulled carts across town, while big trucks wove past them trailing threads of diesel smoke.

Before the Revolution, fur and timber merchants had mined the wealth of central Russia's forests from this city. Now half a million people lived here, and many were out of work or forced to work part time. Having recently been in Poltava, in the farm-wealthy Ukraine, I was conscious of the poverty here. Ivanovo had a textile college, a medical school, technical institutes of chemistry, energy, engineering, and agriculture. But everywhere we saw people poorly dressed, buildings especially run down, streets, for all the sunlight dappling them, especially neglected. Young North Vietnamese and Russian women straggled along the sidewalks. When there had been more jobs, they'd worked long hours. During *perestroika*, the mills had slowed. Uzbeki cotton had gotten expensive. Interrepublic discipline had slackened; distant raw materials no longer reliably flowed into town. And with future income uncertain, Soviet citizens all over the nation were making do with what they had and buying less clothing.

Our greeters drove eastward along potholed tar roads. The city was ringed by depopulated villages growing up to Maine-like pine scrub and by poor collective farms. Rainfall was adequate, but the region's soil was what Russians politely termed "non-black soil." It was mostly clay. The area had short seasons and hard winters. Spring and fall sometimes touched. In Ivanovo region, grass grew well but grain yields were half those in the Ukraine. Regional administrative power came from the mills and from secret military industries. The region's strength in the disorder of *perestroika* was that it had cloth to offer to the barter economy. Farming was not a major regional force. We drove through big fields of wheat and oats and flax, and then through miles of stunted pine and birch forest to the regional town of Shuya, thirty kilometers to the east.

◆

My host was Aleksander Aleksandrovich Sorokin. Sorokin (no relation to P. P. Sorokin, my translator on my 1988 trip with Yuri Chernichenko) was about fifty, with a high, wild, Don

King–like haircut. He was a presence, given to vital, chopped gestures, sudden points of a finger, probing chin-first glances, and blazing smiles. Sorokin was bearish in girth and build, thick neck leading to a square face, a face that could have been carved out of a stump with a chain saw in just a few strokes — it was a plank of flesh almost concealing piercing eyes. His enormous, catching smile was cut into it. The smile reached across rooms — people far down the train platform had to smile back at Sorokin. I found myself beaming away at him even when I had no reason to do so.

Sorokin was professionally hearty. He was a rising force in town, and could have made it as a politician in Boston, too. In 1989 he was a middle-level bureaucrat, supervising chairmen of a score or so of collective farms. By the 1991 coup he would be second in command of agriculture in the entire region. And when regional politicians would blossom after the Party's fall, he would be the one who had made it to the top.

He offered a handshake and a practiced intimation of honesty: "People conceal three things," he shouted, crushing my hand and holding my gaze. "Their own stupidity, their excessive wealth, and a stone in the pocket. But I don't have any of those things. I'm not stupid. I am not rich. And I'm not broke." It was an Ivanovo version of "Trust me." He smiled. I liked him.

He was a practical administrator. "I admit how bad things are," he said. One collective farm's yields were "shameful." The ratio of crippled to working tractors on another farm was "pitiful." A season earlier, and certainly two seasons earlier, such conversation with an American might have marked him as disloyal. I quickly distrusted him as much as I liked him. We would keep in touch. I would visit him again in 1990, briefly in 1992, then in 1993. He would call once from Texas, while on a junket with a well-known international fur dealer. I would even run into him at Professor Ray Goldberg's pioneering international conference for high-powered Russian agri-business leaders, at the Harvard Business School early in 1995, and he was still thriving. And planning for the future.

In 1989 he was confronting impending hardship. Winter was coming. Ivanovo had to feed itself. But the food sharing and stockpiling mandated by central planning for many decades was breaking down. Sorokin was, at the time, first deputy chairman of the district soviet — a civil office. And he was also the Party official in charge of area agriculture. "I have power to run the district's agriculture even without the soviet title," he said, "but I have it." He had previously been a collective-farm chairman for ten years.

Gorbachev's reshuffling of local agri-government to make "Agricultural Production Associations" — creatures of soviet, not Party, authority — left Sorokin head of this new organization after another official, uncontested "election." The new scheme, formally shifting local power from Party to civil administration, followed an edict of the Nineteenth Party Congress a year before. Its informal effect was that those already in power hung up new organizational shingles and sat at the same desks.

One major but unintended result of the restructuring, as *perestroika* moved toward demise, was to entrench the "ruling class" of Party bureaucrats. Holding two offices set Sorokin up for a long stint. His task in 1989 was still supposed to be the enforcement of the *zakaz* for subsidized grain, to be delivered to the government at set prices. The system's authority had so weakened that Sorokin felt impelled to take special steps beyond those long planned to make sure his city had food for the coming winter. Although bosses who fooled with quota obligations used to end up in jail, things were surely changing. Sorokin could ignore part of his formal *zakaz* with impunity. The change *perestroika* brought amounted to a shift in the flagrance with which administrators did what they'd always done. Eventually, the flagrance approached de facto practice of what the administered economy explicitly prohibited: trading in response to demand.

◆

Shuya is one of a few words that, when written, is shorter in Russian than in English: ШУЯ, three letters. It was a scrubby little city in a bowl of woods, muddy all over. Curiously, it looked almost Spanish, because the lopsided one-story houses and few shops were stucco, painted pink and light khaki and a pale institutional green, and some of the roofs were of terra-cotta tile.

Sorokin's agricultural bureaucracy worked from a requisitioned mansion at the end of town. Inside, an astonishing old man sorted himself from a pack of gray-suited officials. His own gray suit was tattered, and a crown of long hair flew about his head as if a private wind blew on him in the ornate vestibule. Lev Abramovich soon let it be known he'd done a lot, little of it having to do with farming. He'd fought in the Second World War. He'd edited a Siberian newspaper, *Amurskaia pravda.* He'd passed seventy, and had easy duties as foreign relations officer in Gosagroprom, including tagging along as my keeper in this region. He had a Gyro Gearloose, *Popular Mechanics* mentality, a notion that all things could be fixed by inventions. But his interest was not in major breakthroughs, like fusion reactors or superconductivity. He was fascinated with humble gadgets, like better-shaped hoes and sheet-metal windmills. Lev chattered nonstop about Chinese walking tractors and solar collectors hooked up to deep pumps, about refurbishing all of Russian soil through the miracle of earthworm farming. Were he a rural American, he'd have set out to make big bucks raising chinchillas in his spare time, and for all I know may have raised some in Shuya by now. He was a Sancho Panza to Sorokin.

Sorokin was a heavyweight, whether doing business on behalf of the Party, the soviet, or himself. He'd hung Gorbachev's portrait in his office in 1989, when such an expression of allegiance was rare. By the time the fashion spread a year later and farm officials started taking down the Lenins who had frowned from their walls for six decades, leaving bright patches, it was almost too late. "We're coming to the trivial conclusion, only now when ideological power is dimming," Sorokin said in 1989, "that real power is where the money is. It's a new discovery for us. You Americans probably think this is obvious." He flashed that alarming smile. I laughed as involuntarily as a baby smiling back at a dad.

He was excited by one place from which money might pour forth, an enterprise he was setting up "for our profit, outside the plan," a farm that raised blue foxes for their pelts. We drove out through long stretches of woods and shrubby grown-back farm-land. Shuya district was not farming all its cropland. A dry July was partially to blame for the poor grain fields we did pass, full of bald patches, bunched-up plants, thin stands, and pale spots. We crossed the Teza River, passed tiny A-frame *dachas* and the prim garden plots of factory workers. At gates marked ANIMAL FARM, we turned in. "So it's real — 'Farm Named After Orwell'!" the other Mark whispered to me.

In four long, roofed rows of outdoor homemade cages lived hundreds of foxes, mothers and growing progeny curled up, long snouts nestled in draped tails. A few paced the paw-step or two between cage walls, wheeled around, and paced again. They watched us through deep, furious eyes. Winter cold would thicken their coats. A man busily shoveled under a line of cages. No workers lounged about. In the context of my scores of other farm visits, the place was so simple and so workmanlike that it begged explanation.

"We had to make the cages ourselves. It was hard to get that much wire cloth. Only one plant, near Moscow, makes it. I went personally to the place. The manager said he only had permission to supply a set list of collective farms. I had to struggle with bureaucrats for an exemption," the farm manager, Valentin Aleksandrovich Kulikov, said. "Fortunately they needed a tractor. We could get an extra tractor through the state supply system and they could not. They could get wire for cages and we could not." The exemption turned out to be the universal unapproved barter.

Sorokin said, "I do such trades often. I find out what they want that I can give, and I hit hard on this point."

Lev agreed: "This is a good area for such trade. We have resources — two meat-processing plants, skins from cattle and pigs — quality leather."

Kulikov had set up in a room in an abandoned peasant cottage and gone about making cages. This was not a high-tech assembly site. He didn't even have a worktable, just a few pairs of pliers, a pile of clips, and a couple of rolls of wire cloth. He'd sat on the floor and worked. And with no more than that beginning, and the high authority of Sorokin, he'd gotten a profitable private farm going.

Animal Farm wasn't a collective. Sorokin had taken advantage of the new, ambiguous "Law on Cooperatives" to offer Kulikov a share of the profits for his management, and let Party colleagues know that he could turn a profit "for Gosagroprom as well," as he put it. He'd assembled capital: getting the land was easy — we'd passed plenty of unfarmed fields and nonprospective villages in Shuya district, and Sorokin himself was the main authority determining use of such resources. What little ruble funding he needed floated about the upper reaches of the bureaucracy. The tough part, Sorokin said, was getting access to barter goods — the tractor and who knows what else. That was the hard currency that was making his Animal Farm work. The line between barter and bribe was described by Sorokin's wide-eyed, open-lipped smile. He didn't tell me how he'd arranged access and title to the tractor.

Boris Q. Citizen surely could not have done what Sorokin did. The Russian heartland had not yet become a new frontier along which anyone could make a fortune starting an entrepreneurial farm cooperative under newly permissive *perestroika* business regulations. This was virtually the first time that even powerful people in the right places could set up enterprises from which they might directly benefit. It was another misdirected baby step in the constrained liberalization that had begun. It followed a pattern typical right up until the Party's impending demise and for some years afterward. Connections, as much as ambition and economic sense, prefigured entrepreneurship. Many a boss bridged the ideological chasm between departing and arriving regimes with such commercial constructions. Still, connections could only do so much. The enterprises the influential managed to start in 1989 were mostly tiny, homely places, and their results too minor to attract much notice. The handmade cages of Animal Farm still defined the possible.

The cement aisle running between the cages stopped halfway along the fourth shed. "We ran out of cement," Kulikov said with a sour face, hands rising, palms up, big and theatrical, comically heavy-hearted, communicating chagrin, whimsy, and fatalism. "And no matter how hard we've tried, we cannot get the rest of our delivery." Had the cement workers extracted the customary sort of tithe — a few loads of the requisitioned cement to sell to their own customers on the side? The farm manager repeated his gesture and wearily nodded.

As a result of the lost cement, at feeding time an assistant rolled a big cart of meat slurry — they'd converted an industrial washing machine into a mixer — along the paved aisle, shoveling supper out to the foxes, until the cart arrived at the end of the cement. Feed for the last two hundred of the twelve hundred foxes the assistant hauled slowly by hand; the cart wouldn't roll in the mud beyond. And the helper couldn't collect the fox droppings beyond the cement for fertilizer. So about fifteen percent of the available fertilizer was lost right there. And in spite of a strong breeze, the place reeked of urine.

The undelivered cement was a small and usual problem. But it demonstrated the crucial link between infrastructure and farm efficiency — if no cement, then no path, slow barn chores, and wasted labor and fertilizer. Sorokin planned to build twenty-three more sheds the following year. Perhaps more cement would arrive with them, but so would similar problems. Looking out at the cloudless, broad sky, I pictured fox sheds stretching back to the treeline.

Kulikov radiated an amiable, quiet competence that made his success managing a twenty-four-shed fox farm seem certain. Sorokin showed how much he adored the guy by yielding him center stage, which he rarely relinquished. "On a trip, I saw a blue-fox farm and got the idea to copy it," Sorokin had said. "But I knew I'd have to find a strong leader or the enterprise wouldn't make sense. High profits would influence my own salary." Sorokin was a fully vested member of the cooperative — to my Western eye, a clear conflict of interest: a public official had used his position and resources to enrich himself. But in that year and place, probably no commercial enterprise operated that had not begun that way, precisely because only high position enabled an energetic person to assemble what his self-interest suggested.

Kulikov had trained as a veterinarian, then worked for a while on a collective farm. In college, however, he'd been astute enough to undertake a special study of how to aid the propagation of wild boar. It seemed at first an exotic choice of topic for a farm vet. But it was a strategic choice. There were many hunting lodges for the delectation of Party higher-ups, who characteristically loved to hunt. Kulikov's specialty brought him into the right places. Soon he was managing a forest and boar preserve of thirty thousand acres (a sixth the size of Manhattan) for officials' hunting parties. For all that, his nominal pay was 210 rubles a month — what a farm bookkeeper might get, and the sort of salary scale that helped explain the disappearing cement.

Sorokin had met Kulikov on a boar hunt, discerned his straightforwardness and good sense, and kept an eye on him. They had some conversations about business. By coincidence, Sorokin's mother had raised foxes in a shed behind the family's farm cottage. She hadn't been able to buy animal feed legally. Sorokin knew a bit about fox husbandry. At Sorokin's prompting, Kulikov studied up on commercial fox farming, toured the few fox farms going, and offered his humble commercial plan. They started things moving. These foxes would be killed in November, after their fur had turned white. The fox meat would go to local chicken farms. The furs would be processed locally and made into coats for the luxury market. They would bring a fine return.

"In the wild, the fox is a vagabond. He doesn't live in a foxhole, but just runs," Kulikov said. "No home at all. He's a native of tundra and needs no winter heat. He preys on the lemming. In winter I feed each one half a kilo of meat a day. They'll live seven months and then weigh five kilos. The economics are very good. These sheds cost only eight thousand rubles each to build. So every time we sell just one hundred animals, we'll have profit for three new sheds. The first batches of foxes will also pay for a proper shop to help us construct the other sheds. We do have a few dangers. Foxes sometimes devour their young right after birth, so I must be wary. I also have to watch their health."

The co-op employed six workers, covering three shifts, a pair at a time. They lived in another abandoned peasant cottage past the sheds. The crew had ringed the sheds with a tall chain-link fence topped with barbed wire. Might foxes escape the wire cages and then leap three meters high? "No," Kulikov replied. "Foxes are valuable. A lot of people would like to take advantage of this place." The fence to guard against people was a familiar feature of Soviet farming, from Lithuania to the Ukraine. As we were leaving, Kulikov pointed to the joke of the farm — two pet rabbits. They hopped around uncaged, guarding the foxhouse.

Out of nowhere, back in the van, zany old Lev enthusiastically exclaimed, "Yes, managers of joint ventures should meet foreigners! New opportunities are for the thinkers!" Sorokin, his boss, had surely made it his business to meet foreigners. He'd even vacationed in Hong Kong and gone on agricultural missions to Egypt (where he'd picked up a bit of French) and India. As soon as the Eastern bloc fell away, Sorokin was in there dealing tens of thousands of raw Ivanovo sheepskins to Hungary for processing. He'd brought back samples of Hungarian-made shearling coats, and set up shop in Ivanovo, imitating them. He was, among his other offices, head of the local "agro-industrial conglomerate."

He was thinking about profitability. The foxes were his third or fourth side-project, and just a tiny aspect of Ivanovo's business. But as the Soviet empire tumbled, that unlikely combination of state and private ownership, built on official privilege and personal ambition, made sense, and money. The homemade fox farm paid half its profit as tax, and was protected from further predation because Sorokin was an owner. But it was a precarious and idiosyncratic arrangement, not the sort that would appeal to outside investors. The year after, no more sheds did get built, although the four already turned up a profit of more than two hundred thousand rubles, with a million projected for the following year, along with a slower building plan. And Sorokin was talking mink.

12

LIKE THE terrapinesque Kosiak down in the Ukraine, Aleksander Aleksandrovich Sorokin had wrestled in school. Presiding at a lunch in Shuya's dusty roadside restaurant Teza (a new, already faded, cement-block establishment about which a farm manager had whispered to me, "No one visits here but transients, our upper crust, and the corrupt"), Sorokin mused grandly, "I stopped fighting, but I still have the appetite of a wrestler. All day I work with people, and almost never eat. No lunch, late suppers . . ." He sighed mock denial and ostentatiously pounded his gut.

"Who'd deal with a fat man?" his wife asked, and the attendant officials laughed. A lot of people in Shuya dealt with Sorokin. Sorokin was a big man. His lieutenants came to him and went from him looking alert, laughing whenever he quipped. The food set a standard for grimness — curled gray cold cuts, collapsed brown bread, oily, musky soup. This was not the Ukraine. We ate in a pine-paneled side chamber while a motherly waitress hovered shyly in the hallway, peeking at the foreigner who only sipped his way through the toasts. This restaurant would have benefited from competition down the street.

In the main hall a wedding party was assembling, and before the end of lunch an electrified accordion shoved booming polkas under the door to our dining room. I wandered out to look and was hustled by both elbows across the room into the arms of a capacious bride who whirled me around briefly and briskly.

Then I was out across the bleak landscape again, driving toward Farm Gorky and its near neighbor a few miles down the road, Farm Trudovik — Toiler — in another smoky van. I'd repeated my request of the year before to spend a week on a farm. The earlier deflections hadn't ceased, but had eased. This year it was possible. Sorokin had arranged a stay with the family of Nikolai Petrachkov, chairman of Farm Trudovik, and his wife, Taisa Stepanovna. I'd asked to board with peasants in a cottage; he'd arranged board with a college-educated Party member who administered fifteen thousand acres of land and five hundred workers. In retrospect, I suspect Sorokin followed a sound public relations principle: give the client what he needs, not what he wants.

A Gosagroprom van brought the other Mark and me, amid a retinue of greeting, policing, and advising minions, to the front of a small house made of glazed brick. It sat midway in a row of a dozen houses strung along a road. Its half-acre yard notched into a large potato field, which ran back toward the flat horizon. The houses, like many in Ivanovo, were trimmed with gleaming blue wooden filigree. This small village was Afanasyevskoye, Shuya district, Ivanovo region. It stood by the narrow potholed main road between Ivanovo and Gorky, about a hundred miles to the east. A convoy of battered, omnipresent Kamaz trucks roared past, on which were balanced farm machines and stacked crates, bales, pipe, and even smaller trucks.

A high bell tower stood across the road, gutted and ruined. Right after collectivization, the many citizens who'd remained secretly religious must have found it a taunt. But to the current generation the tower had become just more mess in a messy country. Villagers had picked over the rubble and built little garden borders and steps out of scavenged bricks. The tower looked like bomb wreckage. The dilapidated church beside it had been a grain storage since the thirties, altar destroyed, windows boarded over, wooden walls bulging, roof sagging from years of strain. "In the next town, the church is restored already," Taisa Stepanovna said, "and there is talk about this one." Would she go? She smiled wanly and said, "I don't think so."

My hosts' cottage had a clean yard — a rare country virtue in the Shuya district, and not one all the neighbors shared. Its neat flower border, fresh paint, and kempt pathways signaled wholesomeness, as it does in country villages at home. The family, all bows and smiles, welcomed me in through a mudroom — "good in countryside without pavement," Nikolai Petrachkov said, laughing with genial unease of the sort new guests often prompt. He pointed out the board platform he'd built so that Dima, who was twelve, could bunk in privacy, at least during summers. Dima nodded shyly. A narrow hallway doubled as a cold pantry. Taisa had lined it with canning jars. The kitchen was nearly filled by a bulky, shoulder-high *pechka*, a brick oven the size of a small car. Taisa Stepanovna slapped the top and said, "Dima slept here when he was a baby." They'd crammed in a gas stove, gas refrigerator, and a kitchen sink that lacked faucets.

For a week I was to wander the two collective farms: Gorky, where Taisa worked as economist and where Nikolai had been born, and Trudovik, a few miles down the road, where Nikolai had been chairman for a decade. I fell into their routine. Taisa worked on budgets and allocations all day, came home and cooked. Nikolai drove back from workdays in his farm office, tended his own cow, pig, and few sheep, fed his ornery cur (which lunged against its chain just inches shy of me every time I approached the outhouse door). We ate supper in the small room where Dima slept in the winter. Off it were Nikolai and Taisa's bed-sized bedroom, and a living room with the standard bric-a-brac–filled breakfront, a gold-colored couch, and a portly television that always would have been on if Dima had had his way. It was a room they'd made too fine for daily life, a farm parlor, where the American delegation slept.

This was a dwelling in transition, neither peasant hut nor yet suburban house. Its occupants had been sophisticated by television and technical college, and by the loosening of the government's grip on information. They made the expected awkward apologies about their humble abode. Taisa contritely showed off the tin tank from which they filled the sink. Nikolai showed the pile of wood he'd split to fire the *pechka*, and then the coal furnace he'd found and installed for the coldest months. Dima showed the goldfish he kept in a big old aquarium; he'd stitched the toe end of an old stocking onto a wire armature, making a serviceable fish net. But they were also triumphant about what they'd made for themselves. The house felt cozy and organized. It had rugs on floors and, in the Russian manner, more rugs hanging on the walls.

They were house-proud and comfortable. For a month or two in early summer they might have regretted the general lack of screens in Russia. And Taisa often apologized for the lack of running water. Every few days, Nikolai found fifteen minutes or so and pressed on with a tedious project he'd been at for years. With a big, long-shafted hand auger, he'd drilled down many feet out by the barn wall, prospecting for water, striking mud and rock. Meanwhile they lugged pails from the community well and visited the outhouse. The outhouse leaned against the sheep shed. The shed leaned against the barn for young stock. And the barn leaned against the house. Nikolai composted animal and human waste from all three, which Taisa dug into the big garden.

We ate glistening fresh tomatoes and sour new pickles, and slaw variants every night. I was amazed by our first supper. Taisa brought out a big bowl of mushrooms. Russians hunt them avidly, fry them nicely, but just when they look done, drown them in gobs of viscous oil. She laid out sturgeon, bread, *pirogi*, potato and beef stew, fried chicken parts, cheesecake, wine, beer, two sorts of bottled water, and tea.

Her table reminded me of childhood feasts at which my father's mother, Mildred Hindin Kramer — whose grandfather (she'd told me) had been "an ironmonger who built the gates around the King's Palace in Moscow," and whose father made jute potato sacks there — also laid out too much Russian food. At Taisa's table and my grandmother's, choices extended beyond anyone's capacity. It was guilt-inducing to choose chicken and sample beef only to find there were also cold fish and hot fish, and to ladle in peas and carrots and lima beans and then lose heart before getting back for spinach, too. Taisa had fried potatoes and boiled potatoes and even reminded me not to forget the dollop of sour cream. She just kept bringing out dishes. But Taisa kept on for a reason that my grandmother never had. "The Communist Party keeps the foreign guest supplied," she said in the middle of the meal. "A car came today with a delivery of special food." This was no farm family's typical fare, not even a farm chairman's. The car restocked the larder several times during our visit.

Most mornings that week it poured, and along the footpath by the side of the house workers sloshed toward undemanding jobs in fields, barns, and potato warehouses of Farm Gorky, skirting the fierce cur, Bruno, who strained at his chain and snarled. Many nevertheless waved at Nikolai, watching him take full, easy swings with a big scythe, laying down a day's ration of wet rye and clover for his sheep, bundling it, wheeling it across the big field behind the house to the shed in a homemade barrow.

After breakfast, Nikolai slung on a shoulder yoke he'd carved from a tree limb and hauled home buckets of water from the community well by the road, a few houses down. It had recently been electrified. He filled the tank above the sink, watered the animals, and went back for a final load. An ancient leaned out of the window of her log hut, just by the well. "My son has died," she whispered. It was her eternal bad news. "My husband used to live here. He died." She was black-and-blue about the face and elbows. A few mornings back, Dima had gone in to check on the old lady and found her on the floor, tumbled down from the sleeping platform atop the kitchen hearth.

"If you want neighborhood gossip, I'm not interested — even on my own farm," Nikolai said. "She hasn't been abandoned. Her relatives buy her food and haul her water. But she's always complaining, and Dima offers help. She refuses, but he keeps going in." "She loves to complain," Taisa said later. "She opens that window and complains twice a day — when I walk by on my way to work, and when I walk home. I sympathize, and she feels wonderful."

Returning from work in the afternoons, villagers often saw Taisa and Dima kneeling by their staked cucumbers and tomatoes, inside improvised plastic greenhouses, even in July. In the absence of further deliveries of sturgeon from the Party's Foreign Section, that's what they would eat all winter: "the pickled vegetables and meat, and we have the potato and cabbage patch," Taisa said, "otherwise we'd have a hard time. We go to the store only to supplement our home-grown food. People who won't do some of their own work but just want to shop have a harder time. Even a factory worker in Ivanovo can have a garden plot."

Nikolai and Taisa favored work, worked hard, and dealt with me with dignified straightforwardness. They commented that I also worked hard. They were dead set against poky work, and measured the world by standards that made me think of American farmers. Sorokin had chosen adroitly. I found few other farm chairmen like Nikolai in other Soviet and post-Soviet travels.

At breakfasts, with the rooster still muttering behind her, or late at night, washing up after one of the lavish feasts, Taisa Stepanovna was assertive, quick to kid, alert and wholehearted in her answers, curious about my world, speculative about the news. Her husband, a few years her senior at forty-six, had the looks of a country-and-western star, his long, still-black hair neatly laid back, comb tracks showing. On his square, lined face he habitually wore the disarming, equable, slight smile of a man requesting that you trouble yourself on his behalf, say by removing your hat in the theater or speaking up a bit. He was patient and approachable. Even while he was eating, workers drifted in at will, joked, posed small operating questions, and got amiable, serious replies. He drank tea in the day and vodka at night, and enjoyed a chat.

Two of his brothers and a sister lived right in Shuya. Taisa's kin lived just over in the city of Gorky (now Nizhny Novgorod again). Stalin had displaced entire populations, but here in the heart of the nation was a clan. Blessed with industrious parents, they'd both always known how to work. They were used to it, they said, and therefore their lives had had a certainty, at least until recently, because they had always known what chore to do next. But now they were befuddled. Society's rules and regulations were lurching this way and that. Nikolai had become more cautious about how he directed workers because of "contradictory influences."

The greatest puzzlement, unsurprisingly, was about the few farm workers who'd begun to hold and benefit from private property. "I want guidelines," Taisa said to us, all business. "I want to know how to calculate rents for these lease-brigade farmers, for example." There were no state guidelines, yet she still faced blame by off-farm superiors if she set the wrong policy. She asked me in detail how rents were figured for American farmland, and I told her, but I think too much was different for her to find much guidance in the information.

Our late-night talks went on all week. The rooster crowed, outside the parlor window, sometimes soon after I'd gotten to sleep. Everyone straggled awake, and after a few minutes the perfume of frying potatoes and the murmuring of morning conversation drifted in, followed by Dima, who stopped to offer a little bow to the stranger, then flipped the TV on, too loud. Starting the day with news had become family habit. Nikolai was glad that news reports had grown franker and broader throughout *perestroika*. The voices washed through the house, bringing tidings from the outside world.

Over the sound of the television, we almost shouted when we spoke at the breakfast table. Taisa was full of opinions, moored in her experience. The cottage stood on land administered by Farm Gorky. She'd worked at the farm for the twenty years, since finishing at Ivanovo Agricultural College, and had been chief economist for most of that time. Her chairman had been at his post since a year before her arrival. Stable management was part of the formula for successful collective-farm operation. He was approaching retirement — an incidental fact that would figure in events soon to change their lives. That chairman had long ago been "brought here and recommended" by the combined district and city Communist Party committees, and, said Nikolai with what I took for circumspection in speaking of his counterpart on the next farm down the road, "He hasn't been a poor chairman. He's a mechanic, a technician. He built potato warehouses, a complex of apartment houses. He has 200 workers on the farm, and a village population of 320. But in his villages, the young people have moved away."

Nikolai had been born on that farm, also went off to Ivanovo Agricultural College, came back and drove a tractor for years. He was suddenly pulled off the farm, elevated, made chairman of Farm Trudovik, next door: "It wasn't my initiative, but I felt my duty deeply. I am a Party member. I got my education free. Given a government assignment, it was my duty to fulfill it. I was appointed, but now democracy has come to us.

"People now are even elected to management, and recently, for the first time, another candidate ran against me — the farm agronomist. I got 170 votes and he got 40. There was a quarrel — why were there 210 votes when the number of people with the right to cast votes was smaller than that? We never figured that out." Nikolai laughed. "My rival had no program. He was nominated by his friends. It was semilegal. Every worker brigade on the farm could nominate a candidate. Only I was nominated, though, until in the general meeting the chief agronomist jumped up, and his friends nominated him. They hadn't put him through primaries. I think it's good to have two or three candidates, but best to nominate each in the regular way. Still, his name stayed in the voting. His defeat influenced our relationship at first — I felt awkward. But we got used to it. We had no habit of such struggle, and both of us had to adjust.

"Everything has been difficult running the new farm," Nikolai said. Taisa teased him: "The previous chairman could thump his fist and say, 'This is it — this is my decision!' but you can't. The workers have a big voice now. Running a farm was difficult under the old system, and difficult now."

Nikolai scolded back, "It would be easier to be a bad chairman — or to go back to driving a tractor!"

She came right back at him. "If you were a tractor driver, you'd have time — and we'd already have running water!"

And Nikolai answered wistfully, "If I had money, and the law on land changed, I'd *buy* Collective Farm Trudovik. Then I'd be a real boss. And I wouldn't have elections — I would appoint managers I wanted. Obviously there should be no role for elections in choosing an efficient manager. The popular man is not necessarily the best running things. When elections started, frankly I felt uncomfortable. Now I accept it. I even feel it is necessary." I didn't quite believe his last statement — I was always impressed with those dutiful doublings-back on meaning.

He returned to his fantasy of autonomy with animation: "I'd like to buy the land myself and be independent. I *know* how to take care of land and how to hire good people to tend it with me. I don't think that's a big contradiction with being a Communist, for me, because I'm prepared also to work myself — maybe harder than my workers."

Taisa, laughing, broke his monologue: "It's words! He couldn't work as he used to. He's not as strong." Nikolai laughed with her and said, "But Taisa, I still have my head on my shoulders — I can think clearly. Twenty years ago I took the system for granted. Back then, we didn't think at all. We had the clear and correct road, and without any thought just moved ahead. Whatever the official zigs and zags were, we always said the same thing: 'We're moving along Lenin's road.' We said this even when the road made sharp turns!" He laughed.

I asked Nikolai if he'd heard childhood stories about how his family had fared during the time of collectivization, which was one of those sharp turns. "I know everything about that. My mother always told me, during private moments, that before the collectivization, people had lived better. Peasants worked harder and were dedicated. They had food. You know, around here, getting rid of the *kulaks* lasted for years. It started back in '24 and continued into the thirties. It was a big mistake — we pushed out the most productive, honest workers."

Taisa said, "The authorities just arrived and killed his mother's cow, and left her with no milk for four children."

"They grabbed the sheep, the horse," Nikolai said. "We became very, very poor. We worked, though, and survived and nobody died in my family. All are now grownups and doing fine — except my father. He died in '41, fighting in the war."

Perhaps aware that he was asserting that private property can be run more efficiently than state property, and that the taking of farmland had been violent, Nikolai doubled back again: "Now our political situation isn't as bad as that. It's more animated, but we've run up a blind alley. I find the frankness of the press irritating — a reporter writes one thing, and someone else criticizes him. Who is right? We're not used to this. One or the other must be lying openly in a million copies of the newspaper — I don't think that's fine!"

Eventually after each breakfast, we remembered to stop talking and set off for work. The Five Year Plan listed Trudovik as a dairy — although there were so (relatively) few actual Soviet dairy cattle that dairy farms were meat farms. The farm also raised pigs and sheep, and grain to feed them and to keep residents in bread.

"I'd prefer to deal with big cattle only," Nikolai said, "but that is not our state plan. We are still very much under the control of the Agricultural Production Association. Your host, Aleksander Aleksandrovich Sorokin, controls us. And he only follows a state order issued still higher. He is controlled by the district Party committee. So control at farm level still comes from the Party. Power still travels down to us from the commission on agrarian policy of the Central Committee in Moscow. What Yegor Ligachev decides, we immediately feel. We still have a mandatory crop delivery order and must follow it. Pigs and sheep are in the order. So I raise them."

Had Nikolai peered up at the authority structure towering above him, he would have seen the familiar disorder he'd grown up with compounded by new disorder set off by Gorbachev's programs. He was subject to regulation by newly hopeful democrats, technocrats having their day, and purist ideologues who felt their convictions trampled by every reform we in the West found cheering. Nikolai was a compromised mediator. He owed allegiance to neighboring families with whom he'd grown up, and also to the diverse officials above him.

The usual old troubles were still there. He spent more time getting his hands on the right tools, animals, seed, fertilizer, machinery, workers — on setup — than on operations. "I'd love to eliminate bulls and breed only by artificial insemination," he said, for example, "but I can't. We haven't got a qualified vet. And I'd need a far more careful staff than we have, to notice when cows were in heat — now the bull does the noticing. Our artificial insemination isn't world class, because our country does not search for the best bulls, the way they do in the West. So all in all, I can't eliminate bull breeding."

And he had troubles caused by ideological differences on new possibilities: "Our laws are too general. They allow too broad interpretation. I want very much to offer private farmers land for rent. But we don't yet know how much to charge, because we don't yet know the price of land." Would the long-awaited, much debated, much delayed "Law on Land" help? I asked. Taisa answered, "I'd have a frame of reference."

Nikolai wondered. "Most people's deputies never tilled land, so how can such guys write a law about farm property? I could suggest criteria for establishing the correct size for a piece of rental land: whether or not it's being used, produces income, could bring in rent, what is its geography, what area is it in — that list is a starting point. A law on land could allow us to calculate and have guidelines — if one ever passes." Nikolai said later, "But nothing about the new laws is ever clear. I read Gorbachev's speeches. I think he pursues the right line of development. And then we receive our orders — supposedly from the top, but actually through the local bureaucrats — and they are absolutely distorted."

◆

Taisa took me to see her special project — Zhanna, Farm Gorky's lease-brigade farmer. Zhanna received us in a spotless but tumbledown wooden barn far back on the farm. She stood there, hands clasped behind her, in her best blue, high-collared dress. She'd lavishly applied blue and gold eye shadow. "I saw my chance when Gorbachev proclaimed that land could be leased to small groups," she said. Formerly a milkmaid, she'd felt frustrated that the barn where she'd worked was badly run. She'd had "tens of ideas" how to improve it.

The year 1989 was that window when farm chairmen often felt enthusiastic about having a lease brigade or two around, and cheerfully — and cautiously — complied with Gorbachev's directive. The danger in allowing a gung-ho work team to strut its stuff on a collective farm was, of course, that they'd show up regular brigade workers. Farm chairmen knew about the reformers who'd tried such "experiments" over the decades, and knew that the Party had always sensed approaching danger and brushed it away. The chairmen I asked had heard of the Khudenko debacle (he was the farm chairman in Kazakhstan who'd paid special brigade workers well to outproduce normal workers, and died in jail). As Zhanna was organizing her lease-brigade barn, a play celebrating Khudenko was drawing audiences in Moscow. It was an idea that had come of age — in Moscow.

In Shuya, the problems with lease brigades remained. *Perestroika* was localizing power some and had opened the media to frank discussion of inefficiency. But back on the farms, unequal pay would still infuriate residents. Soviet children were trained from kindergarten on to favor obedient group efforts. *Individualist* was a Bolshevik pejorative that still stung. Gorbachev's edict was unenforceable on a large scale.

Still, chairmen were delighted to comply a little bit. Some were certainly interested in the good results. Others must have noticed that lease-brigade bookkeeping offered a way to hide private sales of farm crops. Many chairmen shifted group property to their own cousins, in-laws, or buddies. Others played it straighter: I found early lease-brigade farmers who were just plain ambitious, seizing new opportunities.

Zhanna's crew did its job right. Her cattle gained more weight each day than any other on Farm Gorky. And indeed, Zhanna had become the highest-paid worker on the entire farm. At least in front of the American delegation, farm officials and one passing neighbor adored her.

She was controversial local news, though, because her efficiency and high pay had split the community. She had often spoken to reporters. Her account was polished: "Collective farms have their troubles — just try getting wooden boards and you'll see. I managed a regular work brigade in a cow barn a few years ago. We needed a new floor. Finding boards was hard but a truck finally delivered some. I asked a brigade member to carry them in. 'I don't touch wood,' the guy said to me, 'I'm a *skotnik* — a cattleman.' For some reason, that was the last straw. I asked to be transferred back to being just a milkmaid. Why should I be the boss who pushed people around if I didn't get anywhere? Then the idea came to me — I wanted to work better, and calmer."

Zhanna was from a peasant family and had never strayed from the village. Her mother and grandmother milked cows too. "It was surprisingly easy to organize a lease brigade once I'd realized what I wanted. We took over the same barn I was managing. I chose new people — ones I wanted to work with. The old regular brigade had fourteen people who didn't want to do much. The first new lease-brigade worker I selected was my husband, then six friends, all young, all hardworking. We eight do more work than the fourteen. We get good pay. We get envy from other farm workers but no confrontations, yet.

"Now the same person will feed cows and also shovel behind them. That never happens on the main farm. There, that's got to be done by two people — this must sound amazing to a foreigner. In our cooperative, our salaries are the same and we rotate jobs and shifts. Only one of our group, by the way, is a Party member, just by chance. The Party never comes up in our discussions. We talk about cows, barns, the farm."

She voiced several delicate denials of a sort that must have helped tactful folk keep their lives simple during the previous seventy-five years: "I myself don't think I'm mature enough to join the Party. Maybe someday I will be." And she said, "Journalists came and asked if I wanted to go further and *own* a real individual farm. I can't think about that now. I have too much work to do. And I earn seven or eight hundred rubles a month, triple my old salary, so I am not unhappy with the pay."

Zhanna was a winner, but to some extent she was in the Stakhanovite tradition, useful as a moral lesson for laggards, more a pro-authoritarian workaholic Hero of Socialist Labor than the vanguard of some dangerous, renewed, autonomous, rural, *kulak* bourgeoisie. She herself seemed genuine in her pleasure at making good pay and at a workplace that worked. She was in the *artel* tradition — the rural farm workers who, before the Revolution, negotiated the price of their labor and worked more or less democratically within their groups, following strict bylaws, like trade unionists.

In 1990, a year after this first visit, when I stopped back briefly she'd still reported happy cows, contentment with the shifting new order, and contentment with her lease brigade. In her second year, Zhanna sounded even more like a Western farmer: "We're looking forward to a new decontrolled market for milk. We went three winter months with no feed grain. Now we've found grain. Our housekeeping in the barn is a lot of work because we still lack simple mechanical equipment. We have no better animals. The bull semen we get puts height on the calves but not weight. Milk price is the constant issue. We graze the animals in pastures, forests, fields, but we don't have fence wire, so we have to watch them when we could be off working. Last year our men made 540 rubles and the women made 450 rubles a month, still the highest pay on the farm. A few groups raising calves have now imitated our lease brigade. That's made the villagers' envy worse — people who don't work much are angriest. They don't see you sweating. They just see you in the store with money in your hand."

13

"I ASSURE YOU," said Lev Abramovich, Gosagroprom's ancient official greeter, keeper-in-line of foreign delegations, apologist for Ivanovo region agriculture, and would-be earthworm farmer, "I travel around, and the barn you are about to see is the worst in the area."

The delegation piled in and Nikolai drove an old jeep across a bumpy wheat field on Farm Trudovik. He stopped and spoke to several men who lounged beside a halted combine — a standard work brigade on a standard day. This was expansive, flat country. Even in midsummer the air felt thin, a breeze away from the Arctic. Far across the big grain fields, a ribbon of low pine woods underlined the broad gray sky. The vista reminded me of Maine's potato counties. We drove on.

We pulled up in front of yet another tumbledown cattle shed. We'd passed worse barns on the forty-five-minute drive out from Ivanovo to Shuya, but this one was the barn that Nikolai Petrachkov had given over to the lease brigade headed by Volodya Kurikhin. Lev the greeter was not above spin control. "The barn sags," he said. It did, but the roof looked sound. I was naive enough to feel excited. Nikolai had praised Volodya Kurikhin so strongly I felt as though I were about to meet the hope of Russia.

He wasn't prepossessing, which was proper for a savior. Volodya Kurikhin's gestures were restrained — a shy glance at the visitor, a hand barely proffered. Compared to the charismatic and routinely hearty Party men with whom I'd been keeping regular company, Volodya seemed a faint hope. He stood just under six feet tall, with short sandy hair and a completely cock-eyed grin — a right-sided smile that he delivered with head listing to port.

How long, I asked, had he been a member of Farm Trudovik? He shook the listing head. "I'm not a member. On my residence papers I am still registered as an electrician from Shuya. I worked on many new barns, including the new barn that sits here." He pointed at the building. "I was finished and I moved on to other farm wiring jobs. But in May I came back here to milk cows."

We strolled across his barnyard and at my suggestion clambered up ten tiers of hay bales to the tin roof of the big, open shed. It was clean and quiet. We had a good view. I arranged a bale as a desk, opened my laptop, and wrote looking out across Volodya's fields. It was a splendid, sunny afternoon. Nikolai drove off to see some other work crews. Volodya, the other Mark, and I were high above Lev, who, in his seventies, didn't climb bales but hung out down below, hoping to hear the conversation. We spoke quietly.

"I spent five years as an independent builder," Volodya said. "I started working with my father during summer vacations while I was still in school. He taught me. He built everything with his own hands. But he is a stronger personality than me. He has great stamina and strong will. I have a long way to go to rival my father. He's a pensioner now, sixty-nine years old. But he's still as strong willed as ever. One time, years ago, right in the middle of celebrating the anniversary of Soviet victory in the Second World War, he said, 'I won't drink anymore.' And he never had another drop. There was no big fight. No party got too wild, no sickness, no legal incident. He had simply made up his mind. And he did his work the same way. I hate working eight to five, with a time card. I'm like a Cossack — independent. Everyone has to find what is right for him. I think I was influenced by my dad.

"That's why this new lease-brigade announcement was interesting to me, because of my dad. I didn't know much about how to farm. I knew barn building. I have no information about how independent farmers in the West work. Television shows some Western farms for a minute now and then. I've picked up a little from that. And I met some Swedish farmers who were on tour here, but that was back when we were just starting. We are learning as we go on this farm." Far below, I saw our keeper, Lev, pacing in the sunshine, looking up in our direction now and then, but mostly just watching others in Volodya's brigade coming and going at their work. Volodya laughed.

"We depend on Nikolai Petrachkov, because he is the chairman here on Farm Trudovik. We stay dependent as long as we can only rent this place. We can't own it. The collective farm still has authority over us. If the chairman of the collective farm became unfriendly, it would be hard for us to survive. Nikolai Petrachkov has provided us with good land, a tractor, other equipment. At the beginning I felt he was the only guy who supported us here. Now I feel the situation is becoming more normal. Other people in the community who were envious are getting used to us. Their tempers have subsided. They are paying less attention. I'm still wary that politics will change in the whole country, or even here on the farm."

In retrospect, these words of Volodya's appear prescient. Had more damage befallen him in the years after he uttered them, they'd make a fit start for a tragedy. Volodya's fate would teeter soon. But the tragedy was Russia's and had been written long before Volodya came on to play his small part. When Volodya's life would change, his small subplot would move toward the comic, not tragic.

"The problem is that everything, that includes the cows, still belongs completely to the collective farm. We're not even allowed to rent the cows. They're supplied for free, but only because Nikolai Petrachkov says so. The farm can take them back, and controls all decisions about them. We can't cull out a single bad cow and send her to be slaughtered without the collective-farm zootechnician's approval. We have a cow as big as a railroad car who gives hardly any milk. She just eats. If I had my way, I'd sell her for meat and buy a calf of good breeding with the money. We wrestled back and forth for months before the zootechnician let us get rid of ten terrible cows. There are ten more we would sell if we could.

"They have their own politics on the collective farm. This country has a meat shortage and a milk shortage. My big problem is a lack of high-protein feed. That would make my cows give more milk. The zootechnician here is just looking for a big cow population so she can write down the census number and fulfill her quota. But she's not looking for quality. The chief economist doesn't care about growing high-protein cow feed. She's just got crop quotas to count. But you take this old peasant lady I know here, with a cow of her own, and she gets 9,000 liters of milk a year! The regular dairy brigades here on Farm Trudovik never even get 3,000!

"After just a few months, I have proved that a higher yield is possible. We're already above 3,000 liters in this old barn. But it will take us three years, not one, to make a good herd — if they let us. I'm pushing the collective farm to double my land. With our number of cows, the norm is about two hundred fifty acres, and we don't even have half that. I think Nikolai Petrachkov agrees with me. What I need is the chance to grow my own feed. I don't want to depend on the poor stuff the others here produce. I want to grow other types of grain than what they grow here — several fields in a rotation. I want to grow turnips, and perennial grass, and vetch. And if we had the right equipment, we could manage the whole hay crop with one worker.

"We can't buy feed grain — we don't have money, and anyhow, none gets sold here; it all belongs to the farm. But we could grow it! And if I grew oats, which are in short supply, I could sell them and maybe use the money to buy other feed. There also isn't enough technical information for a small operator like me. We need foreign sources on that. My father-in-law teaches English at a college here; he could translate. I hear American farm magazines advertise good breeds of cattle. But where would I buy such a magazine? I'll tell you a mystery. We have lots of okay Russian handbooks about how to farm, but still the situation doesn't improve. It deteriorates!"

In the midst of Ivanovo district's agricultural mayhem, Volodya Kurikhin burned with a fervent ambition unusual in the USSR. He was near to winning the rarest privilege in the nation: a chance to do a complex job very well. We clambered down from the haymow, and there was Lev right below us, hustling away lest we imagine he'd been trying to listen in.

Volodya had organized a tiny office for himself inside his rundown barn. Cows lowed and munched cud outside the doorway. He'd slept there the night before — a greasy old quilt and crumpled newspapers spotted with food lay on a cot. Farm records were strewn on a board table. He was attentive to his job. I told him he was the first ambitious guy I'd met in weeks. He smiled grimly and said, "Some of my crew feel as I do, although one or two think this work is just a job, same as everywhere else."

His next line could have been scripted for a U.S. Information Agency propaganda film: "But even if someone is interested only in money, he'll still work hard for us. Because he knows that if he does, he'll get much more money. In this lease brigade our salaries are equal. Because I work hard, and even sleep here at night next to the cows, I'm in a good position to say to others on the crew, 'See here, I work hard and so should you!'" Volodya sounded like a manager.

His confidence was backed by a document filed in the office of the quota-conscious farm economist. Volodya and Nikolai Petrachkov had made a contract for the use of this barn, a kind of folk-lawyerly attempt to set down the rights and duties of both parties. It essentially created a mutually imposed zone of law in a nation with little business law. Contracts with workers were rare, and when they existed, often amounted to no more than a sentence or two asserting that workers would work and be paid. This mongrel, homemade, topsy-turvy manifestation of both sides' wish for law was Nikolai's attempt to back himself, to render more legitimate and safer his authorization of an ideologically iffy and locally unpopular enterprise. He'd courageously gone ahead and supported Volodya in a time of new possibilities and continuing uncertainty. And he had done this in a place where private effort for private gain was considered selfish and immoral. That was doctrine drummed into children all through school.

The contract was redolent of the time and place. I include much of it, and trust that even skimmers will stop and regard clause 7 of section III, a spot presaging change for Volodya. The contract, dated May 10, 1989, was sloppily typed on sheets of yellowing paper. I've left the language and the careless indications of numbers intact:

AGREEMENT ON RENT SUBCONTRACT FOR MILK PRODUCTION WITH BOARD OF FARM TRUDOVIK

Collective Farm Trudovik of Shuya District, Ivanovo Region, which we'll subsequently call "the holder of the rent," represented by the Chairman of the collective farm, N. A. Petrachkov, acting according to rules of accounting inside the collective farm, and the employees of the farm, represented by Mr. Vladimir Kurikhin, whom we will subsequently call "renter," signed the following agreement for the duration of 1989–1994, and the subject of the agreement is as follows:

I. Obligations of the renter

1. The renter undertakes an obligation to produce and sell to the holder of the rent the following output: 60 heads of cattle, milk calculated from annual yield per cow 3,000 liters, total delivery of milk 1,800 centners [180,000 kilograms], number of calves [by weight] 27 centners, dung 600 tons. Price: total: price per unit, per centner, 35.23. Price for meat of calves 3.08 kg. Dung: 1.50/ton.

2. Total price: of produce they deliver annually, 72,630 rubles. The expenses of the renter are assessed at 53,600 rubles. The income of the renter should be 19,000 rubles. The renter also undertakes the obligation to use effectively 60 heads of cattle, which he undertakes as part of his rent.

3. He undertakes the obligation to inseminate the cows. He has also to follow the health manual and adhere to veterinary and sanitary demands. Also he has to comply with demands of fire regulations. He shouldn't allow pollution of the environment.

4. The renter has no right to sell, or to pass to someone else, the things he has from the rent holder. He has to be careful of the property he rents, and use it effectively according to this treaty, and also fix it at his own expense. He also has to do everything for the health of the

cattle that the zootechnician will order. The lease brigade has to pay a rent of 1,839 rubles per year, or has to pay rent every month in the sum of 153 rubles 26 kopeks. They have also to pay for all the materials supplied to the renters by the holders, and for all services rendered by rent holder. They also have to order on time from the rent holder all the equipment, material, transport, and help they need. They also have to pay attention to the production of dung, and sell it to the rent holder for 1.5 rubles a ton. They have to move the dung on their own up to 2 kilometers, or pay to move it in this radius. They have also to do initial accounting of their activity.

II. Obligations of the rent holder

1. We are passing to the lease brigade for the duration of our treaty the following means of production: cow shed, open shed for hay, well, and water heater. Total price: 1,839.07 rubles.

2. To pass to the brigade land, total price 2,400 rubles.

3. To self-feed, using the internal price within the collective farm, that which is necessary to supply the cow in a way that will produce 3,000 kg. of milk/year . . . [The document details what sort of feed, and what prices: hay, silage, concentrates, potatoes, grain mix, salt, and precipitate at a total cost of 34,839 rubles, and suggests that in the calculations two measures of haylage equal one measure of processed grain.]

4. To use veterinarian service to serve the cows . . . [for some specified charges].

5. To fix the barn and the shed [as specified] . . .

6. To help the renter with transportation and other types of services in a way that was already coordinated — electricity, transportation, use of tractor park, use of veterinary medicine, other services . . . [in return for specified fees for each].

7. The collective farm undertakes an obligation to instruct the staff on proper use of equipment, firefighting rules, special uniform supply if needed, and special boots according to the norms.

8. We'll buy from the renter all produce according to this agreement in quantity and quality, and we undertake to buy his produce above this agreement at the following prices: . . . [prices follow].

9. The value of over-quota dung goes up too.

10. The milk should have content of 3.7% fat. If lower, we will adjust price.

11. If renter gets sick or goes on vacation or something else, the

collective farm will find a substitute, but the renter will have to pay the salary of the substitute.

III. Other conditions

1. Agreement will be valid from 5/10/89 . . .

3. Electricity will be paid for at one kopek per kilowatt-hour . . .

4. . . . treaty could be prolonged and both sides could agree to change certain parts of the treaty . . .

6. If a member of the lease brigade gets hurt on the job, the collective farm takes care of him, and compensates him if he loses the ability to work.

7. After every year, the treaty should be looked into again and some changes can be made.

IV. Still additional conditions

1. The renter can open his own financial account. [This was a major point. Control of spending means decision-making autonomy. No normal brigade had it.]

2. If one of the sides feels the agreement has been violated, it should be looked into by both sides not later than three days after notification . . .

5. During the summer period, the renter can hire additional workers, but the renter has to pay them himself.

6. The rent holder gives the renter cropland where he can produce feed for the cattle, but the renter has to farm it himself and has to pay for the feed he collects on this land.

V. Final conditions. Appendix.

. . .

2. The treaty is concluded in two copies and each side keeps a copy. It must be signed by the farm chairman on one side and every member of the lease brigade on the other. If we have a disagreement over the execution of the agreement, we can bring it to the attention of the Shuya Court. It becomes valid after we sign the act transferring the cattle . . .

7. The lease brigade has to collect a special fund, 10% of its income, to have money to pay for the vacations, sick leaves, etc., of brigade members.

8. The members of the lease brigade can count their work as part of their work for the collective farm [for computing pension benefits].

VI. Responsibilities

1. If both sides violate this treaty frequently, then they may feel it proper to make it void before it expires.
2. The lease holder has to pay a fine of 20% of the price of the feed that he doesn't deliver on time to feed the cattle.
3. If the renter won't deliver the produce as described, he has to compensate by paying money for it.
4. If something from the property is stolen from the renter (the tractor), he has to pay the full price of the property to the holder.

Signed, Nikolai Petrachkov, and 6 members of the brigade, firstly, Vladimir Kurikhin.

"Volodya is a good farmer now," Nikolai Petrachkov said as we worked through a new delivery of special-guest food at supper with Taisa. "He was not when he started. An electrician I'd never met helped wire a new dairy barn for me. Then he came to me and proposed a small farm, in line with Gorbachev's edict permitting lease brigades. After many meetings I felt he was serious, so then we worked out the contract you saw. We gave them the old abandoned barn. Our zootechnician selected sixty animals. I admit that they were the worst on the farm, but that's what she gave them.

"This summer, for the first time, Volodya and his brigade are working 107 acres with two tractors we also gave — no, *rented* is the word. They pay rent to Farm Trudovik. The farm economist knew how to figure out the rent for the tractors and barn. This is not completely new. As for renting land, that is confusing. In the end, the lease-brigade members earn about twice what others at Trudovik earn, but work longer, harder hours. They produce more. We buy all their milk, for an average of thirty-five kopeks a liter. The state supplies us with thirty-eight kopeks for each liter we deliver. We get another subsidy that makes it fifty-four kopeks, so we actually profit almost a ruble for every five liters we buy from Volodya and sell to the state plant, which by the way gets seventy-four kopeks when it sells the milk.

"I don't understand the fees I myself set these people. I don't know why we pay them thirty-five kopeks for milk when we get thirty-eight. And why doesn't Volodya share our subsidy? Is the overall amount too little or too much? I don't know anything about land rent either. We charged fifty-five rubles a hectare, because that's the amount our farm records show we profit from each hectare of the farm. But I suspect even that's wrong — somehow not the right logic. For one thing, we have fewer headaches than before. They perform so well, we seldom hear from or see them. They take care of growing and finding their own feed. They've already improved the building, which was poor. They've got the tractors running, and they maintain them. They have almost never shown up in my office with unexpected problems.

"On our books, we still pay out exactly the salary that we did before for maintenance of those sixty cows. But we pay six people instead of twelve. And I have to say, that makes some of the people in our town angry at them, and at me. 'Look,' the people say, 'the land belongs to the collective farm. The cattle also belong to the farm. So why do you allow those people to make a killing out of our common property? They don't share their money with everybody. How can you allow that?' Not everybody complains — the old babushkas don't care. They have small, fixed incomes. It is not hard for me to handle. This experiment should be here."

Taisa was more direct. "The complaints come from loafers, too lazy to work hard," she said. "They're a kind of union of sluggards, young and old, men and women, paid all their lives not for the quality of their work but for literal execution of their orders, without a care in the world about quality."

"Unfortunately," said Nikolai, "some people don't like their good work or their high pay. It bothers people who earn half as much, and don't see Volodya in the barn fourteen hours a day, then sleeping right there, getting up during the night to tend new calves. Envy has no logic. These others could work harder and earn more, too. Volodya and his crew are the only ones who have asked for a lease brigade. I hope more people will see that this way is good for our farm and country.

"Our industry will have to do some *perestroika*. There is untilled land that should be given to small farmers — I can't say that there are huge sections in central Russia, but there are some; in Siberia, of course, there are more. But as long as we don't have basic laws on land or property, I am not even sure that what I have done is legal. Volodya's crew can't own cattle — they can't even buy a cow that the collective-farm zootechnician doesn't want. She, not Volodya, is still in charge of Volodya's lease brigade's herd. And I am still in charge of their barn and land. The whole situation is undefined. That's why the envy remains."

◆

After breakfast, in the middle of my week's visit, we again sat in Nikolai's office at Farm Trudovik. Nikolai read mail, responded to questions from crew chiefs and aides who ran in and out. He planned his day. He had to keep the harvest going and construction projects working. "Volodya's farm has been in operation just three months. The contract is a real agreement," he said. He wanted to review its production numbers, and gave a few commands over the phone.

The farm economist strode in. Liubov B. Zotina sat with a straight back and spoke, the other Mark assured me, with clipped, precise speech: "To date on the special unit: Milk per cow: consistent 15 percent overfulfillment of their plan. In May, June, and July projected average yield per cow was 325 liters. Actual average was 364 liters." What she did not say — although Nikolai looked up the numbers later — was that Volodya's group also outstripped Farm Trudovik's production. In May, June, and July, Trudovik cows averaged 284 liters of milk. And, given the worst cows and the worst building, Volodya started out doing 25 percent better, and three months out was a third better. Increases in yield on dairy farms are hard won. The numbers were impressive.

Nikolai called in the chief zootechnician, Nadezhda A. Shashkova. She sat, ankles crossed and face stern, and reluctantly recited her digest of Volodya-related facts: "He's got basically the same quality herd we have on the rest of the farm." Nikolai had just said that this very person had assigned the lease brigade the worst cows. "On my authority we have sent for butchering ten of sixty cows, and I am looking at eliminating another six. Our average cow lasts six or seven years. By regulation, we may cull only barren cows or those with 'atrophy of the udder.' Otherwise we are required by law to keep every one and push milk production even in less productive animals." This amazing regulation made no sense for any farm wanting to maximize milk production. American cows last about four years in herds. Such turnover is a part of high production.

So I asked the zootechnician a question she may have found bold, or even rude: how did she feel about doing her job less well than she knew how in order to make the record look good; how did she feel morally? Surprisingly, she smiled. "I feel frustrated and terrible after many years of work in our agriculture. We've always had to follow certain procedures contrary to science and common sense. In the past few years, under Gorbachev, we've started to breathe a little more freely."

I asked if she was surprised that Volodya had gotten good results so quickly. Nikolai was a kind man; he saved her embarrassment by answering. He said, "I hope it's the first bird of summer. I can't encourage others yet, with no law to back me up. When there is, I'll start more lease brigades. We can't raise productivity following the old path. Lease brigades seem like the surest available way toward change. Look at those statistics — in labor productivity, these city boys already do as well as our most experienced milkmaids! They even harvested and stacked their own hay, I see, which somehow isn't part of their productivity data — and which milkmaids don't do."

"I'll add hay activity," the economist said glumly. She saw me studying her and offered a slight, strained grimace. The farm zootechnician's face mirrored the expression. They were disapproving underlings. They didn't like Nikolai Petrachkov's sponsorship of Volodya, and had every reason not to be pleased with this candid discussion.

14

IN FEBRUARY 1990, *Farm Journal*, one of the most widely read American agricultural magazines, published an article about Volodya. Under the headline "Soviet Agriculture Opens One Eye," Volodya's cockeyed grin and sharp eyes shined in full color. The hyperbolic caption read, "[Volodya] has been entrusted by the Soviet government with his own herd of dairy cows. Since going on his own, he has about doubled milk production." I quote him saying, "I wanted to build something with my own hands. And I wanted to see what I could do — to show everyone."

That same month, the regional boss, Aleksander Aleksandrovich Sorokin, had phoned from a hotel in Texas. He'd traveled from Shuya, prospecting joint-venture contracts with an old Colorado fur trader and a company that wanted to sell to the Ivanovo government a turnkey factory producing frozen French fries.

That summer, finishing with business in Moscow, and holding train tickets back to Ivanovo, I was laid low by a virus in a steaming, screenless, mosquito-infested hotel room. After four days, a doctor was about to assign me to a cholera ward when the fever broke. I had just a few days for a hurried trip north.

I wanted to see what a year and a half on the job had brought to Volodya's lease brigade — among the first workers in decades at liberty to farm Mother Russia well, thanks to the friendly farm chairman. I'd left Nikolai Petrachkov anticipating a law on property so he could start other lease brigades and Volodya could buy his sixty cows and move clear of the collective farm's adversarial zootechnician and economist. Nikolai also was anticipating a law on land, so he could sell Volodya his land and then enough more for his brigade to sustain its herd. The farm would then be someplace Volodya's children and his partners' children might gladly inherit.

I took the train to Ivanovo with an interpreter named Yelena, a graduate student whom Viktor Lishchenko suggested. We went to Sorokin's office. "How's Volodya?" I asked. Sorokin said, "I've heard he's got family troubles. His wife — I heard his wife complained about his farming."

"But I have an interview on tape. He says how proud she is and that she approves his hard work."

"Well," said Sorokin, shrugging, dismissing Volodya in favor of more important topics, "ask Nikolai Petrachkov."

I listened to Sorokin's talk about the French-fries factory (coming soon) and the blue-fox farm (thriving) instead. "My views on capitalism changed with my trip to America," he said. "Now I know we have had a unique situation here in the USSR." He said it sarcastically. "If you want lunch, you can't have any because our cafés are closed. I want to pay money for food, but I can't. When we have all-night restaurants, you'll know our state monopoly has been killed." How long would that take? He gave one of those confusing Russian responses that support opposing views: "We are very close. We are just at the beginning." That quieted me down.

I drove the forty-five minutes back out to Shuya. At high noon, Nikolai greeted me like an old friend, clapping me on the back, grinning. I'd rarely felt so warmly welcomed anywhere. He still looked like a country-and-western star. His pompadour yet waved, with no gray in it. Without a word, a distracted waitress laid out another cold gray lunch at the Teza restaurant. Nikolai and I discussed America, not business. Then we jounced out of town in his jeep — but not to Farm Trudovik. We went to a ground-floor office in a cement administration building on Farm Gorky, the farm down the road. This was Nikolai's new command post. A reassignment to his home farm had come through.

Nikolai, reluctantly at first, filled in events. The previous May, the old chairman of Farm Gorky had retired, after twenty-one years on the job. Farm Gorky was where Nikolai had lived all his life, even while heading Farm Trudovik. Taisa Stepanovna stayed on at her post as chief economist at Gorky. Local soviet and Party officials, both represented by none other than Sorokin, had consulted (by looking in the mirror?) and jointly offered Nikolai the job: "Sorokin asked me to do it. He said it would be difficult for an outsider to take on."

Nikolai sat at the long table that nearly filled this new, smaller office. The same portrait of Lenin hung behind him. Taisa came in and out, half listening, working at her own projects. "Things have changed," he said. "The Party has backed away even further from daily management, but the soviet won't take up the slack. So I have less dictated to me from above than a year ago." His succession to his new job, he said, hadn't quite been routine. At his election, a last-minute opposition candidate had materialized despite Sorokin's unanimous recommendation. Nikolai had driven a tractor at Gorky before rising through the ranks; his wife was well respected; he'd won easily, but there had been a contest.

"I considered staying on at Farm Trudovik," Nikolai said, "to finish the projects I'd started. But I couldn't resist the new job." Not only had he grown up on Gorky, but it was larger, more fertile, and richer, and he liked the prospect of having his wife guarding his back, in place of the contrary staff at Trudovik. "I lacked complete harmony there" was his polite understatement. Taisa and Nikolai, on the other hand, seemed to like each other genuinely. Their conversations had a playful, needling edge that only solid couples chance. "I've become Taisa's *official* boss," he said, "but still not the *real* boss."

And how did his start at Gorky compare with his Brezhnev-era first months at Trudovik? Had the Party's retreat from supervising simplified transition? "Before Gorbachev, I didn't have to think at all. Now things are more realistic, and more complicated. I have more leeway to decide which fields I will plant with which crops. But we still are part of a command economy. There's no market economy here, only talk about market economy. The state buys our grain. And things are harder. Some Party power has shifted to the soviet, to farm chairmen, and even to workers. In the long run this might help feed the USSR.

"But frankly, the old way was more businesslike. I have big headaches. We've been building small apartment buildings, because good housing helps keep good workers. On some farms only old people stay. A Gosagroprom construction office, strictly controlled by Communists, used to police tardy builders. Construction officials could lose Party membership, so bosses pushed workers. This function has shifted to the local soviet, which doesn't manage things at all. We planned three buildings, each with twelve apartments. Two should have been done by now, the third by fall. The builders didn't even start the third, and I guess they won't. Our soviet has paid no attention — it's as if it doesn't want real power."

He asked what American farmers did, and when I said they hired builders themselves and negotiated payment schedules that penalize delay, he liked it. Details of market relationships seemed marvelous to him, and he did not want to hear that they sometimes got complicated in reality. "We can't influence our builders that way. There's no arbitration, no contract, no law really, just procedures. We didn't need much law when we had strong Communist authority. Now builders will wire a house but not string the wire from the pole. For two weeks, I've struggled to make them do just that. Before *perestroika*, I'd just phone the Party secretary and he'd raise hell. Now builders say, 'Why bother with time-consuming final details?' Their payment is in already, because of reforms — we now build from our own funds, so construction organizations demand payment in advance. They have the power now."

Nikolai finally got around to the topic on my mind.

"The return to my home farm brought just one painful regret — the move let loose troubles that brought Volodya Kurikhin's farm down," Nikolai said. Volodya had needed Nikolai's protection right from the start — that was normal for a reform experiment in the tangle of bureaucracy connecting every job. A Soviet rule: if a corner of the economy worked, it was a protected exception. Like the wealthy collective farms I'd visited whose chairmen had found patrons high in the Party, Volodya's lowly but prosperous lease brigade had worked out because it had special protection. It had started after Volodya impressed Nikolai who'd impressed Sorokin who'd impressed some big boss in Moscow (perhaps Viktor Lishchenko), forming a chain of personal impunity that warded off righteous bosses, bitter zootechnicians, and the envious neighbors who hated communal resources producing private gain. Patronage in the old system hadn't just protected corruption; the islands of progress were even more dangerous to the system and had required more protection.

Nikolai's move over to Farm Gorky broke Volodya's chain of patronage. Farm Trudovik's new chairman was "a careerist, a conservative, normal chairman," Nikolai said, "a good chairman" who "knows how to farm" and who "was educated at a fine agricultural institute." The new boss "had previously managed a collective farm, and is younger, so he'll be able to build Farm Trudovik for years."

Nikolai smiled. Taisa had come into the office and sat down to hear this part of the tale. She stated the sad truth: "Nikolai's replacement did not believe in lease brigades." While apologizing for showing up a system he loved but mistrusted, Nikolai was spilling the beans, and Taisa liked the discussion. She was angry and bold. "The ladies you talked to with my husband in the office last year — that zootechnician, the economist — would have said the opposite if they'd been alone — that Volodya's performance was mediocre, that allowing an outsider like Volodya on their land, especially to make such big money, was improper. The zootechnician had a big fight with her own husband before he joined that brigade. Nikolai couldn't throw his full support behind Volodya. He felt worried with no laws on property or land. Those laws still haven't really come, although we expected them. Nikolai felt the future of Soviet farming lay with the lease brigade — and private land, too. He wanted to transfer Volodya to a better barn."

Nikolai spoke up: "The Germans attacked us; we won the war; but they live better than we do. Maybe with wiser leaders we could have done better by now. Gorbachev recognizes that our main problem is that people can't take initiative. It is crucial. The case of Volodya demonstrated that things can change if you allow people initiative. I'd buy my collective farm if I had money and law permitted. It's a pity that seventy years of Soviet power haven't given the average Soviet man an adequate philosophy so all collective farm members would really take responsibility."

I thought that any "adequate philosophy" shy of universal saintliness would have doomed the experiment.

"Now Nikolai doesn't dare create other lease brigades here," Taisa said. "He was frustrated that he couldn't even back Volodya strongly last year. There was enormous resistance to Volodya."

Nikolai said, "Volodya came to me after his troubles over there were just starting. He asked me to let him lease an old barn on a back lot here at Gorky. We'd had problems with some workers on that farmstead, but we solved them and I couldn't give it to him. I never imagined he would act drastically and suddenly drop farming. He'd done it so well. I told him to be patient, and things would be okay."

"Probably it wasn't the new chairman's direct fault," said Taisa, working up a head of steam. "It was the specialists responsible for managing the farm — the economist and zootechnician. The chairman's actions reflected their influence." "Probably," Nikolai said, adding his pointed but diplomatic phrasing, "the managers there were not interested in leasing relations. It was only the interest of the prior chairman." He may have said it angrily.

"Volodya did not stop by to see me again. We didn't even talk after he quit. I think his hopes were shattered. Maybe if he'd built a house on the farm, and tried to become more a part of the village . . . I said we would help with materials. But he went home to Shuya every night, to his wife there." Taisa would not leave even this hint of shared burden for Volodya's demise. "They would have eaten him up alive, even if he'd built on the farm," she said.

We sat drinking tea, and Nikolai said he was surprised this stranger from the West had reappeared. We recalled my week's boarding with them the year before. We caught up on neighborhood news. The plan to turn the grain storage across the road back into a church — had it proceeded? "Not yet," Nikolai said, laughing. And the poor black-and-blue old lady who gossiped out her window whenever Taisa and Dima went to the well — was she still alive? "Alive and eating better. Her daughter visits more often, and took her into Shuya for the winter. The old lady can't walk as well as last year, but she still shuffles around the house." Had Nikolai's project digging a well by the cottage brought running water yet? "I've had no time to finish the job," said Nikolai. Taisa said, "It's my opinion that he simply doesn't want to finish the job. But I'll stimulate him to do so!" He laughed again, pledging he'd work on it next day off.

Nikolai said abruptly, "I heard exactly what happened, and I'll tell you. The people who envied him just dismantled his farm. He earned too much. Volodya's crew always paid precisely, in accordance with each detail of the leasing contract I showed you. They followed the agreement to the letter. But as soon as I left, the new chairman jacked up the land rent. He added other fees.

"I'd promised to repair Volodya's barn at the farm's expense — it was so old, and was farm property, and he paid rent. The first thing they said was 'You must repair it now, at your own expense.' The new chairman piled on so many conditions that Volodya's lease brigade had to stop work and move away. It was a shame. They'd grown high-quality cow feed. They'd increased production. Well, now he's building houses in a cooperative construction brigade. His ideas were split in pieces." Nikolai seemed caught by the waste of it all. He sat silent for a minute.

◆

I proposed that we drive down the road, find the new chairman and that farm economist and zootechnician, and ask for their accounts of what happened.

Nikolai looked up, surprised. He liked the idea, and he grinned and said, "Let's get in the jeep." The flat, drought-browned wheat fields between the two farms blurred by in a few minutes. We jounced into the dooryard of Farm Trudovik's office. Nikolai held up his hand. He would not go in. He would oblige the American delegation in that time of maximal *glas-*

nost, and enjoy imagining the conversation inside, but he would not witness the second-guessing of a hack chairman ensconced by higher-ups.

I opened the door to the office. The secretary wore a cotton housedress, white with little red and yellow flowers spaced evenly on it. "American journalist here to visit with the chairman," my translator, Yelena, announced. Then I was in his office, and we had stumbled upon the right instant.

The chairman was compact and gray-haired, with a pleasant enough smile. He held out his hand and introduced himself: "Drozhin — Vladimir Anatolievich Drozhin." He was amiable and poised enough to be cordial, even though he must have been bewildered by this surprise visit. Then he introduced the economist and the zootechnician, whom I recognized from the year before when they'd worked for Nikolai, and who by chance now sat at the new chairman's side. They recognized me, too. We shook hands. This chairman kept two likenesses of Lenin in view, a portrait and a statue. The office must have already looked like this shortly after the farm started in the 1930s. It had a linoleum floor and walls thick with drab paint. I'd interrupted a staff meeting. The chairman dismissed all but the two women. I explained to him that I'd spent a week at the farm a year earlier and hoped to catch up on events. How was his new job going?

"It's unrealistic to steer a course before getting to know the people. People here seek order, but a manager can't simply command these days. We must find the instruments to make people do what they want to do. But we must not command them. I am trying to follow their ideals and do what they really wish to do," he said. His formal language came right through the interpretation. I marveled at his rhetorical way of recasting strong-arming as execution of the People's will. This was a proper Soviet voice, that of a standard bureaucrat. Here, in the flesh, was the much invoked obstacle to reform that the official reformers I'd met complained about.

I asked about lease brigades in general. He commenced a lecture: "We try turning people toward leasing so they can earn more, and so they will have to remember where money goes. Leasing evokes the interest of workers in the final results . . ."

I felt cranky. "Where's Volodya Kurikhin this year? I wrote

about him in *Farm Journal,* one of America's largest farming magazines. I called him 'the Farmer of the Future' and they ran his photograph."

Chairman Drozhin: He's not here anymore. He is in Shuya.

M.K.: When I was here last year, he seemed so productive and determined.

Chairman Drozhin: It was that old barn! It was uncomfortable for the calves in the winter. We had a warm winter, so he survived, but there were not proper conditions for milking there. I suggested a new barn at another sub-farm, with two hundred cows. But he didn't agree.

M.K.: You offered a similar contract? Same deal?

Chairman Drozhin: Probably — some differences. They should pay for using pasture to graze cows, which they didn't under the last contract. And the cost of land was not properly valued in their lease, so the lease was not properly valued.

M.K.: In other words, too much of the profit went to them?

Chairman Drozhin: Yes, almost all the profit went to them. The moral effect on the community was bad. Maybe my reason was not just economic.

Nikolai's account of Volodya's lease brigade had included low milk prices, increased production, and no increase in total wages paid. Nikolai had suggested that Farm Trudovik may well have turned a good profit on Volodya's effort. The farm economist spoke up, offering another angle on Volodya's demise: "He left because he wanted private enterprise. He didn't want any connection with others here. When he left, he had plans to buy a house in the village. He wanted to buy his own cattle and not mix with the business of others. He can't even find a steady area of employment now. He works nowhere in agriculture. Nobody knows where — something not very down-to-earth!"

The farm zootechnician, who had denied Volodya cow-culling rights even though her own husband had joined the lease brigade, also spoke up: "My husband has returned to his place — in the collective's tractor-driver brigade. It was impossible to live that way! Everybody envied him. There were rumors. People groused. Was I helping him to get special feed for the cows? And when a cow fell ill, there were cries from everywhere — we administrators are responsible for the illness of every cow on the farm, and that lease brigade put us in danger. I would not have let my husband keep working with this brigade, even if it hadn't halted. He might have made a little more money, but he didn't have time for his vacation, and he interrupted his pension."

Chairman Drozhin interrupted with his own further complaints: "They assumed no material responsibility for what they were doing. Leasing means we should get part of the profit of the tenant. We didn't get any. So we really had no payment for leasing, and if you do not have stable leasing payments, how can you have leasing at all? Still, I can't say it was an entirely economic decision. It was complex, a mixture of circumstances — they'd chosen a farm in such bad condition. But you should understand that nobody drove them away. Nobody closed their farm."

The mysterious deity who opens doors for wanderers chose that moment to intervene. The chairman spoke into his phone, and then announced, "In a minute a visitor will see you." And soon, in lumbered a tall, thick blond man in his thirties with a mild smile and serious, piercing blue eyes. "Loskutov," the man growled, "Aleksander Vladimirovich Loskutov."

"He was on the brigade with Volodya," said the chairman. "He lives here, and he again works on the farm in a regular brigade. You may talk to him. Ask him anything. We have nothing to hide."

I thought a suggestion that we speak in another room would complicate the hospitality. Loskutov also recalled my visit to the barn the previous summer. "What happened to your lease brigade and to Volodya right after Nikolai Petrachkov left?" I asked. There wasn't much room for subtle questions.

"We had worked all year, worked hard," Loskutov said, "and it was an agreeable way of working; the brigade was very strong. We were already discussing how to renew our deal with each other. We were about to promise to work on for at least five years more, as our written contract with the collective farm was for five years. Then, suddenly, at the end of the first year, the farm administration decided on their own to revise our agreement. They insisted we raise the payment for leasing. The economist hadn't changed. She was the same person who had been consulted on the original agreement. But she changed the clauses of the agreement — the same economist." He stared and pointed at her when he said this. Then he looked directly at the chairman. I was moved by his poise. I didn't know why, but Loskutov was speaking candidly, or maybe guilelessly. "That was really strange. We had paid 54 rubles per hectare, times 47 hectares. According to this new arrangement, we should suddenly pay 260 rubles per hectare — five times as much."

I asked if he'd been given a chance to argue about what was fair, or to negotiate the increase.

"They offered their new version. No discussion. We did not accept it. We waited a month and the brigade dissolved. We'd worked from May '89 to May '90, the entire first year of the agreement. Then we worked on into June. Nothing improved. We closed."

And had he felt a lot of envy and angry feelings toward the brigade on the rest of the farm?

"Closing us down did quiet all the people," he said, and if I understood his tone, it was bitter.

I asked if before talk of closing came up, way back when they'd been working only six or eight months, others on the farm had wished to start similar lease brigades.

The zootechnician interrupted: "Interest in this kind of thing has been decreasing all over the country."

Chairman Drozhin spoke up: "A clause in the agreement said it could be revised each year — not all aspects, but lease price could be corrected. The contract said it should be 'accepted by both sides.' My analysis is that pushing this innovative lease-brigade form of enterprise on the collective farm made ordinary people fight it. In all enterprises I've encountered where lease brigades were introduced, we've experienced the fact that it's not proper. For some reason, participants think leasing and earning higher wages should be linked. But why? Leasing should not be a way of raising wages but a way of raising the effectiveness of the enterprise! Some people don't want to work more effectively, just to earn more money." He seemed sincerely to see no connection between wage and ambition. "Because leasing is a fashion, they try it. I've heard of men working for a year, getting ten or twelve thousand rubles but producing nothing, then quitting a lease."

I asked if that was the case with Volodya.

"No, it wasn't the case with Volodya. With him, the trouble was simply that other people on this farm were paid less, and I think that accounting was improper. No more questions about that . . . but if you want my view of Soviet food shortages, it's this: we who farm produce more and more. The big problems are with processing and storage. Journalists focus on farms, but the main trouble happens after food leaves farms. We supposedly have new abilities to solve problems at farm level, not through a command system. But it's not true. We don't. We are still tangled with funding, and with delivery of machinery. And that's all I have time for."

◆

Nikolai awaited us outside. The whole conversation hadn't taken more than twenty minutes. Loskutov followed us to the jeep. He knew where Volodya lived down in Shuya, he said. He would guide us there. We all tumbled in and, as we sped away, excitedly took turns describing the conversation to Nikolai. He was soon laughing. "Is this how American journalists do their work? I like it. It still does not happen here."

We stopped back at Farm Gorky on the way to Shuya. The sun was setting. Yelena and I had to catch a train in Ivanovo in a few hours. Nikolai ran into his office and reappeared lugging a fat black plastic suitcase. He laid it on the hood of the jeep and made me open it. Inside, a brand-new accordion glistened, a small, gaudy vermilion accordion set with rhinestones and filigree. He laboriously wrote out a document that would bring it through customs. "A gift from the workers of Farm Gorky," it said, "to a good journalist." I refused it, and watched him load it into the back of the jeep anyhow.

"Volodya," Nikolai said, standing by the jeep and summing things up with his gentle indirection, "has probably stopped believing our leaders' promises that things are changing." He added a bit of news. "I happen to know he's just been dealt another disappointment. Ivanovo authorities were asked to send a young farmer to West Germany for further education. I suggested Volodya, but they turned down my suggestion."

Still, Nikolai remained a Party defender. "A leader like Gorbachev can introduce a new system. But if the farm managers won't accept it, it won't work. Managers have to support a leasing system and take steps that lead further on." Nikolai sounded pensive, but he was a deeply optimistic man. "You know," he said, smiling, perhaps at himself, "we could make our collective farm a corporation with shareholders. We may not be prepared to give over land to private ownership, but shares could be a step. A shareholder who became a pensioner could get income from prior work. A worker who moved away would have to sell back shares." This was, in fact, what would happen to most collective farms two years later, after the Party fell. It would leave the same men in charge, and they would still have the same problems with individual incentive and responsibility. Few chairmen were like Nikolai Petrachkov. Nikolai and Taisa and I pledged that we would meet in another few years for the next chapter of the saga, and Nikolai's driver drove us off to Shuya in search of Volodya. We had an hour to spare.

Loskutov beamed. "That economist!" he bellowed. "She whispered in the chairman's ear, told him to change the contract on us. Damn! We were doing so well, even with the worst cows, and we were still going up. Why did they stop us? He told you how they suggested we go to another barn with more cows? He didn't tell you it was to join a big regular work brigade, and we wouldn't have had any control over who did things. We'd just be workers there. He told you our barn was unhealthy? Our cows were healthy. They told us all that nonsense, and finally we lost our enthusiasm. Not just us. There were other people on the farm who were thinking of doing the same thing. Their enthusiasm got smashed, too."

We drove past the Teza restaurant into the back streets of Shuya, past factories and warehouses and anonymous blocks of flats, piloted by Loskutov. Opposite the police station we turned into a pitted dirt parking lot. Loskutov disappeared inside a drab apartment building. The sun had set. Heavy clouds edged with pink hung in the sky. Rain splattered for a few seconds. Grandmothers gabbed and tiny children still played around the building. I stood watching. Volodya's neighbors stared back.

Three young men bent under the hood of an old Lada, speculating about its symptoms. The Soviet Union (at least Russia) was the only place I'd been where bystanders avoided chats, all signs of friendliness and recognition, and even eye contact with strangers. They peeked a lot but stayed far away. If circumstances led them into approved contact, they'd warm up. The problem wasn't coldness, however, it was a habit of caution that long preceded *glasnost*. I counted dozens of furtive stares.

Loskutov dashed back. He'd found Volodya's wife, Olga. A neighbor would mind their two sons. She would come right down. She might be able to find Volodya. Olga ran toward us, breathless. She'd obviously just thrown on a sweater and dabbed spots of rouge on her cheeks. She was small and shy and seemed work-weary but eager. "Volodya spoke about your visit last year," Olga said. "He might be at his construction brigade's workshop — it's just a few blocks away." She crowded into the jeep beside Yelena, and we all twisted through Shuya's streets. We stopped before a ramshackle garage and Olga ran in. She came out shaking her head. "His truck headed up to Palekh a few minutes ago. He will be sorry."

"So are we," I said. "But let me ask — do you recall the moment he came home and said his rent was being raised and he'd have to quit farming?"

"He was angry! He yelled. They'd increased production. But then the new chairman raised the price on him, charged more for land, cows, everything. The agreement they were offered would have meant they'd be farming for no pay at all. Volodya said it was designed to make them quit. They weren't expected to sign it.

"It happened just before summer, when the best milk price is set. If there was any way they could have continued, they wouldn't have quit. The herd of two hundred cows they were supposed to get — that was phony, too. They wouldn't have had the freedom to work right. There were other bosses running that barn, and it was a standard work brigade. And those cows were very bad, very old. Volodya was supposed to give back the herd they had improved and start all over again! It repelled them to contemplate going back to working with people they couldn't trust. But the big reason may have been that so many farm residents were against them, and told them so openly. Do-nothings came by. 'We can do without you,' they said and, 'Your cows are hungry.' People came right into the barn and found fault with them.

"But I believe you can't even blame those people — Volodya was doing something new. I blame the farm authorities. The new chairman and the farm economist. The chairman met the economist's demands. Nikolai Petrachkov could keep her in line, but the new chairman didn't. She was against Volodya from the start. They struggled to the last day, and right up until then he hoped to stay. *She* said, 'Stop farming.' The collective farm sent in men to close the brigade. They actually went in and moved the cows. Volodya learned something — he'll never start such a business again."

We drove fast and Yelena and I caught the night train to Moscow seconds before it left. After a while, the rocking train calmed us. Train rides had become intermissions. Yelena, who was a doctoral candidate in agricultural economics, stared out at the passing farms as the scenery faded into darkness. "It's too easy to say Volodya was kicked out by the economist and leave it at that," she said. "I think Volodya's problem wasn't the economist, or the new chairman. The problem is that up to now our people have rejected new structures. Volodya was too visible. Life on a farm is too open. In factories there are successful lease brigades. Our leaders thought the form would fit agriculture best, and it hasn't. Those six or eight workers set a pattern that might have taken away the jobs of half the villagers. A farm has a ceiling on payroll. The government lets them spend only so much. These few guys took sixty cows' worth of labor opportunity, land, and payroll. A successful national farm-reform plan must not require a Nikolai Petrachkov or an Aleksander Sorokin to supervise the community's cooperation. It must work automatically."

At five-thirty in the morning, the train groaned into Moscow. I caught a few hours' sleep, then had supper with Viktor Lishchenko, who sounded more outspoken than usual. He said he was not surprised that Volodya had been thwarted. I thought to myself that when even the last pro-Party idealists supporting slow change spoke up as Viktor now did, bigger changes could not be far off. "The system we evolved rejects innovations the way a body rejects foreign matter," he said, "which has caused our descent in the world economy. That's exactly what's forcing us to change so much. Our country is full of innovators, but the system rejects them all. Volodya's successful lease brigade immediately established a showcase that proved the system is wrong. So he was wiped out. Economic adventurousness is permitted in the USSR again and again, but only on sufferance. And that muddled reach for progress, while still retaining centralized management, leads again and again to the same fate for energetic, creative people. They become organ grinders' monkeys. It's the illogic of pervasive control made manifest." I wished that I'd met up with Volodya again. I still wanted to know how the person with this dual role — both energetic, creative man and organ grinder's monkey — had fared.

PART V

BACK TO
SOMEPLACE NEW

1992

15

I HAD BEEN BACK in Moscow for sixteen hours and had a big choice to make. It was June of 1992. I sat with my American friends Cindy and Vlad drinking tea. We looked down from their kitchen window at a foul canal and some dingy side streets. Cindy wrote for the *Los Angeles Times*; Vlad freelanced, often writing about exotic far corners of the former Soviet Union. Now that things were opening up, he spent some of his days fighting for access to KGB records of the interrogation of his grandfather, who'd died in custody in the late thirties, before Vlad's father escaped to the United States.

"These days, living in this city is like camping out," Vlad said. He smiled. Vlad had a special way of giving weight to his most casual notion. He'd opine distractedly, then, halfway through, engage eye contact, smile hard, and hold your gaze until you had to smile back, letting him know you got his drift. I smiled back.

I *was* beginning to get his drift. A lot had changed since my last visit, in the summer of 1990. Boris Yeltsin had been elected president of the Russian Federation in June 1991. In August, seven high-ranking plotters had attempted to depose Gorbachev, the president of the Soviet Union. And then the Communist Party had fallen.

I'd found a first difference right at Shermetyevo Airport. It was not business as usual. Formerly, tours of older Americans, Europeans, even Japanese, had choked the baggage area, bunching around their Intourist guides and peering with fearful eyes out into Russia. The tourists were gone. So were the jowly foreign business travelers in dark suits too heavy for the season, heretofore slapping backs, bearhugging Russian counterparts, grinning and saying "Huh, huh, huh." I left the efficient Finnair flight from Helsinki regretfully, in the company of just a few brisk yuppies. They were collected and knew what they were about.

The baggage-cart situation had worsened — if that were possible. I'd always thought of it as the first missed opportunity for capitalist enterprise that travelers encountered on Russian soil: the initial face-off between socialist bureaucracy and naive bearers of hard currency. Year after year, baggage carts had stayed scarce, beat-up, broken, and surly helpers had issued them reluctantly, for small tips. The attempted coup had ended seven decades of Communist Party rule but could not nudge the carts forward. Just a few stomped-on specimens sat about, most missing wheels, handles, and baskets, some upside down, one on end, tumbled into a heap behind a pillar and guarded by an inert young man with soulful, watchful eyes. The lead Finnish yuppie, pert in her business suit, laid hand on a cart. The young man jerked it back. "Not take, all broke," he said flatly. "In that case, get some new ones from outside somewhere and I'll *make* this one work," she shouted angrily. She threw a dollar bill at the man, yanked a cart with only three wheels away from him, and wobbled it across the room toward her piled luggage. He bent and pocketed the fallen bill.

Vlad was bilingual by birthright. He'd just returned from adventures in Tajikistan. "Life's no different in Moscow now than out there," he said. "Less works than ever before. Here or there, you need to bring a knife, can opener, plastic sacks, medicines, soap, toilet paper, passport, string. You need to carry everything and be prepared for anything, like a Boy Scout. Plans may have to change in moments." He looked at me and smiled. I smiled. He poured more tea. "The old regulations have not, in most everyday matters, been supplanted by new ones. They sort of mostly don't apply much anymore, and sort of do," Vlad said. "You can probably go where you want and no one will stop you, even though, technically, you still need those city-by-city visas." I was elated that there was no Party to confine my contacts or acquaintances, but neither was there anyone to lead me to revealing places, and to ease life on the road.

I'd stayed the previous night in the apartment of Viktor Lishchenko, who'd overseen much of the planning of my prior journeys. His usual cordial welcome had changed. He was all business. The moment I'd set down my bags, Viktor had let me know that our years of exchanging collegial favors no longer governed our dealings: "I cannot help you as an individual. The director of the company I and my partners have formed with my institute will arrange your stay. The cost will be one hundred fifty dollars a day." And if I didn't sign up for this deal, said Viktor, "you're on your own. I can't help you at all." A Moscow executive then earned about fifty dollars a month. Viktor and I had traded many favors and confidences over the past five years. What Viktor proposed — perhaps it was the monetarization of a seeming friendship — didn't sit well with me, and it didn't make sense in spite of the advantage it preserved of allowing me to see things from the inside. Power was oozing away from those who'd so long been the only insiders, and there was much to see from the outside now.

For the first time, I could ask any Russian I cared to ask to interpret and help navigate. On four previous outings, I'd nearly always had to make do with translators supplied by the "Soviet side." For ten days of my 1988 trip, a fashionable punker from Zagreb, stringing as a *New York Times Magazine* photographer, whispered heretical translations to me. And, of course, the other Mark, my émigré professor friend, had come along from Boston on my 1989 trip and supplied ad hoc commentary to literal translation. But even on two trips as an invited guest of the Institute for the Study of the USA and Canada and the Soviet Writers' Union, my hosts had doggedly supplied me with an agricultural economist, a political theorist, an automotive engineer, and a tractor maintenance engineer — fine people, all of them, but not a poet in the lot.

Anyone who has planned hard travel through forbidding territory knows that the prospect of a kindred guide commutes trepidation into anticipation. For decades, the Soviet government had preempted the privilege of guide selection, along with so many other acts of personal volition, isolating travelers in bubbles of officialness. Even in the absence of the Party, my prior hosts had obviously been planning another constrained, formal, and now pricey tour for the American delegation, as though nothing had changed.

Things had. Vlad had called me excitedly in Boston a few weeks before I left. He'd thought of the right fellow traveler. The gent was, like Vlad, perfectly bilingual. The candidate and I were the same age. His name was Sergei, and he was also a writer. He knew the countryside, farmers, farming, officialdom. He was not one of *them*. He lived on the edge of the system. He was a dissident, a quiet rebel, a Soviet man who'd found a way to move far outside Soviet society.

There was one problem, Vlad had said. Sergei spent time in Moscow, but mostly lived in a tumbledown log cottage in an abandoned farm village three days' strenuous traveling northeastward, up toward Archangel and Perm. And the village had no phones. There wasn't even a road to it. If Sergei had an American correlate, it might have been a 1960s back-to-the-lander, such as I had been. Sergei would be difficult to contact, and I was coming soon.

"I hung up with you and phoned Sergei's girlfriend," Vlad said at the kitchen table, "and told her about my American friend. She almost cried. Sergei would surely want the work, she said. But alas, he'd left two days before for his village and might not return again for months. The American will have come and gone by then. She said she'd send a telegram, but it probably wouldn't reach Sergei — they usually didn't."

Yet here was Sergei Sylvestre Bronislavovich Sossinsky-Semikhat, lumbering into the kitchen of the tiny apartment, fresh from a morning tennis game. A well-used wooden racket stuck out of his briefcase. He was forty-eight, tall, broad, gray-haired, with a big, bemused smile. I'm sure I seemed bewilderingly gleeful, but he represented my liberation after long confinement — as, it turned out, I did for him. I could cease being the American delegation, my encounters prescribed, dictated, scheduled, approved, and frozen by people interested in managing what I knew and thought. I would move around clear of the exhausting role of dangerous, suspect guest of the gracious Party, shepherded, guided, gentled, blindered, made the best of.

Sergei took up the story: "The same day Vlad called — it was just on a whim — I was already up in Kologriv, the last place with a telephone office, and I remembered something I had to tell my girlfriend in Moscow. I *never* call from the road. I was even amazed to get through. 'Come back,' she said. 'An American is coming.'"

After that call, Sergei had gone on up to his village for a few days, long enough to plant a garden. He had just returned. His journey back from his cabin sounded adventurous to me, although it was a normal commute for him: he'd come downriver by rowboat, then by logging truck to Kologriv, by Aeroflot's local biplane from Kologriv back to Kostroma. Sleeping in friends' apartments two nights en route, he'd made his way to Vlad's table.

I had no trouble making my decision. I laid out the trip I had in mind: we'd travel for six weeks, during which I hoped to return to Ivanovo and find my old hosts Nikolai and Taisa, finally speak with Volodya Kurikhin, and see how independent farms were faring after the demise of the Party. Then, perhaps, we could even go on northward and end up in Sergei's distant village. We'd go to inconvenient places. The conversations would be meticulous. Without an approved itinerary, we'd have to fight off authorities and ruffians. Was such travel possible now, and was Sergei interested? "We can do that," he said.

I brought up money. He hesitantly asked, "Would it be too much if I charge three hundred dollars for the six weeks? I could do it for less." From his perspective, this would be a windfall; translators were common, low-status workers. Those fortunate enough to have retained government jobs made about twenty dollars a month. I had a magazine and a publisher contributing expenses, I told him, and we settled for quadruple what he'd requested.

For the rest of the afternoon we all sipped vodka and talked. Sergei had given up on the Soviet system in a stylish way that Westerners would have trouble imagining. In 1984 a collective-farm chairman he'd befriended had helped him find a broken-down cabin in the "nonprospective" village of Astafyevo and gotten him through the local paperwork. Sergei more or less owned the cottage. In late summer, when the Unzha River was lowest, he could approach his new village by logging tractor, in spring and fall by rowboat, and in winter by an ice road loggers plowed up the spine of the Unzha. If we decided to go on to the place after Ivanovo, we'd find a car or train north to Yaroslavl, get rides on to Kostroma, Kologriv, the muddy river outpost of Chermenino, and upriver to Astafyevo. The friends he stayed with while traveling, Sergei said, would be fun for me to meet. They weren't people whom Americans would expect to encounter in small-town Russia. I'd be surprised at their lives and spirits and views. We clearly were not heading out into the authorized Russia I'd visited before.

Sergei's family had been well known in Russia, Vlad said. Viktor Chernov, the head of the Socialist Revolutionary Party, was his grandfather. The SRP had won election in the tumult of 1917, defeating the Bolsheviks. Chernov had convened and presided over the famed and short-lived Constituent Assembly, which had met for just one night, in January 1918. Bolshevik soldiers had closed it down and seized power.

Sergei grew up hearing from his mother stories about the family in the aftermath of the Bolshevik move. She, two aunts, and Sergei's grandmother were thrown into cells in the basement of Lubyanka, the stone headquarters of the Cheka (later the KGB). The Cheka tortured them — interrogators yelled questions at his grandmother for days, awakening her whenever she dozed. This treatment was a common fate of Cheka prisoners, who called it "the Conveyer." Viktor Chernov succeeded in escaping to Paris. The family eventually was able to regroup there.

In 1944 Sergei was born, in wartime France. Five years later his father took a job in New York with the fledgling United Nations, and the family moved to the borough of Queens, where Sergei went to public school. When Sergei was sixteen, in 1960, with Stalin dead and Russia appearing to Sergei's father to be again on revolutionary track, the family relocated to Moscow, after forty years away. Sergei spoke accentless American English by then, and American-accented Russian. Still, he was required to enroll in the regular English class in his Moscow high school.

The teacher, who probably felt threatened by such virtuosity, punished him for using unapproved idioms. Sergei's father's friends were the artists and intellectuals of the brief "Khrushchev thaw," and they had given the family the confidence to return.

"I'd decided in advance to give it the best try I could," Sergei said. But from the start, his background separated him from his generation of Russian children. He had grown up free of Party discipline. His family was bohemian, intellectual, left wing but freethinking. Back in Moscow, he soon came to feel as much an outsider, because of his Westernization and his adversarial lineage, as he had in Queens for symmetrical reasons.

Faced with the rigidity of Soviet schools, he grew rebellious. He continued studying history through graduate school, where he became a "production section leader" of his brigade of Komsomol — the Communist youth organization that all students had to join. Terming it an official Komsomol activity, he gathered together an exhibition of modern Soviet painting. He mounted it in a hall at an Academy of Sciences institute his Komsomol group had often borrowed, and the artists phoned the international diplomatic corps and invited them. A few hours after the doors opened, the KGB swarmed in and closed the exhibition down. The world press reported the event widely. Sergei's Komsomol supervisor was fired. Sergei was reprimanded. His academic fate was sealed. Eventually, he handed in a doctoral thesis that discussed American scholars' views of the Yalta Conference. It was rejected with only one comment, from an irate Party loyalist: "Where are the quotes from Lenin and Brezhnev?"

Unable to get an academic job, Sergei became a translator for Progress, an English-language, international publishing house most of whose books extolled Soviet glory and Party theory. He translated everything, as requested — political history, propagandistic novels, and children's stories. He remembered a particularly dreadful one about Papa Lenin kindly taking poor schoolkids into his study and feeding them breakfast. With a few exceptions (he found that books of early history were often less politicized than those on recent history), he hated the work.

He liked the literary life surrounding the job better. Stuck with nowhere else to go, he stayed more than a decade. He and his older brother, a professor of mathematics at Moscow University who eventually built an international reputation in knot theory that gave him some freedom, spoke English together as an exotic, secret language. Sergei took summer work as a porter on geological expeditions surveying Arctic regions. He married and divorced twice, and raised seven sons. With the advent of *perestroika*, the state's impulse to produce English-language propaganda diminished, and so did its demand for Sergei's skills. That's when, with no hope of applying his sophistication to compensated work, he moved out of town for good.

In the country, he was surviving on odd jobs gleaned in Moscow. He gardened, hunted, foraged — he'd found a sack of dried corn in a disused chicken coop and boiled the corn into porridge. His brother brought home occasional hard-currency honoraria from conferences, and gave Sergei a few hundred dollars a year, which took care of all cash needs. A huge tank of diesel fuel stood above the Unzha, just a fifteen-minute walk from his cabin, abandoned years before when the regional collective farm had ceased tilling the remote fields up and down the river. Sergei got fuel from there regularly for an ancient outboard engine, and traveled the Unzha by boat.

He had carried up from Moscow to his cabin the few boxes of family papers about his grandfather, and without hope of publication was writing a biography. He had dear friends. They'd show up at his door — loggers from downriver who wanted to drink with him, painters and writers from Moscow who'd made the tough pilgrimage to his village. The Muscovites would stay for weeks, then he'd be absolutely alone for months more, writing and hunting. He'd managed to find an old upright piano at a closed-down regional music school twelve miles away, paid a hundred rubles for it, and, trading vodka for the labor of local farm hands, bounced into the cabin with it loaded onto a six-wheel-drive truck. He tuned it up with a wrench and spent dark winter hours playing Mozart.

I sat at Vlad's table and kept smiling. Sergei's Russia was what I'd been looking for. Travelers had been systematically led past such places. I wanted to see my old haunts in Sergei's company, too. I relished the hard trip to Astafyevo. I felt elated, like someone whose clouded vision could suddenly be remedied with painless surgery.

Late that same afternoon came the surgery. We went across town to Viktor Lishchenko's apartment to reclaim my bags from the realm of authorized travel. Lishchenko stared, saying little as I gathered my things. I felt like a new infidel stepping back onto sacred ground. I'd learned a lot from Viktor, and he'd pointed me toward secret places I surely would not have found without him. As I headed out the door dragging my suitcase, Viktor said, perhaps out of concern, perhaps anger, "This is a dangerous decision." In Russian, he cautioned Sergei: "The old regime is still in force here. Watch your step." Viktor was right, of course. I was moving out from the shelter of his office and away from access to the reform efforts he'd fostered. I was closing off safe contacts as I opened others. I left, still elated but full of dread. For the next few hours I felt like a teenager who knows he is heading off to do the wrong thing and feels sure that's just what he wants to do.

◆

We'd be in Moscow for a week. Sergei had some business to complete. We had contacts to make and rides and housing to see about, now that the Party wasn't doing it for me. Planning in Moscow was hard for anyone used to e-mail messages and faxes and phones that were answered by people who knew answers and took accurate messages and called back. In Russia, calls didn't get through. When they did, people said they'd do things that they wouldn't, or just didn't. Add a couldn't to the list. What I wanted to do — wander unofficially in rural Russia (which was always more easily and fully regulated than the city) — was new at that moment. It hadn't been done by Westerners in sixty years.

Specifically, I wanted to go back to Ivanovo, to territory administered by Aleksander Aleksandrovich Sorokin, who now headed all agriculture in the region. One problem was that Sorokin was Viktor's long-time ally on many projects. Sergei phoned Sorokin, and finally got through. Someone in Moscow (Viktor, I discovered a few years later by asking him when I met him at a conference) had spoken with him first. Certainly,

Sorokin said cordially, he would receive me on my own — for just two hundred fifty dollars a day. This fee inflated twenty-five-fold the going rate for Western business travelers. I shifted strategy. I felt freed by the idea of not doing things the way I had up till now. I would make no further contact with Sorokin. I'd just go and see people I wanted to see anyhow, even if they lived on his turf, and even people beholden and accountable to him — farm chairmen, Gosagroprom officials, workers.

With lessons and encouragement from Sergei, I went local. A Russian with private reasons to visit a distant city would call friends of friends and borrow or rent a couch; there were no hotels for personal travel. Official hotels still asked foreigners for passports and city-by-city visas. We tried many contacts at once, as Russians do; three promised to work out. A journalist friend of a friend of mine had a colleague who'd gone to work on an Ivanovo newspaper. A friend of Sergei's with a beat-up Lada wanted to drive us north. He proposed that we find some woods and just camp out. And Sergei had a second cousin in Gosagroprom who would put us in touch with the Ivanovo chief of Gostekhnika, the agricultural trucking and repair services that supplied Gosagroprom.

Finally the Gostekhnika chief's assistant called the cousin back and said he did have a room he seldom used, with kitchen, and it chanced to be right across from Ivanovo Gosagroprom's office building. We could probably stay there. He'd see. Call back in a few days. We wandered around *unofficial* Moscow while waiting. We called on Sergei's friends, who would have been unpersons on any prior itinerary of mine.

Moscow was transforming quickly. Property was still theft, and everyone was stealing. Only about fifteen hundred store-fronts, according to the newspapers, had opened for private trade at that point, just months after the attempted coup and subsequent events had driven Gorbachev and the Party from power. The People still owned the buildings, and there were no legal grounds for allowing private profit from the People's property. Bureaucrats had no precedent, no procedures, no guidelines for decisions on leases or lease terms. There was no one to take rent, no one to take it on behalf of another, nowhere to bank it. Storefronts that would be ground-floor shops in any European city were simply run-down apartments in Moscow. Prerevolutionary postcards show shop-lined streets and thriving market squares. Moscow's streets had been noncommercial for as long as all but the oldest oldsters could recall. People's lives centered on "obtaining," but not on buying.

Abhorring an economic vacuum, the invisible hand now placed *tolkuchkas* back on Moscow's corners and squares — the word might translate as "black market" or even "places of pushing." *Tolkuchkas* were clusters of steel boxes, kiosks about the size of dumpsters, with windows cut in front. Trucks brought them, actually, not invisible hands. Cranes dangled them by eyelets in the roofs, and dropped them into place. And wherever a few dropped — on a wide sidewalk, at a major intersection, or by a park near a metro station — another busy marketplace developed. Some kiosk operators installed steel flaps that opened out like awnings, and most soon added glass showcases and change windows. Owners shuttered them as securely as strongboxes each evening. Common wisdom said gangs controlled them, tithed vendors for protection, dictated suppliers. Occasionally a colony of *tolkuchkas* would disappear overnight, even though they'd been in place for months. Was it gang warfare, bribery, tax evasion, lingering enforcement of anti-middleman regulation? The cranes came and they were gone. New colonies appeared elsewhere before morning.

The *tolkuchkas* were instantly successful. A bold name, in English, the language of plenitude and swank, announced each: FREEDOM, and MY VALENTINE, and WHAT YOU WANT. The names were alluring. They promised gratification. How unlike those pious, orthodox names the state had imposed on collective farms back in the hungry years of collectivization! I'd like to meet the people who named the *tolkuchkas*. I'd often met the sort of person who'd named collective farms.

The stocks of the kiosks were undifferentiated — no special shoe kiosk, soda kiosk, clothing kiosk, gift kiosk, sports equipment kiosk. MY VALENTINE offered cans of orange soda, a few cans of food from Poland, Bulgaria, and Turkey, one smallish beige leather coat, one length of shoelace, two new toilet seats, a few brooms, vodka, and candy. WHAT YOU WANT had about the same — no coat, more candy, three kinds of beer, more vodka. A kabob stand stood apart, selling only *shashlik* skewers. On later visits, perhaps as gang control consolidated, the items stocked by kiosks grew even more uniform, but stayed unspecialized.

The once-sedate squares surrounding *tolkuchkas* looked like post-Armageddon cyberpunk scenes. Around the gaudy booths, poor, sick ancients in tatters ogled new goods, often sexily foreign goods. Shifty toughs hung out, gossiping, protecting, sizing up the shoppers. Stolid babushkas and squat old men with war medals on their wide lapels shuffled through the rubble that no one ever swept. Beggars with abscessed legs wandered in search of miracles, talking to themselves and passersby and God. Commerce had restarted. The *tolkuchka* scene caught some essence of that first post-Party year — a prohibitive, stodgy former Moscow intact all around, and this overlay of cruel, wild liberty just lowering onto it.

◆

Sergei asked around, trying to connect up with the cruel, wild liberty. The journalist friend of a friend who knew a journalist in Ivanovo had another friend who knew a young gangster named Boris. Boris supplied *tolkuchkas*. We went to see Boris. His mother, Alla, grabbed us as we entered — she had her own business. She was dead set on explaining it to the foreign journalist before her son could talk about Moscow's new food supply routes. Alla had just started up a videotape marriage brokerage. It was already introducing, she said, "pretty Russian girls to Englishmen in London who have the good genes that Russian men lack. Women here can't marry and have healthy kids — only three percent of kids born here are healthy. Male genes have gotten weak. No woman here wants an invalid baby."

They made an enterprising team. Alla beamed like a stage mother when Boris talked about his success. He was short, solid, only twenty-nine, clearly bright and made to feel like the man of the house. He spoke knowingly — about friends, sometimes about himself (I suspect the distinction blurred): "I began with go-carts. They are popular. I won some races and this brought me in contact with a stuntman studio, which invited me to work for them. So I took a job in the film industry. Some of those involved — a cameraman, a scenic designer, a director — decided to set up a new film company. They were deeply artistic people, so I did the business part for them. That's how I started to do business. Under the shield of this company, the circle of my interests grew. Later we formed a group of friends, including several 'legal persons' [corporate shells of some sort]. My mother's brother, who is also twenty-nine, is in the group. Some men in the food supply business thought we could help them. I'm also interested in buying land, because everywhere else in Europe it costs a lot and here the price is cheap. The mechanisms of paperwork, legal formalities, however, haven't been established. Land can serve to secure my new enterprises.

"People here are just beginning to be able to work. Someday we'll pour grain on all of Europe. Friends brought computers into our business — selling them made us a profit of three, four hundred percent. My friends took a tourist trip to Cyprus, and for a thousand dollars got a package of papers in a week for an offshore enterprise in their names. The money we take in will be nearly untaxed. Then my friends returned here and wrote up a contract with their own company in Cyprus to supply something — charging inflated, retail prices. The goods got sold here, without profit, at these prices. But the profit showed up in the markup from wholesale, in Cyprus — untaxed and in hard currency. That's one way they got profits into Europe.

"My friends and I concluded a contract recently in Turkey, buying forty tons of goods — shampoo and chocolate. A guy who went with us put up forty thousand dollars. Here's how the money got out of here for that one: We took credit at a bank in the name of a 'legal person.' By means of various banking tricks, the dollars made their way to a private account in Poland. There's a Polish company, owned by a friend here, that seemed to have nothing to do with Russia — another kind of offshore company. The 'legal person' here and the Polish company concluded a contract — any kind of contract, it didn't matter. Under the contract, though, the credited rubles were converted to dollars. Then our friend who owned the Polish company went and took the money from his account and brought it to Turkey.

"Two big trucks drove the shampoo and chocolate here. The

Turkish firm took them through customs, guaranteed delivery to Moscow. We had security men, but shampoo is not an item robbers take from a warehouse. We then broke up our large delivery and sold lots to people who ran *tolkuchkas* — there's a certain circle of people who know one another. I go in my car and show them samples and make arrangements. The *tolkuchkas* are spontaneous — rackets, of course, but not controlled by state enterprises. They're quite civilized."

Before we left, Boris's mom insisted on screening some of her "girls'" videos. She said she'd advertised in London, and had already sold many copies of the tape. "These twenty-four women received three hundred eighty letters, and some are getting married already, but so far the British embassy has refused to accept these girls." She clicked on the tape. A plain woman in her mid-twenties with dyed blond hair undulated into a living room, rock music playing in the background. She stopped, smiled, and said in a thick accent, "Hello, I am Galina. I like Hemingway and Galsworthy. I like to nurse my granny. I like my friends . . . I am a caring and loving person and shy sometimes, but in general I'm easygoing. My star rising is Aquarius. I am romantic and tender . . . I want someday to have a happy family and healthy children. I want to meet that special partner for whom I can devote all myself and make him happy, and I promise I'll do my best for him. That's all. Bye."

A cute bye. The tape continued, other women also dancing, saying amazing things in coy voices: "I have a dream — I want to swim in the Ocean Atlantic," and "As for my prospective husband, his age and appearance are not relevant. Mutual understanding is." I suspected the young women of not quite knowing what they were dancing toward, and Boris's mom of knowing just where she was heading.

◆

On the edge of Moscow a market had come into its own on weekends at the Vernisazh. The same goods that sold in the *tolkuchkas,* and along New Arbat, also sold at the Vernisazh: *matryoshka* dolls within dolls (both sweet-lass-inside-sweet-lass and dictator-inside-dictator styles), soda, and cheap clothing. Sergei's eldest son, Fedya, had bought an Italian home-knitting machine and sold sweaters there, doubling his tiny salary as a factory watchman. The material wealth of careless organizations also passed into private hands there — husky workmen stood before tables decked with a few spools of wire, some gears and some gauges, pipe elbows and a faucet or two, a new pair of pliers and a used sledgehammer, all likely filched from work. Booths at the Vernisazh did specialize. One had piles of fiddles, clarinets, trumpets, and accordions. A few sold cameras — I bought an old knockoff Leica with an enamel KGB medallion embedded in its case. A Russian friend insisted the medallion had been added just to catch the eye of a credulous tourist.

A dozen booths sold off the vestments of the Communist Party. I bought a velvet banner big as a tablecloth, handmade (the stitcher's initials were hidden under the hem), that read, "UNDER THE BANNER OF MARXISM-LENINISM, UNDER THE LEADERSHIP OF THE COMMUNIST PARTY, MARCH FORWARD TOWARD THE VICTORY OF COMMUNISM," and on its reverse side, "TOWARDS BETTER WORK OF STUDENT TECHNICAL-INDUSTRIAL BRIGADES!" A smaller, rayon flag read, "THIS BANNER IS GIVEN FOR HIGH QUOTA-FULFILLMENT IN THE SOCIALIST COMPETITION." An oxymoron of sorts, awarded some brigade that had won a factory or farm production campaign. This was the year to pick up the paraphernalia of the lapsed regime. A year later, in 1993, the Vernisazh banner supply would have dwindled. There would be fewer, they would be plainer and far pricier. No one was making them anymore.

Along the rear edge of the market fields, Azari rug merchants had piled carpets. I offered a lowish price for a Kilim. "Do you theenk I am baby?" the merchant asked incredulously. "Your shoes costing maybe eighty dollar. Your shirt it's thirty-five dollar. Maybe I know the prices in the world!" And he did. He'd been generous in his pricing of the shirt.

◆

We worked, by phone and in person, consolidating plans for our private assault on Ivanovo. And we continued roaming the new, private Moscow. We had surely stepped through Alice's mirror. Our encounters often felt disconnected, horrifying, sometimes touching. There were rules, but they couldn't quite be grasped.

The daughter of Edward, a historian and friend on whose couch I was sleeping that week, had joined the brand-new Green Party. Her father told her nothing political was settled yet; the Party might yet reclaim power and she should stay out of trouble. Masha had gone downstairs one morning a few weeks before and noticed a young tough she'd seen around the building with their next-door neighbor. The tough had spotted two other young men, sprinted out the door to his car, and locked himself in. The two men had smashed the windshield with iron pipes, reached in and beaten the man, dragged him out, hit him harder, and run off. He'd crawled into the lobby and died.

We met up with Sergei's friend, Tanya, on the street. She was a filmmaker, and she was horrified and agitated. She'd just walked out of her apartment as three Uzbek hoods had climbed from a car across the way and menaced a man with their submachine guns. Tanya couldn't forget the terror on the man's face. The Uzbeks didn't shoot him. They drove off. "This is new public behavior," Tanya said.

◆

Tanya took us to visit her friend Natalia in one of the endlessly duplicated shoddy apartment blocks that ring the city an hour's subway, trolley, and bus ride from the center. In the hallway outside Natalia's apartment, someone had scrawled in a large, childish hand, YIDS OUT OF HERE. Natalia was about to follow that advice — she was almost packed, immigrating to New York in two weeks. That, she said, was the reason she could speak freely to me. She wasn't fearful; she was competent and practical and opportunistic. She'd founded a cooperative restaurant downtown five years before. She'd served "Russian, Oriental, Georgian, Jewish food — *stolichny* salad, Georgian *lobio*, and gefilte fish. The main problem was procuring food. There were no *tolkuchkas* until recently," although there were already expensive private markets with meat, fruits, and vegetables. "Inspectors came all the time to check if the restaurant followed the rules. We needed butter for almost all our cooking, but there was a rule against our purchasing any for private profit. We fooled them by making it into Indian-style ghee, which we kept in cartons. They could have jailed us. Even in the months when there was no butter in the markets, we managed to find it. We went through a kilo and a half a day.

"Grains also could only be sold legally in state shops. We couldn't store much — that was automatic evidence you were a criminal. For this stupid reason, we couldn't cook grain dishes. Only this year that craziness stopped. Now everything is sold everywhere, and prices are shooting up. There are gangs, too. People drove up in foreign cars and demanded money. They became our guards. Once we had them, the café also started buying, selling, trading computers and electronics. 'The boys' got paid a percentage of computer sales. I thought their bosses were government officials, but I don't know for sure.

"They did their job. With 'the boys' there, we didn't have any robberies and didn't have much problem with taxes either. We just bypassed taxes — if we'd paid all the ones that were on the books, we'd have been broke. We made enough profit to live a normal life. I spent inconspicuously so the babushkas in the neighborhood wouldn't get jealous. Honesty is in short supply. I didn't expect my partners or workers to be honest; the people supplying us were hardly honest either. One fellow worked in the café and also supplied our meat. He was a thief, but he had the car. He'd spend five hundred rubles in the market and tell me he'd spent a thousand. I wouldn't steal from myself, so I took over doing the shopping.

"The best part of the whole experience was seeing the customers eating and enjoying themselves. Filmmakers came. Actors came. An American journalist came once, a guy who'd found a Russian wife and stayed. In spite of the good income and good crowds, I'm leaving. I don't want my nine-year-old son to live here. You see that sign that says 'Yid' in the hall? A kid downstairs wrote it, but his mother screams the same word at me. There were twenty Jewish families in our block. Now only three remain. Two, after I've gone."

◆

Sergei and I went to Tanya's film studio. It still made documentaries for schoolroom use, as it had for decades before the fall of the Party. They were doing final cuts on a film that until recently would have been daring. It was a remarkable piece of craftsmanship, made entirely from period footage, about the tragedy of agricultural collectivization. This heretical subject had been taboo before 1992. But the makers were still showing restraint: the film did not deal with events as recent as *perestroika*. It would be a few more years before they'd dare catch up, Tanya said. We sat in a small editing room, eating matzo and butter and drinking vodka, and listened to the voice-over explain, step by step, "the destruction of the peasantry."

"They turned everything into shit," said an old woman, standing before a thousand-year-old church. A farm worker termed Communism "paradise for silly men." The film traced one woman's forced journey to Siberia, back in the time of collectivization. Tanya had interspersed footage from a propaganda film in which happy peasants clowned and gleefully signed away their horses and farms for the good of the motherland. The film was powerful, and so was the vodka. Between the two, I was filled with sorrow. At the close of the film another old woman uttered a post-Communist caution: "Before we worshiped idols, and now material things."

◆

I stood with Sergei in front of the dreadful headquarters that had housed the Cheka (the acronym stands for the Extraordinary Commission for Combating Counterrevolution, Speculation, Sabotage, and Misuse of Authority), the KGB (Committee for State Security), and now the post-coup reincarnation, the MVRS (Security Ministry of the Russian Federation). A publisher we'd met with the day before, Boris Likhachev, happened to drive by in a Mercedes-Benz. He rolled down his window and asked, "What are you doing in this dreadful place?" We were in Dzerzhinsky Square, rechristened Lubyanka Square. The statue of Felix Dzerzhinsky, founder of the Cheka, had been toppled by a mob after the 1991 attempted coup, in front of international news cameras. The base of the statue was still strewn daily with flowers — left by relatives of his victims, and perhaps by those mourning the orderly times over which he'd presided. Both strains of public sentiment were about.

We'd come with Yuri Chernichenko, my friend the crusading journalist, with whom I'd crossed the Soviet Union four years before. He was still writing books, had written about our trip across America together, and was active in the service of his new Peasants' Party. Today the MVRS was busy with public relations, of all things. The Security Ministry had summoned the nation's political leaders — "not only the registered ones, but any with influence," Yuri said. The summons was not for questioning by a "conveyer" of tormenting agents — the treatment Sergei's grandmother had suffered at Lubyanka. The reincarnated KGB was playing nice. Yuri had been invited to a public relations meeting.

Seventy-five or so former heretics filed into a posh, paneled conference hall, sat in easy chairs, and cross-examined former KGB ministers and deputies about important issues: access to sealed records, current police monitoring and bugging and scare tactics, visas vetoed by the MVRS on political grounds, and many other touchy matters of the day. The questions streamed from the audience of politicians, one after another. The generals and ministry chiefs delivered, for the most part, bureaucratic doubletalk — it may be one of the few real cross-cultural constants in the world.

The nationalist and extremist Vladimir Zhirinovsky, leader of the Liberal Democratic Party of Russia, was there, and I studied him. His body language reminded me of Charlie Chaplin in *The Great Dictator*, body curved, arm rising, finger pointing, then descending rhythmically for emphasis, as though the finger were the butt of a whip and his words the thong lashing the audience. "There should be seven million KGB staff, not seven hundred thousand!" he shouted. *"Then we'll have order! Damned democrats have destroyed the country!"* A handful of liberal politicians, including Yuri, filed out as he ranted on. We followed, snooping at liberty in the corridors of Lubyanka instead of following directions and going right to the street. We stumbled upon a cozy tan and pink coffee canteen with a working Italian espresso machine, pastries, and the best smoked salmon in Moscow. Here, food was still subsidized. The sandwiches were cheap. Yuri whooped with laughter as we drank and ate. "We have raided Gorbachev's farm, we have seen the futuristic farmlands of California together," he said to me, "but this is the most amazing of all the places we've had adventures together!"

◆

I spent some days with the people I knew around Moscow from my sheltered earlier trips. They'd risen high in the service of a now-compromised regime, and they were all, in their ways, coming to terms with their lives as the framework of values against which they'd habitually made their judgments melted away. I passed an afternoon with Sergei Molochkov, formerly on the staff advising the Politburo on Canadian affairs. We walked for hours through woods and across fields outside Moscow. I'd known him for years, but this time (as thousands of recollections flowed from unsealed lips across the unbound nation) he spoke more freely. He mused about how unworldly he'd been and how alluring the West had seemed. Now that there no longer was a Party elite, he recalled his first privileged trips abroad, decades ago, when only the Party elite journeyed beyond the Iron Curtain. "We went to a conference in Stockholm. I was just a kid. The city amazed me — it was so efficient, wealthy, clean. I had to go find my own lunch. I went into a cafeteria, ordered a cheese sandwich, a bowl of soup (I still remember that it was pea soup, and they stood a spoon straight up in it), and tea. They gave me a little pot, and when I looked inside there was clear water. They also gave me a little bag, and inside was another little bag with a string on it. These damned Westerners, I thought to myself, are so hygienic they don't even want to handle bags that have their food inside! I ripped it open and the fine powder went into the pot and the water turned red and I drank it. As I did, I watched another man fix his tea, and of course he opened his tea packet and dipped the tea bag into the water. I felt nearly faint with embarrassment and realized that this was another fine capitalist invention for making life easier, which we had never even dreamed about."

◆

Edward, the historian of America with whom I was lodging, a lifelong Communist until just before the attempted coup, had also traveled to Europe as a Party representative. "I came back from ten years abroad, was a little bit outspoken, and for fifteen years I wasn't allowed to go abroad again." "It was your big mouth," the head of his institute had told him. "I had a clear thought throughout my career," Edward said. "I wanted to survive — and also to live a decent life." He held up one of his popular books on American history and said, "Only six or eight pages contain passages I would now revise." He held up another, translated into German, and said, "Even at those moments when I said what I had to, my facts were always objective, never manufactured."

◆

I phoned Yuri Zamoshkin. He was a sociologist, an erudite, wry, and troubled man. He told me he had cancer, and he was dying. Zamoshkin had, like the Canadianist and the historian, preserved his worldliness and foreign connections at a price. But Zamoshkin had long since gone public with his past dissimulations. Early in *perestroika,* he'd published an article expressing regret and repentance for having been willing to compromise his sense of truth by speaking scripted government lies abroad. He said frankly that he'd done so not out of fear or revolutionary conviction, but only to preserve his cherished foreign-travel privileges. His conscious tradeoff of public hypocrisy for private freedom troubled him for the rest of his life — as similar decisions had troubled less forthright counterparts.

Zamoshkin's attitude complicated my once-simple identification with only the uncompromising dissidents who were trucked off to the miserable prison camps of the *gulag.* Zamoshkin had a clear sight of his nation's government, but hadn't wanted to go to prison for speaking out. He was a sub-heroic man with an active mind and realistic self-knowledge. He wanted access to the books and minds of the world. On a trip to Canada (his article confessed), and perhaps elsewhere, he spoke publicly in favor of Soviet positions while knowing that what he said was untrue, and even knowing that many in his audience realized it. His were not big military lies that cost lives. He mouthed niceties about Communism, and bought freedom. There was a paradox, and it was a common one.

Zamoshkin said on the phone, "Dying is a kind of orderly procedure." He still had some strength, and when I went to visit, sat with Nellie, a philosophy professor and his wife in a long love match. As she'd requested, I'd brought the handful of pain-killers from my medicine kit. She held them up for Zamoshkin to see. He was gaunt, but that made him smile. His high tenor voice always surprised me for the first few sentences. He was disappointed I'd brought so few pills — even hard currency couldn't buy medicine reliably. He hadn't lost his sardonic smile and remained, this once more, the erudite, self-absorbed, penitent intellectual.

"With *perestroika*," he said, "we introduced, let us say, fifteen percent freedom. And introducing a fragment of democracy was like transplanting an alien organ that didn't take. The nation's whole immunological system started to fail. The country fell apart from the strain." The metaphor of illness and decrepitude struck me — as though Yuri Zamoshkin and his nation were dying of the same malady.

"Some people now become pathologically nostalgic — they want back the good old order. Some become hysterical — they remember, or think they remember, something or other that was fine about the system that used to exist before, but doesn't now — something like, for example, national unity. Well, it wasn't real unity. But when the Party was strong, people at least didn't kill each other. Unwritten tribal languages got written, actually strengthening and preserving differences. Putting all those nationalities together, muting them so they couldn't work out their unease with each other, set up the outburst we now have. Then along came that fifteen percent democracy, and it killed the whole Soviet body. That fact is a verdict — it confirms the wrongness of that system.

"What has happened now leaves our people so afraid. Don't underestimate the fear. I'm an optimist by will. I make myself see the good things. This is a realistic observation: I do see people rediscovering themselves, getting rid of stereotypes, experimenting with freedom of speech and of thinking. This process scares many people, but it is hopeful, because full democracy must allow conflicts and negative thinking. The difficulties, the bad sides of progress, are much easier to see. Enforced optimism was a form of state humiliation, and the wages of such deep demoralization that we are paying back now are severe." Zamoshkin tired of speaking. He tried the new pills. A few months later he would be dead. He was too aboveboard to be a hero, but easy to praise as a thoughtful man.

◆

Sergei and I spent days walking around the city. The Soviets had confiscated some churches from the start, and were still sometimes doing so as recently as the early 1960s. They were made into warehouses, community centers, movie theaters, museums. Sometimes their wrecked hulks sat rotting for decades as monuments to atheism. Now the Orthodox churches had been returned to the patriarchate, and we watched workmen putting a Russian Orthodox cross back atop a half-ruined steeple. A bit farther on, we found a jingoist, racist rally under way in Gorky Park. Demonstrators there had a cross too, and raised it aloft. A hundred or so skinheads, with all the angry menace of hooligans at a Liverpool soccer riot, screamed slogans about the motherland, about their Serbian brothers, about the sullied purity of the Russian race, about the fools who'd misled the once-great nation. They seemed jet-fueled by fierce feelings of national insult. Russia is humiliated, shamed like a beaten dog, and we have no more security. Our virility has been stolen from us.

Someone, of course, had to take the blame for degrading the nation so. They had a little list. "Yids," Freemasons, democrats, Gorbachev, Yeltsin, Gaidar, Lenin, the pope, the illuminati, America, Jeffrey Sachs (for pushing economic "shock therapy"), Harvard, the World Bank (for withholding credit). They had flags, and heraldic symbols painted on sheets and posters, and they shouted their accord with each speaker's dreadful ranting. Like a good liberal, I felt glad there could now be such a rally.

◆

Russians were desperate to mellow out, and so was I. The transit from the dull security of Soviet life to the uncertainty of making do with the unknown was hard on everyone's nerves. I accepted Edward's invitation to escape from Moscow for a weekend. Mos-

cow's sour-smelling squares swarmed with stay-at-home escap-
ists; absolute drunks wobbled about, scanning the harsh world
through slit vodka-eyes. Stepping around the weekend drunks,
Edward and I headed for the hills to his *dacha,* just out of town.
A stream of families abandoned the city with us — babushkas
clutching tiny grandkids in shorts, papas dressed mysteriously
in wide-lapeled suits and fedoras straight from 1930s gangster
films, all of them laden like pack mules with garden tools, bedding, squares of window glass, scavenged boards and tin for repairs, new buckets for the wells and outhouses, a few chickens
squawking in crates. We all trudged downward, burdened, dogs
tugging us through catacombed corridors niched with heroic
Soviet statuary into the still-grand subways, past pensioners
hawking newly unbanned Christian newspapers and young
toughs hawking pornography. Gypsies set pleading toddlers
clinging to passersby, and old ladies genuflected obsessively
with tin cups before them. The trains, amazingly, had gone on
working well.

Colonies of *dachas* ring the city. In Soviet times, one didn't
have to be rich or even influential to get a *dacha.* They were
handed out by the workplace — the socially responsible workplace. Workplace committees decided who could buy a car, take
a holiday, get physical and psychic care (a few years before, a
broiler-factory manager had proudly shown me his plant's "relaxation room," where jittery employees lay in semidarkness
in airline seats while disco music from Squaresville chunka-
chunked from big speakers and docile art flashed asynchro-
nously on several slide screens — sixties American grooviness
transformed into a klunky, wonderless light show).

The newspapers in the kiosks announced that monthly inflation had hit twenty percent. The silver lining was that the
ruble was taking on real-world value: the economic "shock
treatment" had cost widespread suffering and political oppor-
tunism, but did monetarize the ruble.

Leonid Brezhnev had banned freestanding *dachas* for a while
— too like private homes. So construction crews had built tan-
dem and quadri-*dachas* that connected only at the corner of
adjacent lots, joined by a few feet of common wall, minimally
conforming to Brezhnev's edict. Even then, *dachas* remained

private retreats for weekend practice of bourgeois individual-
ism. Cheap *dachas* and cheap vodka had made misery bearable;
they were the substitute opiates that helped keep the lid on for
decades. Now they were making survival tolerable.

After the coup many Russians found themselves poorer than
ever. Costs of production began to matter, and factory managers were shedding amenities — including *dachas*, vacations,
and health care — as fast as the weakening labor unions permitted. Twenty years before, Edward's research institute had snared
a leasehold on about fifteen acres. They'd sliced it into eighty
lots, bribed the construction ministry, and distributed the resulting cottages by draw. Edward had gotten lucky.

He'd always wanted a car, too, but had bad luck in that quest.
In Soviet times, money wasn't money in the basic Western
sense that money buys goods interchangeably. To ensure that
all material goods went out according to the central plan and
to maximize control of individual lives, the Soviets required
case-by-case permission for major purchases. Only with a permit could one pay rubles for a *dacha* or car. This system helped
control the ambitious and reward the meek.

Edward's name rose for a decade until, in 1988, he was first
on his institute's waiting list — he'd get the next Lada to come
their way. But meanwhile, on the other side of town, *perestroika*
was gathering steam. An executive order declared that scarce
goods would thenceforth be issued by lottery, not seniority. For
Edward, it was the earliest pain of the transition.

I'd gone to the car lottery meeting with Edward a few years
earlier. He'd walked into the subdirector's office for the drawing
looking downcast. His suspicions were correct. A secretary —
one Edward never got on with — plucked the short straw and
soon was driving around Moscow in Edward's new car. By
chance, years before, she'd also drawn the *dacha* right across
from Edward's. After winning the car, she moved her cottage's
front fence three feet forward, breaking the bylaws of the compound (once enforced by the now fallen Communists), to make
room to park the Lada in her yard every weekend.

Edward and I lugged supplies the fifteen-minute walk from
Kikoshina station to the *dacha* compound; the secretary's car
across the street was the first thing he pointed out. His *dacha*

looked good. Two stories high, with a foyer and two small bedrooms on each floor, it was now salable. An open market in
dachas had sprung up, and one nearby had gone for about five
thousand dollars.

It was Edward's only remaining asset. He'd stored up a nest
egg during a frugal lifetime, but savings that would have lasted
through a sheltered old age wouldn't support him for even six
months. He'd turned sixty, and he had high blood pressure; his
salary suddenly seemed shaky. The institute had fallen a month
behind in issuing paychecks — the banks that controlled salary transfers now floated funds for their own use by delaying
transfer.

Through my Western eyes, these hard conditions did seem to
hasten the advent of economic efficiency. The evidence was in
Edward's new life, he explained over supper: for the first time, a
dozen books into his career, Edward was writing history in a
style he hoped would draw readers on the open market. He'd
found work for an international foundation, and earned fifty dollars a month in hard currency. So he'd just hired a carpenter to
repair the *dacha* — privately, by the hour. Past the compound's
gate, a farmer had split a few acres away from a collective farm
and sold milk to Edward and his neighbors.

But for all the wonder of free expression, private carpentry,
and local milk — and these new things were wondrous to Edward — the economic transition also had brought uncertainty
and moral confusion. The small traders who were buying up
soap, tea, soda, meat — whatever they could get from corrupt
clerks at controlled state prices — resold their stock on the
streets. They were the ones in this crazed economy who got
appropriate goods to appropriate people. But their work seemed
immoral to most Russians; even educated Russians who avidly
supported reform muttered about these "middlemen."

At eight P.M. Edward's wife, Ina, was still at work, compensat-
ing for hard times. In the garden, she hoed, watered, and weeded
nearly a quarter acre of squashes, cucumbers, radishes, tomatoes, and onions, potatoes and oregano and mint and watercress,
gooseberries, cloudberries, and other berries we couldn't find in
the Russian-English dictionary, including one sort that dangled
on bushes whose pale green leaves and olivelike branches waved

in the night breeze. Their dog crouched and barked at the jerking branches.

It was buggy. Edward had covered the windows with cheese-cloth — Russia was, as ever, a nation with big mosquitoes and no screens. We scrubbed off city grime and ate sorrel soup and black bread in the freestanding summer kitchen at the back of the garden. I lazed for an hour, reading in the sun. A few neighbors drifted in. We poured pepper-flavored vodka. The talk soon turned to the subject of love — mostly failed love — and it went on until midnight, when the sky at last dimmed into twilight.

Love was an escape this crowd put to hard use. Around Moscow, only infants and lovers still smiled.

Edward held up his glass and told of marrying Ina thirty-eight years ago on a dare, a few weeks after they'd met. Natasha, a neighbor who recently had turned to selling Western office equipment to foreign embassies, had just bailed out of five years of tragic infatuation, "as pure as in one of those American romance novels," she said, "with a Moslem boy from one of the Muslim 'stans.'" His parents, who were on the Communist Party Central Committee, forbade the relationship. But Natasha had flown down there whenever the boy's parents flew up to Moscow. Between illicit visits, the family chauffeur had posted letters for the lovers. Near the end, a friendly uncle had taken Natasha aside and said her only hope of marriage was to conceive a male child and then confront her lover's parents. She'd realized then that she wanted to be loved for herself alone, and had torn herself away. Someone new would turn up, she was sure. We toasted the future. Down the road, a family dined on their porch, shouting out Russian folksongs. "These songs are always sad," Edward said, "complaints about lost lands, lost family, lost love."

A friend of Natasha's showed up. She was divorcing. Spurned by her one true love, the friend married an old suitor. At twenty-five and severely diabetic, her condition poorly controlled by Russian medicine, she was hurrying to conceive a child. Her husband moved from academia to business right after the attempted coup, made money, but started keeping fast company and drinking heavily. One night a few months before, he'd told her not to come home for a while. "If I don't come home tonight,

I won't come home again," Natasha's friend had answered, and hadn't since. There were more tales, as sad and romantic as the neighbors' songs. I added an old one of my own. We headed for bed late, and by then we had slit vodka-eyes too.

In the middle of the night I listened in on a long dog dialogue. The nearer dog had only one thing to say: Ghrrrrrough-yap. He said it incessantly. Ghrrrrrough-yap. His neighbor answered variously: Yip. Yah. Whine. Wa-rup. The nearer dog never changed his tune. Ghrrrrrough-yap. It went on until dawn.

In the morning, blinking in the sunlight, I saw a neighbor out in her yard, a few cottages down, hoeing potatoes for the winter while her old dad staked tomatoes. Ina stood in her own garden, back by the water spigot, scrubbing her face with whey. "Cold cream's best," she said, "but we haven't any. Whey is second best. We struggle for everything we find, and that gives it meaning. Maybe it's not so bad to live this way."

For the hard winter everyone expected, Ina's garden and countless others outside Moscow would once more provide for even professional families. Collective farms close to the cities had been ordered to make plots available to city dwellers, thousands of whom were commuting out to potato patches. The gardens answered the riddle of why Russians never fell into famine during their wild transition — with the collective-farming system in such disarray and the politics of land privatization stalemated. In that sense, everyone in the country had temporarily reverted to peasantry. No one was many relatives removed from a garden patch, nor many steps from an old uncle who stole from the fields of the collective farms themselves. *Dacha* cellars bulged with potatoes, and Moscow apartments, crammed with cans of hoarded food, looked like warehouses.

Back in Moscow, Sergei told me that he and his brother Alyosha, the mathematician, on a lark once had driven three thousand miles to Lake Baikal in a car the size of a baby carriage, often on roads like horse paths. They'd camped by the shore and written up a journal — in English. The journal records an afternoon when they'd sat by their tent and watched an Armenian engineer working out his dreams. In true Soviet fashion, he'd built a catamaran; he'd told them he had dreamed of sailing on this deepest and once purest of inland waters. And in true Soviet fashion, he'd paid little attention to reality. The open pontoons were far too small to float the weight of the boat, crew, and supplies. Sergei watched the craft sail about twenty-five feet into Baikal's choppy seas and swamp to the gunwales.

The trip in from the *dacha* cost three rubles. In front of Edward's Moscow apartment a woman sold cucumbers for a free-market price, twenty-one rubles. So the state had priced an hour's comfortable train ride at one seventh of a cucumber. In the West, the ride would be worth about seven cucumbers.

16

WE FINALLY HEADED off to Ivanovo on the night train. I rattled the door to the toilet and was no longer surprised to find it perpetually locked. Of course the car lady did it. She scolded Sergei for requesting tea at two in the morning, which was when the train left Moscow. Five minutes later he looked into her compartment. "She was in there drinking tea," he said.

Outside Ivanovo's central station, a huge, stainless-steel Salome head of one Olga Genkina, a now-lapsed heroine, balanced on a pole forty feet in the air, her metal scarf streaming sideways like a platter. She'd been caught with ammunition and guns in 1905 and killed by an angry mob of "Black Hundreds." The lineage of heroism goes to the victors. How long would she keep her perch?

We found a working pay phone. I was more surprised that a few things still worked than that so much didn't. But no one at Gostekhnika would admit to knowing our contact, a Mr. Mogilny (whose name contains the root-word meaning "tombstone," so that's what we called him). Sergei said, "The solution is always to go anyhow." The taxi driver steered with a tiller. He had no legs. A few months before, other cab drivers had stabbed him for stealing their fares, he said by way of making conversation. Gostekhnika, the trucking and repair section of Gosagroprom, turned out to be in the same big brick building as the offices of Aleksander Aleksandrovich Sorokin, whom I hoped to avoid.

"Tombstone" Mogilny, Gostekhnika sub-chief, was indeed there, predictably blocky, hearty, and cordial. Sergei's influential cousin, Yuri Kormilitsin of Gosagroprom in Moscow, had appointed Mogilny to be our pal. We appeared to have successfully gone around Sorokin. In the building's cafeteria, Mogilny fed us porridge with butter, meat with butter, milk soup with butter — in his organization, the shoemaker's shoes got fixed. He led us to the office of Aleksander Ilyich Novikov, who had the spare apartment.

Novikov supervised a garage. He was a good ol' boy who seemed to know everyone and bend his elbow with them all. His division had held on as Gosagroprom hypertrophied. They had the capacity to ship things and fix things — to do real work. So they shipped textiles, foods, and vacationers, and took in return whatever was up for barter. Their secret business would fascinate economists. Fortunes were quickly made and concealed by the right cronies at the right strategic sites all over the former Soviet Union that year. Unsurprisingly, my questions about such business met with evasive answers.

Novikov was short, almost collegiately dressed in an ironed shirt and creased pants — rare in a nation where washing and ironing were inconvenient. "My son, Sasha, is in a wheelchair — he was in a motorcycle accident," Novikov said. We were offered his apartment for a week. And by the way, could American medical miracles help? And no, he told us, he was not bartering. He stressed that. This was universal, international good-ol'-boy business. He was following a code I recognized.

Novikov would bunk out on the edge of town, at the family *dacha*. We drove out with him and ate supper there, shouting into the ear trumpet of his frail, stooped grandfather, who looked constantly surprised and said "I've never met a foreigner. First one in my village" many times before the night was over. Sasha could not walk, but he held his baby in his lap and talked computers with me. His wife was a schoolteacher. We all made many mandatory toasts to Sasha's baby, and to motherhood and fatherhood in general, and of course to international friendship. Some months later, a rehabilitative surgeon, who was a friend of my cousin Susan's husband Bill in Texas, read Sasha Novikov's medical record and wrote, regretfully confirming that there were no American miracles to reverse his paralysis.

◆

We set out the next day to find Volodya Kurikhin, ex–"Farmer of the Future," fired by Farm Trudovik's replacement chairman, Drozhin. We tipped a Gosagroprom driver, who drove us out to Farm Trudovik. With a few questions to passersby, Sergei discovered that Volodya's partner, Loskutov, still worked on the farm. He was off somewhere, but a series of peasants pointed us toward the door of the *promtovarny*, the industrial goods shop, anyhow. "Ask in there," one said. It was closed. We pounded on the door. Finally it opened, and Loskutov's wife was inside, head wrapped in a babushka, taking inventory. She said, "You're those Americans who visited Volodya? I've heard about you. I'll call Olga, his wife — she's my best friend." She excitedly told Olga that we were standing by her side. Simple as that. We drove back to Shuya. We stood in Volodya's apartment house courtyard, where Loskutov had led us in 1989 and where I'd chatted with Olga. And there, as if materialized from a dream, stood Volodya, waving. Finding just the person I wanted to see, after so many controlled trips, had been straightforward. Without political escorts (we were not the American delegation any longer), we'd just gone and done what we'd set out to do.

I remembered Volodya's puzzled, lopsided smile the moment I saw it again. He'd filled out. He'd prospered. His apartment was surprising. It was furnished with leather couches and beautiful oriental rugs — not what I'd have expected of the hardworking would-have-been farmer. Fine icons hung on the walls. His wife served us liver, which was costly and "fresh from the market," she said — a lavish gesture of hospitality. She carried out tea and a bottle of Metaxa, sausages and bread, Swiss chocolates, and cakes. Sergei read out the *Farm Journal* article, and Volodya laughed and shook his head and said, "My life has changed so much. I'm another Volodya now."

And he was another Volodya. He'd struck me during our earlier visit as more directed than the average farm worker, but I'd missed his eloquence. He recalled the events of May and June 1990, two years earlier, leading to the end of his lease brigade: "The culprit who ruined my farm was Drozhin, the replacement chairman — not the chief zootechnician or chief economist, although they also didn't like what we were doing. Drozhin was the kind of chairman who got irritated if he merely heard something new was going on. We had worked hard the whole winter. The cows milked well. They all got with calf. And then the new calves were born, and none died; we'd given the farm excellent new cows. We'd replaced a quarter of our herd, and we were ready to go on working.

"There was a big meeting. The collective-farm board came. Drozhin came. The city Party committee came. Sorokin, the big boss — even he came. He just listened. He didn't speak. All board members opposed us. But they accused us of just one thing — getting paid well. I told them, 'In that case, we will just throw everything away and start drinking like your regular collective-farm workers do. Then you'll be happy, because our wages will go down.' I was angry.

"Near the end of winter, the collective farm began dumping cow manure into our fields one day. They didn't spread it, just dropped truckloads of it. I asked, 'Why do you want to ruin our fields?' The chief agronomist said, 'You won't be working on them anyhow.' I went over to Nikolai Petrachkov at Farm Gorky. He's a very serious man, the one I still respect among the area's chairmen. Couldn't I move with my crew down the road and join him again? He was friendly. But he said that he didn't have room.

"I made up my mind to fight right to the end. I aged ten years from the experience. My contract with the farm was for five years. I was ready to go to court. I'd fulfilled my half of the contract completely. At that point Drozhin said if we didn't get out of the barn, they'd simply flatten it with a bulldozer and kill the cattle. I'd taken care of those cows for a year. I felt sorry for them. I yelled at him, 'You're a Communist — you should be thinking about the workers' prosperity, but instead you're thinking of murdering a good herd of cows. How can a farm chairman say words like that? What kind of master of a farm are you?'

"I drove right to Ivanovo and saw the deputy Party chief of agriculture in a big office. I told my story and got all excited. He pretended to listen, made a show of writing something down, and that was the end. I worked exactly a year, May first to May first, International Workers' Solidarity Day — but solidarity with whom? They closed up our barn and drove the cattle back to a bigger barn in Putich. Someone told me that along the way twelve cows stopped and drank water into which ammonia fertilizer had fallen. They died. Even after that, I saw Drozhin once more and asked if he'd *sell* me the farm — not the land, just the farm and a small plot. He said I didn't have enough money. I told him I had enough to buy his whole damned collective farm. I was pissed off, but after that I just went away."

If I'd missed Volodya's intensity and eloquence, I'd also underestimated his ambition and navigational skill. He turned out to have been a poised, worldly trader, Russian style. A wheeler-dealer. He'd worked hard at the lease brigade because he'd seen it as an opportunity. It had failed, but just as Volodya had spotted the chance to farm under Nikolai Petrachkov, he went about finding a next opportunity:

"I have a family, kids. I needed to work. It was still *perestroika*. Cooperatives were suddenly allowed at that point. So we started a small construction cooperative called Kommersant. We repair schools, nurseries, the invalid home — only public buildings. We pay our workers good wages. So far, the state's reimbursements to us for our work are coming through okay.

"The enterprise also now has a 'commercial section.' We're middlemen — I'm not ashamed; a middleman takes risks. Our laborers did maybe 300,000 rubles' worth of repairs at a cloth mill. In exchange we got textiles worth that. We trucked them to Voronezh, where there is not much fabric but there's a candy factory. For each kilo of candy that sells in stores (if you can find any) for 120 rubles, we traded 60 rubles' worth of fabric. We sell the candies here for 80, 90 rubles.

"Our business is growing. That Moscow firm Hermes — they advertise on TV now — we brought them textiles in Moscow and they gave us a requisition for payment. It cleared in two weeks, shrunken from inflation some, but we've got half a million rubles in our account. Now no one wants a requisition form. Provincial banks don't take Moscow forms; the country's falling apart. Someone else wants us to trade textiles for grain. We'd have to make a preliminary payment. We can't, because the banking system has blown up. There's also not enough bread in Ivanovo. This grain barter would help — small enterprises like mine can now legally help supply the city. Maybe we can do it.

"We have other troubles. Some companies that approach us are phony, and we can't tell. There's no basis for mutual trust. And consumers aren't buying things, because they have no cash around. People line up at banks, and then the bank gives them only five hundred rubles apiece from their own accounts. In Moscow they can get five thousand, with a day's notice. It's chaos.

"For seventy years our government tried to invent new economic laws. You can't. The world lived according to definite economic laws already. We are making the transition to what the rest of the world knew — or at least we will if the government isn't taken over by people looking backward. There is a danger — maybe not from Moscow, where there are only nine million people. There are millions of babushkas and workers in the provinces, where big decisions are also made, and they remember Brezhnev's era as a good time. It's so hard now for them to live. Everyone has to make money."

And then Volodya showed yet another side of himself: "I have no scruples about the ways I make money myself — except for criminal things. I've worked so hard that I have hardly been home for the years since I lost the farm. I'm slowing down a little now, but never on weekends. Then, I'm always in Moscow doing business.

"All my life I've been fascinated by icon paintings. Tsar Peter the First visited here once to worship a certain icon. I almost went to jail for my interest in icons, so I stopped. But now you can do anything. Look at these icons — sixteenth century, nineteenth century." He pointed at the wall. "I travel around. People bring them to me and I buy them. I knew what I was doing. I confess — I'd go to Moscow and sell them. The Communists destroyed an enormous number. Now they're getting harder to find." So my noble peasant dealt in stolen icons. He was up to speed on the latest business opportunities.

He also had a sense of wanting to do sound business, if only that were possible. Just as top collective-farm chairmen had, Volodya wanted to manufacture his own building materials:

"I'd like to produce something, not just be a middleman. But it absolutely can't be done now. I wanted to buy a brick factory, but land isn't being sold. You still can't get to own the land under a factory, never mind what Yeltsin decrees. I'd like to start a quarry. I know that the state's cost for producing bricks is very high. State structures would be no competition for us. I figured it out. I am also trying to start making flooring materials. I met a Pole in Moscow who was in a joint venture with Germans producing parquet flooring — high-quality products. There are empty warehouses just outside of town. We have equipment. We went to every official. But they wouldn't let us rent or buy a place to put the machines. You can't set them down in the open air. You need quarters, and land. We finally got space as part of a state enterprise, but I'm sure they'll soon see we're prosperous and keep cranking up the rent. They'll add their workers in with ours. They'll demand a share. We'll see. I'm just doing what I'm doing. And I'm doing pretty well." He laughed. It was a businessman's excited laugh.

Back at Novikov's apartment, I felt downright flummoxed that I'd taken this adept businessman for an earnest hayseed while he was running down to Moscow and trading in stolen icons. "I paid over a thousand dollars for this," Volodya had said, handing me a small icon of a doleful Mary. "Russian customers paid a lot — they knew the good ones. Italians fell in love with them and showed it, but the Americans wouldn't show emotion. They'd just wander back three hours later and act cool." That a black-market icon trader seemed to be a man disposed toward constructive action and clear sight was a measure of the confusing moral context that Soviet power had installed. They'd banned property and religion and they'd stifled art, and Volodya had found a bold way to traffic in all three. I took it as a sign of a lively spirit in a tough spot.

The "Farmer of the Future" (as I'd called him in my old *Farm Journal* article) had landed on his feet. In fact, he'd been nimble all the while, conversant in business, eyes fixed on the main chance. How differently I'd read him in 1989, sitting high up in the hay shed, talking quietly so my keeper, Lev, wouldn't over-hear Volodya's criticisms of Soviet farming. Volodya made more sense this way. A man who would seek out the opportunity to farm independently, years before most citizens even understood the possibility, would notice other rewarding outlets for his in-dustriousness. I was confident that he had a few other fallback positions in sight. Let me, then, redub him "Businessman of the Future." "The effects of bad laws in Russia are lessened by their bad enforcement," Marquis de Custine wrote one hundred fifty years ago.

◆

A day later, we drove back out to Shuya to hunt up Nikolai Petrachkov on Farm Gorky. He turned out to have left that morning for Voronezh, to scout for a new pump, but Taisa was there. She was just back from a meeting of the district's collec-tive-farm leaders. Again I enjoyed the straightforwardness of driving out to Farm Gorky and finding her without having to sit through state dinners and hold monitored conversations. Taisa Stepanovna, however, barely responded to my greeting. She said she was rushed. She'd seemed so cordial and open as my ap-proved hostess, but was hesitant and uneasy being visited un-officially. As she spoke, however, she seemed to forget her hesi-tation: "Now shops have opened in the cities. I said to you years ago, I don't need shops. My cellar was full of canned food then, and it still is. I have my own sheep, cow, pigs, chickens, rabbits. We still provide for ourselves completely. Most commercial life now isn't proper. Here I fatten two pigs. I eat one and I sell one. That's honest. I take two pitchers of milk from the cow and sell one. I myself make something and I sell it. That's what is right.

"But middlemen — people who take what one person makes and sell it to some other person and keep the money — that's what we're now calling business. We're against such business!" Taisa's strictness surprised me. She felt in her bones the fairness of the old system's best ideals. When I'd stayed with the family, she had seemed rebellious and feisty in the face of silly reform-Communist regulations. But even in her indignation she'd been dedicated to an essence of justice that the system had, to some extent, enforced, even as it failed so spectacularly in producing a just society.

"We have a nice household, we both work, and we buy nothing," she said. "Nikolai can fix any machine. I can manage a farm. But we don't. The government wants to destroy the whole farming system now, and that is wrong. These days the government gives us practically nothing. Our farm is no longer even state owned. We had to make it into the Afanasyevskoye Joint Stock Company, named after our village. However, it still works as a collective farm. We pool our dividends — one-half million rubles last year. It's almost impossible to farm individually. Our joint stock plan is common. Remember Zhanna? Her lease brigade is still working well. Maybe in five, ten years she may own that farm, but it will come slowly, gradually — that makes sense. Let's not rush privatization. There must still be a leader who will take care of such workers, while it's their job to work. You have to proceed stage by stage."

The enforced discipline and support Party-planned agriculture had provided the nation were collapsing, and Taisa did not see a realistic alternative rising in their place. She saw greedy opportunists acting as middlemen, now that nothing prevented them from doing so: "The government ignores agriculture now. Inflation causes us terrible trouble. The value of our crops has gone up eight times, but the price of a tractor has gone up a hundred times — it was four thousand rubles, and now it's four hundred thousand rubles. All farm construction is frozen. I go into Ivanovo and fight the officials, but I get nowhere. There's a sales tax now, a value-added tax, a pension fund tax. The farm pays it all. Where does it go? I like Vasily Starodubtsev and his Agrarian Party — he's also a peasant [and was one of the seven anti-Gorbachev putschists]. Russia's grain production is down by half — but our farm's is steady. So is our production of cattle and potatoes. No one helps us now. We do it on our own. The market economy is no good. It needs to be regulated." Here on the farm, Taisa had a strong and close-up view of the results of what Western economists such as Jeffrey Sachs were calling "shock treatment." The old system had withdrawn too quickly, in her view. I guessed that Volodya might well have comprehended her concerns, although he'd already understood what lay beyond them.

"You can't hold on to money now, of course, because of the inflation. We buy goods immediately. A year ago we bought a crane for three hundred thousand rubles. Now it's worth three million. Nikolai won't sell it for cash — he wants to barter it for commodities — fodder, mixed feed, sugar. There's a Russian proverb: If you want to live, you have to keep moving. It's a pity there are millionaires. They haven't been working, just buying and selling. If you work honestly, you can't earn a million. Us, we can't buy an apartment, can't buy a car. Those *tolkuchkas* are not right. When the nation has reached abundance, maybe then. I'm not for planned distribution — the socialist economy. But they shouldn't change so fast! Those old bosses who have access to production, they are the businessmen." She was close-mouthed after that. Her principled world didn't work right anymore.

◆

Late in the evening it was still light. Again I walked through Ivanovo. The state market had chickens, fatty beef, good cucumbers, and moldy tomatoes. Outside the door, a peasant woman sold fresh mushrooms she'd gathered herself. This, Taisa would have approved. A few *tolkuchkas* had set up — for slightly lower prices they sold what Moscow kiosks sold, but they didn't have English names. Taisa would have disapproved.

Drunkards tottered up and down the streets, leaving long shadows. I felt as anonymous as I did in any American city. I marveled again that I was at large in Russia, with no official approval. Sergei recalled that in his graduate school days, an order came through requiring all students to report meetings with foreigners. Sergei had argued the principle of the thing with his professor for two hours, after which the professor said, "Just *sign* that you'll do it, don't *do* it." Sergei had signed. "There was no need to break my spirit," he said to me. "I was a passive person — I had already learned to keep my opinions to myself. I didn't like Party types. It seemed silly to try to be loyal. I liked hard-core dissidents less — they were so fanatical. So I dropped out more and more."

◆

Over the next few days we visited farmers who, like Volodya, had ventured off on their own. A few were still in business. I was hunting for a success, a replacement "farmer of the future" now that Volodya had gone on to the building trades, but I never found one. I found a few of the young men limping along in the midst of local hostility, as hemmed in by bureaucrats as ever — bureaucrats who may well have shared the intelligible attitude Taisa Stepanovna had revealed, or who wanted to hang on to their own dominions. The individual farmers were routinely denied credit, supplies, machines, and markets. They were going nowhere, and would not go anywhere soon, although their nation would continue to need their sort of help.

What strong character and what general alienation it took for a farmer to go it alone in that atmosphere. Nikolai Kryukov, age thirty, was skinny, sinewy, rough, and serious. He talked to me shirtless in an old cottage he used as an office, interrupting himself to yell at his lolling, drunken helper: "Go take a hike, you bastard, you're sitting with your back to an American." Kryukov had worked on a poultry farm, driven trucks, done tractor work. Back in 1989, like Volodya, he'd figured out the advantages of farming for himself, as Gorbachev had urged. He'd spotted an abandoned Young Pioneers camp, and managed to get a few acres leased to him around the buildings.

He used that land about as hard as land can be used. He'd rigged up a slow homemade sawmill that would make any Yankee sawyer shake his head in wonder, sawed out joists and rafters, and sold the lumber (he'd discovered the building-supplies trade too) to make some spending money. Twenty or thirty geese ran around honking outside the office. They were for sale. He fattened a few bull calves for beef and milked twenty-two more or less dairy cows. He'd sawed up some stumps and set them neatly in a dark cement garage. He dampened them from a pail many times a day, and harvested a handsome crop of mushrooms every morning.

He came the closest to independence of any of the farmers we'd meet, but he'd failed in accomplishing what he'd first intended. Right by the Young Pioneers camp, beyond a low wire fence, stretched a big field. Wild grass grew in it — the sort of low-nutrition pasture grasses that take when a plowed field is let go after a crop is harvested and nature, not a farmer, chooses the seed. That field was what had excited Nikolai Kryukov about the former camp. It still excited him, although now the sight of it caused him aggravation. It remained unused. It belonged to the adjacent state farm — which, since the attempted coup, had been turned into a "joint stock company" on paper — like Taisa and Nikolai's farm — but went on as before. Its chairman, like most, had no sympathy for an independent farmer and wanted nothing to do with helping one out.

"If we graze on their land, we'll pay a very high fine," Kryukov said. I asked if the collective farm would mow it themselves. "Maybe. They didn't bother last year. Meanwhile, we have to survive for three years here on the small plot granted me or we'll owe big taxes that will destroy us. So I want it a lot. It's a district executive committee decision, and the local authorities just don't like us. They're a case of the goat guarding the cabbage patch — do you have that expression? We can't even protect ourselves against thieves — lots has been stolen from me already. Look at my shotgun there, behind the chair. I can't call the police. They are robbers too. If they guarded this farm, nothing would be here in the morning except the robber, and he'd be drunk.

"Yeltsin read out his independent-farming decree. I laughed. What comes down to us little guys is completely different from what he read, changed a hundred times until it means the opposite. They don't give us land. They tax us. I can't get equipment. I have eight employees — a vet and a bookkeeper both moonlight here. A milkmaid tends the twenty-two cows. I buy the cow feed from all over the place, however I can. I'm able to survive only because I have a big sponsor, the huge broiler-chicken factory across town. They want cheap beef for the staff and cafeteria. They help me with supplies. We also deliver milk to a truck repair depot. The manager is a personal friend who helps. And that's how I have survived."

◆

We walked into the tiny storefront office of AKKOR, a semigovernmental reform association, part of Yeltsin's mandate to help independent farmers with loans and battles against local officials. Russia watchers in the West say AKKOR spends a good part of its budget on its own salaries and isn't very effective. It would, of course, take more than a storefront staffed by a few do-gooders to reform rural infrastructure and win battles with the web of officials who have managed Ivanovo's farming for so long. The local head of AKKOR, Viktor Chesnakov, admitted all that. He drove us out to meet a few other small farmers.

They weren't even as far along as Kryukov. Yuri Vassileyevich Yermolayev had insisted on leaving his collective farm under the new laws. "I'm almost the only guy who left there with land," he said. "I work with another man who got equipment right before the price went up. In this whole region there are just six small independent farmers. I asked for forty acres; they refused." We sat in his tiny kitchen. He had twelve acres of wet clay. He'd just come in from his field. "They won't let me own this house. I had to go to court to get the land. It has been hard going. My friends on the collective farm are still friends, but the administration doesn't like me at all. I was doing some work for them, but they fired me for missing one day.

"Then the local procurator helped. He was different. I was surprised. I've owned the land now for only a few months — since April — and after ten years I can sell it. Still, I have no tractor. I bribe drivers from other places with bottles from a case of vodka. I have no horse. I can trade a ton of meat for a workhorse, the collective-farm chief said. I have no seed, no machinery. I could buy them, but I can't afford the high prices. So I just have land now, and a truck, five brood pigs, thirty sheep, two cows, sixty chickens, and no money. I have made a small clearing and diverted a stream for the sheep. There's a power line over there, so I can put electricity in when I can afford it. But at the moment I have to sell some animals to buy feed for the rest."

Chesnakov took us across town to another of the five independent farmers, Mikhail Kurnayev, in the village of Ignatikha. His story was similar: "I was a senior sergeant in the fire security police. I can tell you that life was easier then. After that I joined a lease brigade on the collective farm and milked cows. It seemed like a good opportunity. The chairman of that collective farm helped me register this place — it was one of the first, in 1990. He thought everything I grew would go to him — which is why he let me register it. But that year, I made money selling potatoes somewhere else, and then I sold winter wheat also. So then the chairman went and planted *my* land himself. Chesnakov, here, and AKKOR helped me get the papers together for the procurator, and they warned the chairman he was using my land illegally. The chairman harvested the potatoes on it last fall anyway. But he hasn't touched it since. They were my potatoes. I went to an official in the agriculture office. He said, 'Do you have your round stamp? Do you have such and such a form?' Things like that. 'Why does it say "Union of Peasant Farmers" and not "Department of Agriculture" on this form? Since it says that, go to that union, not here.'

"I have some equipment, but it is bad. The very first time I used that baler out there, the tying needles broke. That's what Soviet equipment is like. You see that modern dump trailer out there? The hopper wouldn't go up when it was new. At the factory, someone had carelessly soldered a bead of metal right across the hydraulic line. But I've made gradual progress. I'm an optimist; I'm going to struggle on as long as I can." He laughed. "Recently, some jealous neighbors poisoned my dog."

◆

We'd gotten the idea. In post-coup Ivanovo, there were as yet no farmers of the future. In the evening we ate a festive supper in Viktor Chesnakov's old log *izba,* which was surrounded by factories and settling slowly into a sandy field on the edge of Ivanovo. His tiny kids, I remember, were particularly meek and liked everything all evening — they liked being held, being put down, eating, watching. They smiled from their first spoonfuls of borscht (made from kitchen-garden beets) right through to sweet cake and tea.

After dinner, Viktor told a sad story that showed something about at least one of the region's collective farms: "Last fall, Tatiana and I went and lived in the summer *dacha*. We were gathering mushrooms one day in the woods. From far off, we could see a green patch through the yellow and brown autumn leaves. It was grain piled up. It had fermented and heated itself up, smoldering at the core. But the crust had sprouted bright green shoots. I counted eight piles, each a truckload, four tons. Next day I mentioned it to a woman who worked in a shop nearby. 'Go farther in,' she'd said, 'the whole forest is full of these piles.' Last year and the year before were good harvests. The elevator couldn't store all the grain, so they threw it in the forest. They could have sold it directly to the peasants, but they wouldn't."

We discussed the long day of visits to small farmers, and their prospects. "You met three farmers," Chesnakov said. "The first was tossed out of the collective farm. He didn't get the land the law owed him. How is an individual's share of land determined for someone who leaves one of the joint stock companies that was a collective farm? The method isn't fair: the total amount of land on the collective farm is divided by a number that includes everyone there, not just farm workers — fellows who work in the kindergarten and the shop are counted. That way, the farm has to give away less to anyone leaving. Then they're no threat. The farm keeps its power. It's a trick. Small private gardening plots are no danger to the system. Why? I think I know a good answer. We've always had small plots because they don't generate middle-class citizens, which farms would. The thing that's dangerous to the old system here would be rich, independent people. The risk was taken from our lives. We need it back."

17

WE HEADED UP toward Sergei's hideout, hitchhiking. The rides we found in the Russian north seemed to comment on the theme of waiting and blaming. Poor, out-of-the-way workers driving bashed-up cars, jeeps, and tractors that for the most part belonged to their ruined collective farms and state logging concerns — they were all waiting. They were waiting for a strong leader. They wanted order and shelter and they felt ignored, and that insulted them, and they blamed various demons: democrats, bosses, Lenin, the United States. We rode out from a logging settlement sealed in the rusty rear cabin of a battered panel truck that unfortunately, on a summer afternoon, had its coal stove blazing. We sat amid a sullen crew of heavy-equipment mechanics who rolled cigarette tobacco in newspaper and smoked until the hot air was thick and gray while the truck yawed down an endless, deeply cratered logging road. The crew just wanted vodka. They had passed beyond blaming.

Later, an old man driving a polished black 1984 Volga limo picked us up. He'd spent his life on a local collective farm, first driving a grain truck, then the boss's car. "I was a 'shock worker,'" he said — one of those Stakhanovite role models held up to other workers (who generally hated the overzealous workers). "I never refused to do any work, whether or not I had slept. They gave me this car as a reward. Oh, I had to pay, but they gave me the privilege of buying it." The old man told us he had once expected a lot from Russia. But with the fall of the Party, "I'm just waiting to see who will run things next," he said. "We've lost our savings. I can't cultivate land with just a spade. They don't even have horses anymore. And if you could buy a horse, you'd need a harness and a wagon, and where would you get those? If we still lived as our fathers had, on small farms, we'd be living well. Our lives have been ruined. We lost the old farms. Now we've lost socialism.

"My parents started out farming for themselves. My father had a horse, a cow, sheep." Somehow the government pushed them away from work. The old man and his five brothers built themselves houses, four kilometers up a tributary to the Unzha. Together they tilled a hundred acres. Then collectivization came, and later the government moved everyone off the small farms. The brothers all went to different places. Then collective farms started restricting them. "Don't touch that. You mustn't mow this grass, mustn't cut any lumber. So those things went to waste, because you couldn't take any for yourself. My parents were sent away. They weren't *kulaks,* just working people who earned a little bit of money and had two cows. That's why our farms work poorly — the real workers got sent away. My father used to have lots of bees. He told me 'Get bees, I'll give you hives.' But I didn't have time. I was working. There's forest there now."

◆

Sergei had undertaken the rough commute between Moscow and his village five or six times a year for a decade. Following his habit, we stayed with his good friends along the route. Our road adventures brought us to Susanino late in the afternoon. The town was named after Ivan Susanin, who became a Russian hero in the seventeenth century. Poles had occupied Moscow, and the tsar fled to a monastery near this place. Polish soldiers demanded that Susanin, a wily peasant, lead them to the tsar. Instead, he lured them into the swamps. Deep in the mucky maze, the troops realized they'd been had. They tortured Susanin, then, having killed their guide, died themselves. How we know, if no one remained to tell, is not part of the story. Mikhail Glinka's opera *A Life for the Tsar* beatifies Susanin, and

Russians sometimes call someone they see leading others the wrong way "a Susanin." The post-coup Russian national anthem, not so strangely, is a theme from the opera.

We passed through Susanin's swamp on a rough road and were waiting by their building when Sergei's friends Tanya and Aleksei Kurayev came home from work. Sergei had met Tanya years before. He'd hitched a ride in a car full of Young Communists she was organizing, and it got stuck overnight in a mud hole. She taught elementary school. Aleksei was the local procurator. He was tall and lean, with a pencil mustache. She had auburn hair and delicate blue eyes with smile lines around them. They were handsome enough to have been a propaganda poster couple — and their pretty kids should have been in the shot: Alyona and Vanya, five-year-old twins, and Denis, a few years older. The twins clung to Uncle Sergei from the moment they spied him until the next morning when we traveled on. My English startled Vanya, who'd never heard a foreign tongue before, and he stared expectantly when I was quiet, and giggled when I spoke.

The family was technically *nomenklatura*, but we were far from Moscow and they acted like ordinary folk, of the relaxed, funny, and nice sort. We walked down the street to a bookstore that stocked a few hundred volumes — trashy novels, Pushkin, classics, Lenin (still), and a recent government pamphlet called *Agrarian Reform*, containing Yeltsin's unenforceable decrees favoring independent farming. By way of unintentional explanation, the pamphlet had been misbound, nestled inside three identical, askew, badly stapled cardboard covers.

Tanya and Aleksei had been zealous; they'd risen as successful Party members. Tanya's enthusiasm for building a just society had taken longer than Aleksei's to dwindle. "During *perestroika*, the press at last provided frank information about Soviet activities and history. That changed us," Tanya said at supper. "I remember how strongly we'd approved of the Russian invasion of Prague, because we thought Russia was defending 'the people' there. So much bloodshed! We knew nothing about the labor camps, either. I miss *being certain*. That feeling probably will never come again — the time I really believed in something.

"Mark, you have traveled to many places here, but you can't

imagine how difficult it was for me as I grew disillusioned and the Party was still in charge. We had to meet every month and discuss an idea passed to us from above. The meetings were so boring, and those in charge were absolutely the dumbest. It was a good idea not to accept their conclusions in your soul, but to keep silent."

Aleksei said, "I knew all along that few other people really believed. There was *official* opinion — what you said when you spoke at that meeting — and *personal* opinion, which you spoke with friends like this, at supper. I've known my convictions for years but couldn't show them. The soul was divided too, but by 1985 my opinion was formed."

"I knew he had opinions I didn't share," Tanya said. "I was doing Party work, and believed everything. Still, my husband was the procurator! We were officials. My grandmother had told me the *kulaks* had been arrested and sent to starve. I hadn't believed her. Textbooks said collectivization had been necessary, and *kulaks* were class enemies, and they got what they deserved, and that's what I believed. Starting in the middle of *perestroika*, after I'd read more history, I knew she'd told the truth. New books and films came out.

"When a person grows up being told only one thing, she can't compare it with anything else. It's mother's milk — I was nourished by only one food. Had I known contrary opinions, I could have taken into account my experience and education, and judged. But with only one, I grew up ideologically and conscientiously pure, and ignored my experience. The Party view was called the view of the people. We young folks quickly and consciously absorbed this. We wanted to."

Aleksei knew all the rowdies in town, the way a state's attorney in a rural Maine market town would. Returned vets who'd fought in the Afghanistan war caused trouble. Prisoners let out after *perestroika* prison reforms caused trouble. Teenage boys acted up more than they did when Komsomol was the approved teen activity. Yet Susanino was a peaceful place and a beautiful one, with rolling hills and long vistas. A few private farmers, like those we'd visited around Ivanovo, struggled on the fringes of collective farms. Aleksei had helped some of these rebels extract their land and equipment from reluctant farm chairmen. For the most part, the collective farms went on as though nothing had changed.

"I might become a feminist," Tanya said, washing up after breakfast. "Russian women want attention. They have a hard time, and still do all the work. I even grow all our vegetables myself. There's a market in Kostroma, but that's too far. Maybe I'll open a Susanino food shop and start the market economy here!"

◆

A day's hitch nearer Sergei's village, in Kologriv, lived another couple, also close friends of his, Zoya and Vladimir Osipov, a generation older than his friends back in Susanino. They'd met, Zoya said, "in Siberia, in a far-off place that took a month to get to by airplane, train, and horse. Vladimir worked in a gold mine there." She was a Kologriv native, and they'd come back. He'd taught high school shop and agriculture, and was a minor functionary concerned with river safety. He was also an artist, a wood-carver. His goblins and demons crawled around the apartment shelves, laughing and leering. She'd taught school and was on the village Party committee until she'd retired. She'd been part of the historic, nationwide, final disassembly of rural Russia that had attempted to transform the last holdout peasants on the most remote farms into workers in agri-industry, smothering country traditions lingering on in the tiniest villages:

"I was on the district soviet's executive committee in Brezhnev's time, which combined the small old collective farms here and closed the nonprospective villages, moving almost everyone out. There were more than a hundred collective farms during the war. Now there are nine. About 1964 or 1965, following Party orders, we got the chairmen together. Some farms were poor, but others weren't. Many farms refused to be combined at first, so we had meetings all day and all night. Still some resisted. They said they already worked well, they liked their present chairmen, they thought poorer collective farms would undermine them if they linked up. We kept the meetings going, day after day. Finally, when a lot of the people went away tired, leaders forced rank-and-file Communists there to vote according to the Party line. The Central Committee order to combine had come down, and we fulfilled its order.

"While this process was going on, the regional Party secretary contacted me on weekends. He always asked, "How much land have you 'released'? How many hectares of 'new plowland'? We had to put cows where no cows belonged just because it looked good on paper. The Party closed the schools in the little villages, so the families with children had to move down to the central farm. Then they shut the shops. They cut off the electricity. This went on for ten years. A few old folks, mostly single, stayed — and only in a few of the small places.

"My arguments with the bosses never led to anything. If I looked at the facts and spoke up with my own opinion, the bosses said, 'You're pursuing an anti-Party line.' I had troubles with them. We wrote a 'bureau decision,' *On Increasing Milk Yields at Collective Farms in the District*. It called for a big program: milking three times a day instead of two, feeding extra green feed, constant watering, ice to chill the milk. 'Why do we need this?' I argued. 'Peasants know how often to milk. Why does the Party committee need to say this? I won't write it down.' I had troubles then. I was forced to leave.

"There had been a time when I believed I was part of an exciting plan that would build a strong future. Definitely. I first had some doubt way back in the era of Khrushchev, when the Party organization was split into separate agricultural and industrial parts, and then they were treated differently. That seemed wrong to me. I felt manipulated. Now I know much more. I have learned more history. And I am torn apart, devastated, killed. I feel I've lived my life in vain, for nothing, and I see no future for my country. They told us to think of the motherland first, yourself second, and we did. That's why I feel so betrayed. My husband never believed in the Communists. He refused to join. So he doesn't feel this now."

Like Procurator Aleksei Kurayev back in Susanino, Vladimir had pushed away from the Party line while his wife had plugged along at her Party job. Vladimir had been a wild man, a rough customer. Zoya laughed at her memory of him: "He used to brawl with other men. Oh, he had a temper! He once threw a whole cake out the window, he was so mad. 'You're a bandit!,' I'd say to him. He told wonderful stories, too."

And he did. He knew every stream and overgrown field in the terrain around Sergei's village, fifty kilometers upriver from Kologriv. Ironically, there had been empty huts in Astafyevo for Sergei to move into precisely because Zoya's earlier work cleared people out.

"The river was navigable then," Vladimir said. "Big steamships went almost all summer. Kolokhta was a beautiful place. People fished. No logging. The riverbed was all plants. Then the loggers came and the plants got torn out. They put log beams across the river, and the lines of logs backed up and ruined the riverbed. The only plants left are by rapids. Slow tugs drew the old log rafts, with no wakes. The small workboats now leave big wakes, travel at low water, wash away the riverbanks.

"Crews cleared the forests. That changed the runoff. With no trees to even out the flow — a lot of rain and the river goes up. Then it goes down. At the mouth of the Pezhenka where I once saw beautiful meadows, bulldozers leveled the fields. They store lumber there. Same for the mouth of the Kolokhta: that entire area was once covered with wild onions. Along the Pezhenka I remember huge birds — a hundred grouse were around, mating. A good fisherman could catch seventy-five pike a day — five hundred, eight hundred grams each. Now no one catches anything. They've destroyed the Unzha River.

"I was teaching agriculture to schoolboys at the time Khrushchev had his campaign to grow corn everywhere. The order came: plow under all clover, destroy it, plant only corn in its place. All the schoolchildren and personnel from organizations — everyone — crawled through the mud and dust planting corn by hand. They had strings and stakes. They dropped each grain in, or sometimes they'd make special hills. Green leaves grew, but never ears, except right next to livestock pens where there was manure. Many fields were soon mud, with nothing growing. Groups of Young Communist League kids had to run around chasing away the crows. One teacher — she taught biology — got the Order of Lenin for saving an experimental corn field. I have a photograph I took in '61 or '62 showing the kids harvesting corn. To make it look like the corn grew higher than a kid's head, a boy was made to hold cut-off stalks behind his back."

After supper, Vladimir had something he wanted to show the writer from America. With a gleam in his eye and an air of grandpa showing his special treasure, he pulled out an old school ledger and explained what he was about to read:

"There was a man from here who was covered with hair. He was born before the Revolution. The Hairy Man of Kologriv. A teacher brought him up, displayed him, and took him away to display in America. No one from here heard more about him until, near the end of his life, the hairy man sent a letter to his village. 'Is my mother alive? Does she need something, and can I help her?' He sent a photo from America. There he was, all dressed up in a suit, with a waistcoat and a cane and a top hat. The photo is in the local museum." Vladimir opened the old ledger. "'This is written by Pyotr Nikolaevich Smirnov, a local teacher,'" Vladimir read. The account is idiosyncratic — like Genesis, reiterating the same tale while appearing to move ahead:

"'The father [of the hairy man] was Andrian Yevtikiev. The hairy man was born in the village of Bereznik, Manturovo district. The baby was all covered with hair. His mother was believed to be a witch. The local people thought he was born from the devil — the devil who flew to the mother through the chimney in the form of a black dog. They wanted to kill the baby, but the local curate didn't allow that to happen. He reported to the head priest and asked what to do. The Kostroma archcurate answered: "Under no conditions should you allow a murder to take place. The child must be christened. If the child is from the devil, he will not be able to survive the christening. He will die." Of course the baby didn't die from the christening. He was called Andrian Yevtikiev. But the local people didn't like him. So he had to go away. As he grew up, he went away into the forest. He made a dugout and lived there. He begged. And the people gave him alms because they were afraid of him.

"'In the village of Korovitsa there was a woman. She was a virgin. She was insane. They called her Mavra the Foolish Girl. She was also a beggar. But she dreamed of getting married. She met the hairy man and became pregnant by him. Then she came to beg in Kologriv. In the *banya* [bathhouse] of the Yevchevsky estate she gave birth to a boy, a normal boy without extra hair. The boy was christened Fyodor. And he was a recorded, accepted member of Bereznik society. One small landlord, Förster, took care of the son. He taught him to read and gave him an education.

"'Then the hair began to grow. At twelve, Fyodor had a mustache and beard. By sixteen, his whole body was covered with hair. Förster, as an impresario, took him and displayed him in all the cities and villages and earned a lot of money. Then they set out for the United States, from which the hairy man wrote a letter asking about his mother. He said he would pay her debts if she had any. The letter was signed by the Russian consul, and there was a stamp: Consulate of the Russian Empire, Major General Grader. The letter and photo are in the Kologriv Museum.'"

Back in the States a month later, I uncovered Barnum's publicity for him: "By special permit from the Czar of all the Russias, we exhibit for the first and only time in the New World THE MOST PRODIGIOUS PARAGON OF ALL PRODIGIES SECURED BY P. T. BARNUM IN OVER 50 YEARS. THE HUMAN–SKYE TERRIER, THE CROWNING MYSTERY OF NATURE'S CONTRADICTIONS. This Incarnate Paradox, before which Science stands confused and blindly wonders, was found about thirteen years ago in company with his Dog-Faced Father, living in a remote cave in deep Kostroma Forests of Central Russia. They were first discovered by a hunter, and a party was formed who tracked them to their cave, and, after a desperate conflict, in which the savage father fought with all the fury of an enraged mastiff, their capture was effected . . ." Circus folk (according to *Freaks: We Who Are Not as Others* by Daniel P. Mannix) seem to have rechristened him Jo-Jo, and found him "a mild-mannered, quite intelligent young man who spoke several languages. The only trouble Barnum had was getting him to bark and growl at the audience as a dog-man should. Jo-Jo considered such behavior rude."

Over breakfast, Vladimir told stories of the devils he'd carved. He hadn't yet made a dog-faced man, nor even a "black dog who flew to the mother through the chimney." But he was driven to carve wood. He did so constantly, even when he gardened. He was showing off his early tomatoes and I noticed that he'd whittled ridges and fluted ornamental edges on the stakes holding up the plastic cold frame, and on the tomato stakes, too. His rows ran true, and the plants grew exuberantly. Back behind the garden, against a neighbor's wall, Vladimir had built a lean-to roof supported by large poles. He'd put a big, beat-up leather chair under there, and draped carpets and raggedy fringed blankets over the rails. He'd made it a placid, cozy place, an Ottoman gazebo where a man could sit and think and smoke and watch his garden grow. A worn-down tree stump stood in the middle. This was his summer carving studio. He worked there every afternoon, shaping his demons.

My green American vision of the lives of provincial Russians had not included the complications of Vladimir — teacher, state inspector of riverboats and drownings, carpenter, farmer, artist — a playful, imaginative, good man leading a dignified life in a hard place. Nor of Zoya, penitent after a lifetime of zealous Party work. Nor of the parallel situation of Procurator Kurayev and his wife.

"Zoya always made fun of me for this woodcarving — 'Why are you doing these silly things?' Now, finally," Vladimir said, "after I have sold stuff to the museum, she realizes my work was not all silly. But I'm afraid she only realizes because of the money. She still doesn't get that I'm doing art."

◆

Zoya and Vladimir got the four-page triweekly newspaper *Kologrivsky krai*, the "Kologriv Area" (which used to be compliantly named after Lenin, *Zavety Ilyicha*, "Ilich's Tenets"). Here's local news from May and June 1992 issues:

• From an interview in which Nikolai N. Kudrinsky, former collective-farm chairman, reconstructs himself, post-coup, as an anti-bureaucratic friend of the people: "It's not true people have stopped working on the collective farms. Officials didn't let them work, gave no incentives. . . . The peasant was oppressed, everything taken away. . . . I was not favored by the bosses, because I always tried to protect the farmers. I got many reprimands. . . . We fulfilled our quota and had grain left over.

They didn't give the peasants more, or keep any for seed. Instead we had to send it to the state. . . . When I refused, I was called up to the district Party committee, which forced me to do it."

• From an article about reorganizing collective farms as government subsidies diminish: "In Mezha district, a seminar to exchange experiences in reorganizing collective farms was held. They [local zootechnicians] visited production sites and became acquainted with the Canadian method of livestock fattening. The experiences are of particular importance for our rural people, because with rising prices of construction materials, equipment, and machinery, they can hardly build new facilities. The method involves simple structures, grazing livestock in fenced areas without cowherds, a more economical and simple method suggested by life itself."

• From an article (reflecting new post-coup candor) on widespread cutbacks of major public-works projects: "Fortunately the crazy plan to divert northern rivers southward through the Unzha has been dropped. Nevertheless, the Kostroma Forestry Industry Enterprise is now surveying for a project to straighten the bed of the Unzha, to ease the passage of log rafts. If this project is implemented, the meadows of the Kristilov individual peasant farm would be ruined. Current would speed up and undermine the right bank where all the fuel tanks are, and ruin the fish-spawning area. The work is being carried out under a veil of secrecy."

• From an article on one of the many new taxes that the subsidy-starved local government levied on the few private farmers: "The local soviet has decided to approve a tax on improved and unimproved lands, the tax being ten rubles a hectare. . . . If a person's meadow is farther than twelve kilometers from his village, he may pay no tax."

• From an article surveying collective farms' readiness for the coming hay-mowing season: "The agricultural authorities in the district are preparing their machines for the campaign to make feed . . . 64 percent of the rotary mowers are functional."

• From a delightful column called "If I Were Head of the District Administration," in which petty functionaries say how they'd handle the boss's job, the director of the district's House of Culture wrote: "I wouldn't like to be in his shoes. Wherever you look there's darkness, because you need money and don't have it. Or we do have some, but in such small amounts you can't decide where to channel it."

• From an article reviewing transport regulations, asserting that the prior rigorous state control over all commerce would still be enforced, and that those attempting free enterprise still must satisfy intervening officials: "Anyone who wants to do any commercial transport activity has to register at [address given]. . . . Here is a list of things you have to present to get a transporting license:

a. a copy of the order that assigns a person responsible for the motor vehicle activities of the enterprise.

b. a copy of a document that confirms that an enterprise is registered with the state.

c. a list of all the vehicles and trailers with licenses, including the make and model of all trucks.

d. a short summary of all work to be done by the vehicles, including the amount of freight to be conveyed, the main itineraries, and specification of the freight."

• A note on spring planting at a collective farm (the one with official jurisdiction over Sergei's village of Astafyevo): "The tractor drivers of State Farm Chermeninsky are going full speed ahead in spring fieldwork. As of today, 98 hectares are completed, of a total of 250 to be sown. The rain that has just passed slowed planting somewhat. They're still plowing the soil with two tractors [there were actually forty or more tractors, nearly all broken, on the farm, Sergei said]. It's intensive work, but V. Zhukov and A. Sabenov are working diligently and responsibly. This year the farm got no mineral fertilizer. They have nothing with which to dress the sown grass. But so as not to reduce the harvest, the soil has been harrowed. The tractor drivers are in a stalwart frame of mind, so if the weather holds, fieldwork will be performed on schedule."

◆

We were close to Sergei's village, but it was usually hard to travel the final leg of the journey. In Manturovo, a railhead and the remote last paved place before the wild woods, we were prepared to wait all day, and Sergei thought we'd eventually find a ride in a logging truck, or else bunk with a shopkeeper he knew. But as soon as we got to town, we saw a jeep pulling out of the station lot. Sergei flagged it down. Two teenage girls dressed in Sunday-best skirts and blouses sat behind the driver. Yes, he'd take us onward for a couple of hundred rubles — two dollars for a few hours of driving.

We pitched up the deeply rutted dirt road. We were thrown back and forth across the cab. The driver was wiry and dimwitted. He was hurrying in order to get the girls to the funeral of a cousin who'd died on this road, driving a motorcycle. "He was drunk," shouted the driver. "His father went to get hay yesterday morning and found him. He saw something white on the road . . . about here . . . and he came up to it and it turned out to be his son." The jeep driver kept on about the funeral's starting in an hour and his mission to bring the girls there in time. The jeep blew a tire. "Get out in seven seconds," he shouted. He was big and rough and had the spare on with the speed of an Indy 500 pit crew member. The girls made it in time.

Chermenino, after the jeep roared off, was a quiet hamlet — a few cabins, a schoolhouse, and a big old barge, sunk into the Unzha River and used as a dock. A few drunkards sat on a log above the barge. They wore filthy jackets and looked like street scoundrels out of Dickens. One was wide-eyed, short, wire-haired. One was bearded, stooped, red-eyed, worn out. They were Sergei's buddies, and they greeted him with shouts of joy. Whenever Sergei went to Moscow, the one also called Sergei — Sergei Ivanovich — made it his business to guard Sergei's outboard engine, after dropping it into a buried metal drum with a big hasp lock and metal strapping on the lid. Sergei Ivanovich was an ex-con. He liked to get drunk and tell jail stories. He trapped beaver for their pelts and had given some to Sergei to sell in Moscow. Now Sergei handed him fifteen hundred rubles.

We unchained Sergei's battered rowboat and horsed the old motor out of the pit and onto the transom. It started. Soon we were skimming along between palisades of poplar trees, watching ahead and dodging half-submerged logs jammed into the bottom by passing log rafts. After half an hour of pounding up the choppy, chilly river in a rainstorm, we came to Astafyevo. We pulled the boat onto shore and dragged our baggage up the steep bank and then far up a grassy meadow toward the little cluster of log huts high above the river.

We climbed through the fields in slanting evening light. Before we could see the only permanent residents — two old women, both shepherds — we could hear them, cussing their animals up and down the fields. Then there they were. The scene was a pastoral from the underworld. Cows and sheep milled along the slope, hustling and trotting when they had to. The women ceaselessly ran at them with sticks, shrieking their curses. Horseflies as big as thumbs spiraled in a buzzing snarl, stinging the animals' faces. "The women fight each other, fists and teeth, sometimes," said Sergei, "and then they love each other. In winter the sheep move right in with Tyotya [Aunt] Masha. So do her cats."

Sergei's chinked log cabin could have served Abe Lincoln. It looked cozy. Smoke came from the chimney. He'd paid two hundred rubles for the house in 1984. We opened the door. The house was full of smoke. Sergei's second-oldest and second-youngest sons had come up from Moscow to tend the garden — the garden was serious business, a part of Sergei's plan for surviving the coming winter. Sergei got angry almost at once. He fixed the wood stove so all the smoke went up the chimney. The garden he'd come up and planted before meeting me had sprouted, and so had weeds, but his sons Vasily and Yuri had cleared up only half of two rows. There was no spring water in the jugs for spring water. We hauled water. Eventually we weeded. The cabins all around stood empty. Sergei's brother the mathematician had bought one of them, but almost never used it. The brother's cabin had become a museum of artifacts from around the village — a spinning wheel, weaving implements, old carpentry tools, an iron with a hopper for live coals, pottery pitchers and plates, all found lying about. We had vodka and kasha for supper, and Sergei played his piano.

After our travels, we settled in for a few days. We walked to the next deserted villages, Vialtsevo and onward to Paunino, on a back trail through abandoned meadows growing up to brush.

Dead tractors and combines, rusting through, gutted for parts like the hulks in America's slums, sat by collapsing barns and sheds. The Soviet government had put out millions of tractors, and many had moved almost directly from factory to fates such as this. The few area residents had gutted the farm buildings at will, appropriating floorboards, windows, beams.

On the way back through Paunino, we stopped at another cabin. A hale doctor sat chopping vegetables in her kitchen. She'd hunted here when her husband was living, and, in her sixties, she kept coming back for summers. "Now that your friend asks me," she said to Sergei, "I wonder — what *am* I doing here?"

We took the rowboat downriver and visited the chairman of State Farm Chermeninsky. "Just two of our forty tractors work," he said, confirming the half-true *Kologrivsky krai* article on spring field preparation at this farm. "Spare parts have disappeared or become unaffordable, and only a few of our hundred workers bother to report; they're busy tending their private plots." I saw cows — the few remaining cows that hadn't been stolen or slaughtered or sold, and they were so underfed their ribs showed. They stood in a corner of a huge barn. Half of its roof had been torn away in the prior few months by peasants taking building materials.

The demoralized chairman wore a tweed sports jacket. Nearly a year after the attempted coup, a picture of Lenin still hung in his office. "We need state support, and they're abandoning us," he said. I asked if orders came, as usual, about what to plant, and when, and how. "No, they've stopped almost altogether," the young chairman answered. Well, wasn't he glad — he could do what he saw needed doing now. "No, I'm not at all glad," he answered, sounding forlorn. "I don't know what to do."

Was he thinking up ways to market his goods locally? No. Might he try to clean up the organization, work with a few good people? No. Even clean up the rubble in the barnyard? No, no one would follow such an order. Meet and find ways to work efficiently, and try to make enough money to pay good wages? These, he said, were not his problems. Above him, a few towns to the south, the old agri-bureaucrats still were there to do the worrying. The chairman's initiative would not have been welcomed. Sergei and I climbed back into the rowboat and cruised on downriver.

We moored the boat where Kolokhta Stream drains into the Unzha. The flat fields there had become a base camp for the River Logging Authority. It was just as Vladimir Osipov had described it: a boozy, Klondike-style log village, with bunk rooms for transients and cabins for dozens of workers with families, a one-room store (well stocked — the River Logging Authority had money), a one-room schoolhouse, a bakery that turned out tasty sourdough loaves, and a broad bulldozed arena where millions of birch logs were yarded, bunched into cubic rafts, waiting for spring when the Unzha would swell and the big tugs could push them out of the forest.

That night, a few come-from-aways showed up in Sergei's village. The retired doctor knocked. She had figured out why she was up here. "I felt, when I was hunting alone this afternoon, that I was still with my late husband," she said. Near midnight, a whimsical art professor named Khetagurov arrived with his lanky mistress, after having bribed a tractor driver from the Chermeninsky farm with a bottle ("He needed to smell it right away, before we even set out"). The driver had had to ford the river and churn his way up the convoluted logging road. We spent the rest of that midsummer night celebrating.

Next evening, we went to visit one of the shepherds, Tyotya Masha. She was about sixty. Because she'd been an early widow, and childless, she hadn't moved away when the school closed. She hadn't left when electricity had been cut off, nor when the closet-sized shop she'd run had been ordered shut. Local loggers, Sergei said, got aroused just hearing her name. She'd stocked vodka in her shop, and sold it at any time of day or night. The loggers used to come by boat, by tractor, by horse, from Ponga, from Chermenino. They'd knocked on her door. "I used to open the door to anyone at night, but now I'm afraid — that old man was killed down the river." The loggers had paid her above the state price in those premarket days.

Whenever she got a shipment of food in, everyone had soon heard about it, and for a day or two, until the supply dwindled, people had shown up out of the woods at her house. She'd stocked sausage, butter, canned fish, canned meat. When she hadn't known the price, she'd guessed, and after finding out, she'd given credit. The social scene in the woods above the Unzha was thin, and she excited some men half her age, who still came not just to buy vodka but to court her.

She started talking about her cats as soon as we walked into the kitchen of her log hut. A ginger tom leaped onto my lap. She had two on hers. "They sleep on my bed," she said. "I slug them hard, but still they climb up." She laughed in big guffaws, her red face lined into concentric circles around her wide-open mouth.

Her thoughts drifted to the uncertain times. She knew little about politics, but the transition had reached out to change her world, too: "How will I live this winter? There's no transport. Last year they took fifty rubles from me for a trailerload of hay. This year they want a thousand." Big, basic questions were about to surface in her life — who really owned her sheep, her land, her hut, and eventually, whether her small flock made money — questions that had nothing to do with her life or labors during any of her previous sixty years. She'd left the village twice in three decades, "once to see relatives, and once when my husband died."

"That *muzhik* — that's who brought me here. I lived on a state farm eighty kilometers from Moscow. That's where I met the guy. He didn't even have a passport. He married me on his soldier's ID card. When we got out of the army, they didn't give me no passport like they said they would. We came and lived in the house next to you, Sergei. My husband worked in Ponga in 1955, cutting trees for the River Logging Authority. He got that forestry job and his father chased him out of the house after a year. There were a damn big lot of houses left here with no one living in them. We bought one from a old woman with three kids. She went away. The roof leaked, so we covered our faces with raincoats at night. My husband fixed the roof. I moved over to this house after my husband died, after the wood stove in the other house fell in. I visited the old man yesterday, at his grave, and I told him, 'You motherfucker, why have you left me? Get up, goddamnit!'

"He dropped out after fourth grade. But he wanted to drive, so he went down and studied in Chermenino for three years, got through seventh grade, then went to get his license at Soligalich. But right then he got sick. He lived nineteen days in a hotel, and he couldn't eat *kolbasa*, but only could drink tea. Then the hospital sent him to Kostroma, to a cancer hospital. He guessed he had cancer. Ten times I saw him in Kostroma in nineteen days. Valentin had been a handsome man. He turned to skin and bones. Hurt like hell. They operated, cut out his gullet, his stomach, sewed his intestines up to his throat. The stomach was rotted through.

"The chief surgeon said, 'Don't cry, maybe he'll live another month, maybe two weeks. I've done this operation only three times.' But he lived a year and four months without a stomach. He wanted to live very much. Came home by foot here to Astafyevo one day, and when I saw him he said, 'I've walked back here to die.'

"They gave him a piece of paper that said he needed nursing, but they only gave him thirty-five rubles a month to live. He died in the forest, in June 1970. He was thirty-eight and I was thirty-six. He didn't want to die. He said, 'If I could live, I'd even work hard for the state all my life.'

"He'd been a good hunter. He gave the whole village meat. He used to hunt with Police Chief Podubny, a good man, but the guy got mixed up with a gang and shot himself when the law was on his tail — his wife's alive. Even when my husband was sick, he went into the forest. He bagged five muskrats one day. He used to get elk, bears.

"He brought a bear cub home from the forest one time. We raised the bear. We put him by an abandoned house, kept him on a chain like a dog. We had a zoo. People came to look and they brought along their kids. Then the bear began to grow stronger. He wanted to attack me. Valentin was never afraid. They'd play. Bear cubs grow quickly. Bears eat everything, milk, bread, soup — it would always eat. He roared when he wanted to eat. Misha the bear. Then Valentin had to go away to work somewhere. I said get rid of the bear first — it tried to swat me. I had to feed it seven times a day. It liked to eat.

"He took the bear into the town. Came back and says, 'I sold it for one hundred rubles.' 'Where's the money?' I asked. 'Oh, the guy I sold it to was so nice, we drank up the money.'

"That guy kept the bear. It got enormous. A brigade of boys were there from shop class in Oktyabrskiy to see it. They threw cigarette butts at the bear. The bear didn't like cigarette butts. He turned mean after that and almost killed the owner. So he shot it. He skinned the thing and ate the meat.

"My cats go out but then they come in and shit in the stove. This cat knows when I milk. She is always there. If I feed her, she doesn't steal. Tyotya Nura — I thought she'd come over here tonight, but she is sleeping. She grazed my sheep all day. I've got no time to graze sheep myself because I've got the collective farm's cows. I pay Nura two liters of milk a day for grazing my sheep. She goes out with them all day. She has no time for anything else. We used to let them wander free. Now it's too dangerous. The hill is too big to fence. I gave a logger vodka for putting up a little fencing. He drank the vodka and then didn't do anything. No one wants to do anything. He said, 'No, I'm going fishing.' They owe me five hundred rubles, those two. I'll put the law on them. Fuck them.

"I was down at the river washing clothes. The farm bosses and the district chief of agriculture came along in a boat. 'We're waiting for you,' one said. 'What do you want from me?' I ask. 'I want a glass of water.' So I say, 'Okay, I'll give you tea.' I gave them tea up here and something to eat. Since they'd left Kologriv, they hadn't eaten nothing. They wanted to see the herd of cows that eat here. I told them Tyotya Nura hasn't even got any bread flour. The chief knew how she'd worked — she had a medal, a Red Banner worker. She's strange. She didn't tell him she didn't have no flour. She has a suitcase of awards and nothing to eat. If I was in her place, I'd take the awards and go see Yeltsin. So the chief himself said to the farm chairman, 'You yourself have to bring flour.' Two days later, she got a message: 'Come to Chermenino, get your flour.' Before the reforms, all us pensioners received flour.

"I talked the riverboat captain into bringing the flour to Chermenino. And I managed to find a tractor driver to take my flour to the village here. The guy came with it. But he didn't give me the flour. He sold it to me. And the river was deep — he was the first of the season to go over the ford, so the flour got wet. But finally we're baking bread. I don't know why the bosses came. There's a Moldavian woman wants to buy this land maybe. Maybe that's why the bosses came. They brought this vodka from Chermenino. Is there any more left now?"

AFTERWORD

NEWS FROM THE country is as hard to come by as ever when the former Soviet Union is the place in question. So this afterword, written in the fall of 1995, is spotty. But there is some news.

The Belgorod seed-corn plant is partly up and running. Viktor Lishchenko is healthy and living in Moscow, connecting business people with regional powers and administering a training program for prospective Russian agri-business executives. Yuri Chernichenko is still head of the Peasants' Party, which, although it has remained small, has gotten feisty enough to challenge its founder's rule. He's also the oldest elected representative to the Duma, the upper house of the Russian parliament. My translator Pavel P. Sorokin is now agricultural consul at the Russian consulate in Washington, D.C.

News from Ukraine is even spottier. Savely Golovko is a member of the Ukrainian parliament and a regional boss. My keeper Vitaly Chuiko lived long enough to see his country's independence, and died in 1994.

Aleksander Sorokin, the agri-boss of Ivanovo, is, following the attempted coup and the fall of the Party, still agri-boss. He remains head of the government agricultural bureaucracy, and of the region's agricultural bank, and of several private concerns doing agri-business. He says that Nikolai Petrachkov still runs Farm Gorky, and that a number of the smaller farmers who had started up have quit, but that Volodya Kurikhin still administers a construction company.

No one had pried Tyotya Masha out of Astafyevo yet, as of the end of summer 1995. But Sergei Sossinsky has come to America, completed a Ph.D. in history (with a thesis about his well-known grandfather Viktor Chernov), and joined the doleful hunt for an academic job, meanwhile driving a truck in Boston.

The biggest news is how little progress there's been toward agricultural reform. According to an article by Thomas Sigel in *Transition*, the Soros Foundation magazine, in May 1995, farm output has fallen by a quarter since the demise of the Soviet Union. Land reform "has nearly halted. . . . More than 90 percent of Russian farmland is still controlled by large state-owned collectives. . . . Only a handful of new farms were created last year, and farmers abandoned more than 20,000 private plots because of financial problems. Their land has reverted back to collectives." The 1995 harvest was down even further. Since 1991, the *Washington Post* reports, the average Russian consumes 12 percent less meat and 15 percent less milk. He is making up for it by eating 10 percent more bread and 25 percent more potatoes.

Yet reform, which has created genuine commodities markets, labor markets, and credit supply for growers and processors, is paralyzed by the nation's heritage, politics, and poverty. AKKOR reportedly tried to set up a farmer's market in Moscow, but gave up after it was bombed several times (supposedly by the local Mafia, because it interfered with their protected prices and supply routes). The conservative Agrarian Party, including many farm chairmen and regional bureaucrats, pushes for subsidization, not reform of the system, and it is powerful and growing more so. Together the Agrarians and the resurgent Communist Party seem likely to retard land reform. In response, Russians continue to depend on their personal ties to the land — on their private plots and relatives living on farms.

ACKNOWLEDGMENTS

MOST OF ALL and best of all, I thank my wonderful wife, Susan E. Eaton, whose magic and love and patience and song eased the trek to our double birthing.

I'd also like to express continuing thanks and appreciation for various sorts of help, advice, support, and sagacity, to my patient editor, Richard Todd, and to Esther and Sidney Kramer, Samuel McCracken, Sergei Sossinsky, Sean Ploen, Jim Sparrow, Harry George, Steve Biel, Bill Green, Zhores Medvedev, Mark Kuchment (who offered the first suggestion), Olga Genkina and Mitya and Anton Genkin, Claire Grodin, Larry Cooper, Susan Blau, Vlad Klimenko and Cindy Scharf, Viktor Lishchenko, Pavel P. Sorokin, Viktor Novikov, Edward and Ina Ivanian, Elha Vens, Jane and Charlie Butcher, Barry Newman, Noel Perrin, Jim Collins, Earl Ainsworth, Roy Barnett, Joe Filner, Gus Schumacher, Lisa Birk, Delia Cabe-Gill, Susan Todd, Howard Higman, Chip Backlund, Lynn Kippax, Jill Ker Conway, John Chrystal, Jill Delamater, Yvonne Abraham, Laura Hohnhold, Ray Goldberg, Marshall Goldman, the staff of the Geonomics Institute, Fred Hapgood, Sarah Wernick, Robert Weiss, Sonja Hilgrin, Craig Infanger, Lauren John, Larry Martin, Jasmin Krpan, Susan and Bill Keith, Mindy Keskinen, Adrian LeBlanc, Karen Kuwayti, Terry and Judith Maloney, Mary and Angelo Mazzei, Morris and Dorothy Kestelman, Allan Mustard, Yo Maitre, Nick

Mills, Mark Bryant, Bill Patrick, Jon Franklin, Stanley and Pauline Herzig, Lee Totman, Joe and Mary Jane Weisshaar, Don Van Atta, Phil LoPiccolo, Ken Holmes, Kostya Vronsky, Kaye Worsley, Don Robinson, Igor Zotikov, and the many live souls mentioned elsewhere in this book.